DAYS
OF THE
GENERALS

DAYS

OF THE
GENERALS

HILTON HAMANN

ZEBRA

Published by Zebra Press
an imprint of Struik Publishers
(a division of New Holland Publishing (South Africa) (Pty) Ltd)
PO Box 1144, Cape Town, 8000

First edition 2001

3 5 7 9 10 8 6 4

Cover photographs: main photo © Cobus Bodenstein/AP Photo/Picturenet.
Insets (from left to right) © Eric Miller/iAfrika; Benny Gool/Trace;
Paul Velasco/Picturenet; Sasha Kralj/Trace; Benny Gool/Trace.
Author photo © Joy Webber.
Photographs between pages 118 and 119 © Military Archives;
Constand Viljoen; Georg Meiring; Hilton Hamann.

PUBLISHING MANAGER: Marlene Fryer
MANAGING EDITOR: Robert Plummer
EDITOR: Frances Perryer
TEXT DESIGNER: Beverley Dodd
COVER DESIGNER: Christian Jaggers
TYPESETTER: Monique van den Berg
INDEXER: Frances Perryer

Reproduction by Hirt & Carter (Pty) Ltd
Printed and bound by CTP Book Printers

ISBN 1-86872-340-2

CONTENTS

Photographs between pages 118 and 119

ACKNOWLEDGEMENTS

An undertaking like this would not be possible without help. Many people were involved, directly or indirectly, either by giving me their time, searching for documents or just directing me to other people who could help.

There are many who, for their own reasons, do not want it known that they gave assistance. You know who you are and you know how grateful I am.

Then there are people like General Dirk Marais, who acted as a kind of co-ordinator and helped set up the interviews with the former chiefs of the SADF, as well as General Bertus Steenkamp, who offered advice and guidance and twisted the arms of a few people reluctant to talk to me.

And of course the main players themselves, who freely gave of their time and hospitality and never complained about my many unreasonable requests. Thank you generals Magnus Malan, Constand Viljoen, Jannie Geldenhuys, Georg Meiring, Hein du Toit and Chris Thirion.

I am told I am not the easiest person in the world to live with, even when there is no pressure. When under stress I'm informed I am impossible. Life for my wife, Joy, and sons, Bryan and Kevin, was hell for approximately a year while I worked on this project, but they stuck with me through all of my wild rantings. Guys, I couldn't have done it without you.

And finally to my parents, who helped out financially every now and then in the months their first-born couldn't feed his family because he always wanted to be a writer rather than have a real job.
•

ABBREVIATIONS

ANC	African National Congress
Apla	Azanian People's Liberation Army
Armscor	Armaments Development Corporation
BGS	*Bundesgrezchutz* (the border police)
Boss	Bureau of State Security
CBW	chemical and biological warfare
CCB	Civil Co-operation Bureau
CIA	Central Intelligence Agency
CP	Communist Party
CSI	Chief of Staff Intelligence
DTA	Democratic Turnhalle Alliance
EMLC	Electronic Magnetic Logistical Component
Fapla	People's Armed Forces for the Liberation of Angola
FNLA	National Front for the Liberation of Angola
Frelimo	Mozambique Liberation Front
GNU	government of national unity
GOC	General Officer Commanding
GPS	global positioning system
HEU	highly enriched uranium
HNP	Herstigte Nasionale Party
HQ	headquarters
ICBM	inter-continental ballistic missile
IFP	Inkatha Freedom Party
ILS	instrument landing system
Iscor	Iron and Steel Industrial Corporation
JMC	Joint Management Centre
JSC	Joint Security Commission
KZN	KwaZulu-Natal
KZP	KwaZulu Police
MDM	Mass Democratic Movement
MI	Military Intelligence
MK	Umkhonto we Sizwe

MNR	Mozambique National Resistance
MPLA	Popular Movement for the Liberation of Angola
MRL	multiple rocket launchers
Nato	North Atlantic Treaty Organisation
NDB	non-directional beacon
NI	National Intelligence
NP	National Party
OAU	Organisation of African Unity
OB	Ossewa Brandwag
PAC	Pan African Congress
PE	plastic explosive
Plan	People's Liberation Army of Namibia
POW	prisoner of war
Renamo	Mozambique National Resistance
SAAF	South African Air Force
SABC	South African Broadcasting Corporation
SACP	South African Communist Party
SADF	South African Defence Force
SANDF	South African National Defence Force
SAP	South African Police
SASO	South African Students Organisation
SDU	self-defence unit
SSC	State Security Council
Swapo	South West African People's Organisation
TRC	Truth and Reconciliation Commission
UDF	United Democratic Front
Unita	National Union for the Total Independence of Angola
UPA	Popular Union of Angola
Zanla	Zimbabwean National Liberation Army
Zanu	Zimbabwean African National Union
Zanu-PF	Zimbabwean African National Union Patriotic Front
Zapu	Zimbabwe African People's Union

INTRODUCTION

The idea for this book came about when my youngest son, after watching a television news broadcast, said to me: 'Dad, when you were in the army, why did you kill all those innocent people?' He'd seen a report about the Truth and Reconciliation Commission and submissions about the activities of the former South African Defence Force.

I was flabbergasted. Was his opinion typical of the way future generations would see the SADF and the half-million-plus ordinary men and women of all colours, creeds and persuasions who were part of it? Would we former soldiers be judged on the basis of 30-second television news-bites ... on the reports of journalists who'd never been there and who firmly believed in the motto 'Don't let the facts get in the way of a good story' ... people who more often than not refused to test allegations always seemingly made by unnamed sources? Would history be based on the findings of a Truth and Reconciliation Commission that looked as if it had already made up its mind long before the first submission was made?

I suppose it will. That's the nature of wars and political struggles – part of the spoils is that the victors get to rewrite history to suit themselves. But however badly the new historians choose to portray the SADF, I believe that South Africa's new-found democracy and constitution – a constitution held up as a model – would never have been possible without the SADF.

In 1975, as a reluctant conscript aged 17, I entered the SADF. Before that year was over I towed a 20 mm anti-aircraft gun deep into Angola as part of the South

African conventional forces involved there. A few years later, I was the *Sunday Times*'s military correspondent and also wrote for a number of well-known international magazines and newspapers, notably *Soldier of Fortune*. I travelled extensively with the SADF, accompanying them into many battles. I spent time with Unita and long periods with the recces and other units. I probably got to see more of the overall picture than anyone in the Defence Force, apart from the generals themselves, and what I didn't see were the atrocities I now so often hear callers telling radio talk-show hosts they committed in the same battles I covered as a newsman. At the time I was paid in US dollars or British pounds for work done for international publications. Just one picture of an SADF member torturing or executing a prisoner or a local would probably have fed my family for a year. I never got to take such a picture because I never saw any of that.

The fact is, while many were called up, very few SADF members were ever involved in any sort of battle whatsoever. Probably 95 per cent of all soldiers only ever fired their rifles on a shooting range – something that's tough to admit when all your buddies are impressing the girls with (made-up) war stories. One example springs to mind. The guilty party shall remain anonymous. Years after Operation Savannah I sat in a regimental bar in which a sergeant impressed a bunch of new regimental members with stories of his exploits in Angola. He told them how he'd cut off the finger of a captured prisoner and threaded it onto the chain to which his 'dog tags' were attached – he even had a photograph to prove it. I was a part of that particular gun crew with that sergeant (he was a national serviceman gunner back then), and it is true, he wore a putrefied finger around his neck. However, what the 'war hero' failed to mention to his gullible listeners was that our gun position was sited alongside the hospital in Cela. One day, while rummaging about, we came across the hospital's dump containing discarded medical equipment, bandages, swabs and … yep, you guessed it, the finger concerned. This was leapt upon by the sergeant, while the rest of us felt like vomiting. To maintain the effect he threaded it onto his 'dog tag' chain with a nail, and wore it for the next few days until even he was sickened by it.

The SADF I was part of was an organisation that operated according to rules, traditions and codes of conduct. But the soldier on the ground had little idea of the greater picture. That is what this book is about. It is the story of the men at the top who directed us and, by their decisions, directly or indirectly, influenced whether we lived or died. I knew that if I was going to give my children a clear picture of what really went on, the generals – particularly the former chiefs of the SADF and Magnus Malan, the former Minister of Defence – would have to tell their story. I wasn't particularly confident that would happen. As it turned out, I couldn't have been more wrong – all were willing to talk to me with no pre-conditions whatsoever. In a nutshell, we agreed to the following:

- I could speak to anyone I wanted.
- I could ask anything I wanted.
- I was free to cross-check and find independent sources who could corroborate or dismiss anything the generals said.
- They would have absolutely no say in the writing of the book – in fact they would only see what I'd written once it was on the shelves of the bookshops.

In the end I put together dozens of hours of interviews with many of the people mentioned in the book. I waded through piles of documents and saw countless people. It was a strange experience, sitting with these men who had wielded so much power. When I was an ordinary soldier they seemed untouchable, almost godlike in terms of their power and influence – and yet when I sat with them in their homes drinking coffee and dipping rusks I was struck by how human and ordinary they were.

Contrary to popular impression, they didn't always agree with one another; in fact, in many cases, they didn't like each other and had no qualms about firing off critical broadsides at their former colleagues and bosses. For example, Meiring had this to say about Magnus Malan: 'Malan, I think, expressed himself wrongly in politics because he didn't use his power base – that was the military. He tried to become a politician, which he never was. Then, as a minister, he continued to want to be a military commander – [but] he still remained Chief of the Defence Force. I am very happy he was not the minister when I was Chief of the Defence Force, because I wouldn't have been able to work with him. General Malan has not got an operations background. He was never involved as a commander in an actual military combat situation. This means he was very good at a training level, which is his comfort zone, but the training level when he was a training officer was a bloody long time ago. He would also form an initial impression about people which he'd keep for the rest of his life. He would never allow a bloke to progress or to become someone else. He never allowed for the possibility that someone might grow up, become more wise, mature, etc. I think he never grew up. He was always the *stout outjie* [naughty boy]. As a minister he liked to play the fool with people. The worst thing I had to endure was when he took the Military Committee from Parliament up to South West. People would be over-turning each other's beds and pushing each other into the swimming pool. I would just go away and find somewhere else to sleep where they couldn't find me. They liked to throw bullets into the fire in the evening. It was childish. He was a product of the times, where the bloke with the right connections got the right job.'

The generals were men with normal doubts and human frailties, but the impression I was most left with was how, without exception, they had lived their lives according to a code and laid-down rules of conduct.

Why were they so willing to co-operate? Because in their opinion the TRC failed to give them the opportunity to tell their side of the story. I have let them speak for themselves and it is up to the reader to decide whether the truth is being told or not.

Is this the complete, all-encompassing, definitive history of the SADF of the time? No, it is not. There are more stories to be told, some of which – for example the Cradock Four killings and the Anton Lubowski case – I could have included, but wasn't able to get verifying documents in time to meet the publishing deadlines. I decided to leave those stories out. Maybe in another book …

I have no doubt this book will be dismissed by certain factions. There are people who have such a set view of the SADF that nothing, no matter what facts are presented, will change their minds. The truth is I'm not trying to. My intentions are a lot more humble than trying to convert zealots. I merely hope that this will give the people who weren't there an idea of what went on during those times. I also hope it will give the hundreds of thousands of SADF members of that era more of the big picture.

THE MAIN PLAYERS IN THE SAGA

General Magnus André de Merindol Malan

Malan was born in Pretoria on 30 January 1930 and always wanted to be a soldier. At the age of 14 he ran away from home to join the army but was tracked down by his parents and returned to school to matriculate from the Afrikaanse Hoër Seunskool in Pretoria. In 1950 he joined the Permanent Force and was sent on a Permanent Force officer's course at the SA Military College. He graduated as a Bachelor of Science (Mil) from Pretoria University in 1954.

Malan took up a commission at the South African Corps of Marines but within a year this unit was disbanded and he was transferred as an instructor to the Army Gymnasium at Voortrekker Hoogte. By 1958 he had reached the rank of captain and was the aide-de-camp to the Governor General of what was then still the Union of South Africa. A year later he was appointed second-in-command of the SA Military Academy and shortly after became staff officer in charge of planning, operations and training at Army Headquarters. In 1962 he was chosen to attend a two-year US Army Staff Course at Fort Leavenworth, then spent a short while attached to the 35th Armoured Division in Colorado. His commanding officers in the United States reportedly identified him as a possible future South African leader and he was invited to meet President John F. Kennedy.

He returned to South Africa in 1964 and was appointed to the staff of the SA Military College with the rank of commandant (lieutenant colonel) at the age of only 34, something unheard of at the time. Two years later he became a full colonel and the Officer Commanding South West Africa Command, based in Windhoek. He was there for only a year before he returned as OC of the SA Military Academy, with the rank of brigadier. He stayed there for five years before taking over as the Officer Commanding Western Province Command, based in Cape Town, in 1972. The following year he was promoted to the rank of major general. Just a couple of months later, at 43 – an unheard-of age for such seniority – he was promoted to lieutenant general and pushed past many major generals more senior in age and experience into the post of Chief of the Army. He was the youngest man to hold this or an equivalent post in the history of the SADF.

At the conclusion of Operation Savannah in 1976 Malan succeeded Admiral Hugo Biermann as Chief of the SADF. In 1980 he retired from the SADF, became a nominated MP and was appointed to the Cabinet as Minister of Defence – a fact that did not please many of his Cabinet colleagues.

General Constand Viljoen
Constand Viljoen obtained his BSc (B.Mil) at the University of Pretoria in 1955 and began his military career in 1956, rising rapidly through the ranks. In 1974 he was appointed Director General of Operations at Defence Headquarters and then became the Principal Staff Officer to the Chief of the Defence Force, Admiral Hugo Biermann. In 1977 he became Chief of the Army and three years later Chief of the SADF, a position he held until he retired in 1985. Viljoen later became leader of the Freedom Front and a member of Parliament.

General Jannie Geldenhuys
Jannie Geldenhuys was born in Kroonstad on 5 February 1935 and joined the Permanent Force in 1954. After completing a 13-month PF officer's course he was posted to 1 Special Service Battalion as an instructor. In 1964, with the rank of

major, he was GSO2 (Intelligence) at SA Army Headquarters. In 1970 he was appointed Senior Operations Officer at SWA Command and in May 1974 became Officer Commanding SWA Command with the rank of brigadier. That same year he was transferred back to Army Headquarters to become Chief of Staff Intelligence. Two years later, aged 41, he was made Chief of Army Staff Operations and promoted to major general.

In August 1977 he returned to South West Africa as General Officer Commanding SWA Command, which soon became SWA Territory Force. At the end of 1980, after having directed Operation Sceptic – at the time the largest mechanised infantry operation launched by South African forces since World War II – Geldenhuys returned to Pretoria to take over the position of Chief of the Army from General Constand Viljoen, who had taken over the top SADF slot when Magnus Malan moved into Parliament. In 1985 Geldenhuys took over as Chief of the SADF. He retired on 31 October 1990.

André 'Kat' Liebenberg

Kat Liebenberg was born in Upington in 1938. In 1960 he joined the SADF after completing a law degree at the University of Stellenbosch. In 1969, with the rank of commandant, he was transferred to London as Military Attaché and three years later returned as second-in-command of the Army Gymnasium. In 1977 he took over as Officer Commanding 2 Military Area in South West Africa, which at the time was the nerve centre of the main war against Swapo. In 1980 he became Director of Operations at Army Headquarters, with the rank of brigadier, and two years later, at the age of only 42, was promoted to major general and General Officer Commanding Special Forces, a position he held until 1985, when he was promoted to lieutenant general and appointed Chief of the Army. In 1990 he was appointed Chief of the SADF when he took over from Jannie Geldenhuys. Liebenberg retired in 1993.

He died as a result of prostate cancer in May 1998.

Georg Meiring

Georg Meiring was born in Ladybrand in 1939 and matriculated in 1956. After school he studied mathematics and physics at the University of the Orange Free State, where he obtained an MSc in Physics. In 1963, while already a member of the Citizen Force, he joined the Permanent Force, where he received an immediate commission and was appointed an instructor at the School of Signals with the rank of captain. Shortly thereafter he was chosen to attend a 13-month-long technical officer's course in England. After his return he became Officer Commanding the Defence Headquarters Signals unit. In 1970 he became Officer Commanding Wit Command and was responsible for getting the Joint Management System off the ground. He was then promoted to Chief of Army Staff Logistics, with the rank of major general and 18 months later was made Deputy Chief of the Army. In 1983 he became the General Officer Commanding in SWA, a position he held until 1987 when he returned as Officer Commanding Far North Command. In 1989 he once again became Deputy Chief of the Army and a year later became Chief of the Army, a position held until he got the top slot in the SADF in 1993. In 1994 he was asked by President Nelson Mandela to stay on as Chief of the new SANDF, which he did until his retirement until 1998.

1

THE ROAD TO LUANDA

In 1973, when António de Spinola, a hero in Portugal's colonial wars and one-time governor of Guinea-Bissau, sat down to write a book, he could never have imagined that it would help change the course of world history, affecting millions of lives. He probably figured the worst that could happen would be to be stripped of his military commission and fired from the civil service. But *Portugal and the Future* (*Portugal e o Futuro*) toppled the first domino in a worldwide cascade:

- The Portuguese government fell in a coup and De Spinola became head of state.
- The Soviet Union and the United States become embroiled in a conflict lasting 15 years.
- Around half a million South Africans went to war.
- South Africa became a major armaments producer.
- Thousands of soldiers and civilians died and countless more were maimed and crippled.
- South Africa lost the protectorate of South West Africa (Namibia).
- The destruction of apartheid began, with the eventual handover of power to a black majority government in South Africa.

When *Portugal and the Future* was published in Lisbon on 22 February 1974, the timing for maximum impact was perfect. The country was in political and economic chaos.

Portugal's troubles had started 64 years earlier, in 1910, when the monarchy was toppled in a popular republican revolution. Political, social and economic disasters followed in rapid succession and the country quickly slid into ruin. In the 16 years of the republic's existence it averaged three governments and one revolution per year – 1921, for example, saw seven changes of administration.

In 1926 the country breathed a collective sigh of relief when General António de Fragoso Carmona took power in a military coup. The new military rulers' first order of business was to restore the devastated economy – a task they assigned to Dr António de Oliveira Salazar, a young professor of economics at the University of Coimbra, who had come to prominence after publishing a number of articles. Salazar was appointed Minister of Finance in 1928 and immediately put tough economic policies in place. These, although unpopular with the country's workers, resulted in a budget surplus the following year – the first time that had happened in 15 years.

Over the next few years Salazar repeated this feat and slowly restored Portugal's economic and political self-respect. In 1932 he became Prime Minister, and in 1933 he introduced a new constitution that effectively made him dictator of the country. During the 50 years of his rule, having declared a 'new state', and banning all opposition parties, trade unions and strikes, he tightened control over Portugal's African colonies. This he did by vigorously pursuing a policy of closer integration with the mother country and officially designating the colonies 'overseas provinces'. Salazar encouraged immigration by white settlers and decreed Portuguese the only language taught in colonial schools – a situation that made indigenous populations very unhappy.

In 1961 the Popular Movement for the Liberation of Angola (MPLA) began to launch armed attacks against its colonial masters. Its example was quickly followed in Guinea-Bissau and Mozambique. Salazar was under pressure, and countered by introducing military conscription, calling up thousands of soldiers. But the African wars were unpopular. Ordinary mothers were reluctant to send their sons to die in a faraway country, and, increasingly, conscripts were no longer prepared to be called up for military duty. Over a period of 13 years, 11 000 Portuguese boys died in combat (a figure not considered excessive by military commanders), while 30 000 more were wounded or mutilated and became a constant reminder of a war that seemed unwinnable. Draft-dodging and emigration gathered momentum. In 1973 half of all soldiers called up for military service refused to report. As a result of emigration and conscription, Portugal lost half its labour force. This held back the development of industry and saw large agricultural ventures run to waste. Inflation soared to beyond 30 per cent. Moreover, guerrilla activities in the African colonies prevented the country from properly exploiting their resources.

In 1968 Salazar suffered a stroke and was succeeded by a more liberal professor of law from the University of Coimbra, Marcello Caetano, who immediately introduced cautious reforms. The following year, 'officially approved' opposition candidates were allowed to stand for election, although only educated persons – totalling around 20 per cent of the population – were eligible to vote. The colonies were upgraded from provinces to states and given more autonomy. Angola and Mozambique held their first election ever, open to those who could read and write. But it was too little, too late. The tide of discontent in Portugal could not be turned. In 1972 a group of right-wing army officers tried to stage a coup, but it was nipped in the bud by the secret police, who had a reputation for ruthlessness: there were often reports from the colonies of atrocities, including beheadings, crucifixions and mass executions. It was claimed that, at one time or another, up to 10 per cent of the population had passed through the hands of the secret police. In Lisbon and in other major Portuguese cities, workers were restless and mounted a rash of strikes, many of which resulted in pitched battles with the police. Students demonstrated violently at Lisbon University, the Economics Institute and even the Lisbon Military Academy.

It was against this background that De Spinola's book appeared – and it was to be the straw that broke the camel's back. De Spinola wanted Portugal to form a great 'Community of Lusitania' that would include Brazil. He argued that the country should find a peaceful, safe way to extricate itself from the wars in the colonies, which he believed could not be won. It was a sentiment voraciously adoped by Portugal. On 25 April 1974 a group of junior officers who had formed a grouping called the Movement of the Armed Forces surrounded the presidential headquarters after receiving messages of support from garrisons around the country. Three waves of the Seventh Cavalry were sent against them. The first immediately joined their side, the second did the same after the arrest of its commander, and the third wavered half-heartedly, then capitulated after a few minutes. Then the masses flooded into the streets. Caetano, trapped in his headquarters, agreed to hand over power to his old friend De Spinola, who had been asked by the coup leaders to lead the military junta.

It was the start of a new era for South Africa and her neighbours – but in Pretoria and Washington, it appears, no one saw it coming. 'We had no forewarning whatsoever,' said General Hein du Toit, who was the South African Defence Force's Chief of Staff Intelligence at the time. 'The head of the Bureau of State Security, General Hendrik van den Bergh, said he knew everything [in advance], but I know his stories and I doubt it very much. We were taken completely by surprise.'

The fact is South Africa's intelligence-gathering capabilities at the time were crude and inept. Until 1960 the country relied almost entirely on Britain for its military and state intelligence. The local Military Intelligence section – consisting of one or two officers – focused on counter-intelligence and spent its days attempting to identify subversive elements within Defence Force and Police structures. According to Du Toit, after the election in 1948, when the Nationalists came to power, almost all the intelligence files were destroyed: 'From then until 1960 the British, who ran a huge and very efficient organisation, supplied us with intelligence, although in the later part of the 1950s we got less and less from them,' he said. In 1961, when South Africa declared itself a republic, even that trickle of information dried up. 'The Defence Force was very small at the time,' said Du Toit. 'The most senior officer in the army was in fact the Chief of the Army, a major general. Below him were brigadiers and colonels. At the time the intelligence section consisted of two officers for counter-intelligence and two for normal intelligence.'

In 1963 the Minister of Justice, John Vorster, instructed General Hendrik van den Bergh – called 'Lang Hendrik' by friend and foe alike because he stood six feet five inches in his socks – to set up a national, secret intelligence-gathering organisation. It eventually became known as the Bureau of State Security (Boss). 'Van den Bergh staffed Boss with security policemen who knew a little about internal operations but absolutely nothing about how to work overseas,' Du Toit said.

Vorster and Van den Bergh had a long history and personal ties that stretched back to World War II. Both were members of the Ossewa Brandwag (OB), a pro-Nazi paramilitary organisation that used terrorist tactics to oppose South Africa's siding with the Allies in the war. The British concentration camps of the Anglo-Boer War, in which tens of thousands of Afrikaner women and children died, provided the emotional fuel the organisation needed to foster opposition to the British. The OB wore stormtrooper-style uniforms and adopted the Nazi salute. Both Vorster and Van den Bergh were arrested for their activities during World War II and interned at Koffiefontein, where they spent countless hours discussing common political ideologies and developing what was to become a lifelong friendship. After the war Van den Bergh was well established in elite Afrikaner political circles and, with Vorster's backing, rose rapidly through the ranks until he headed the security police.

In some circles it is believed that Vorster eventually became Prime Minister of South Africa because of Van den Bergh's possible role in the murder of apartheid's chief architect, Prime Minister Hendrik Verwoerd. On 6 September 1966, Verwoerd was stabbed to death in Parliament by parliamentary messenger Dimitri Tsafendas, a prohibited immigrant who had already been ordered to leave the country by the Department of Internal Affairs. It is claimed that the security police had four files on him, and Van den Bergh said he was a self-confessed communist – yet somehow he was still appointed to a permanent position in the Houses of Parliament.

Vorster owed his position as Cabinet minister to the timely death of Prime Minister J.G. Strijdom in 1958. By all accounts, Strijdom did not trust Vorster and would not have appointed him a Cabinet minister. But Verwoerd, Strijdom's successor, had no such qualms. In an attempt to heal the rift that existed between the Ossewa Brandwag and the reunited factions of the National Party, Vorster was appointed Deputy Minister of Education and later Minister of Justice.

By 1966 the government was in the throes of internal bickering and appeared ready to fracture. On 28 August 1966, a little over a week before Verwoerd's killing, the *Sunday Tribune* ran a front-page article under the banner headline: 'Verwoerd must go plan: Cape Nats back Anton Rupert'. Ironically, the article (written by Aida Parker, who later had close links to Van den Bergh) read: 'The knives are out in the National Party … And Dr Verwoerd is the target.' The article must have galvanised Vorster into action. How was Verwoerd to be removed – and how would his own position be affected? It was unthinkable that an NP leader would be removed from power by his own caucus, and yet … the only other solution was to remove him physically. A few days later, in broad daylight and under the nose of the Minister of Justice and the members of Parliament, Tsafendas plunged a knife into the Prime Minister and killed him.

On many occasions in the future, General van den Bergh would declare to the media that Tsafendas had been 'more thoroughly interrogated than any other suspected criminal'. Yet on the very day of the murder Vorster issued a press statement that appeared in *The Star*, saying that, as Minister of Justice, he could categorically state that Tsafendas operated alone and that there were definitely no accomplices. Conspiracy theorists believe that this makes Van den Bergh's supposed interrogation improbable. How could Vorster have known so much about Tsafendas before a proper interrogation was even done? They also point to the fact that the police officer originally involved in the interrogation was suddenly removed by Van den Bergh, who took over the questioning himself. The officer later said that his interrogation indicated that other people could possibly have been involved.

Jaap Marais (leader of the Herstigte Nasionale Party (HNP) – a right-wing grouping that broke away from the National Party, and at the time of Verwoerd's assassination a member of Parliament) – writing in *Die Afrikaner* of 10 September 1999, said: 'Within half an hour of the murder he [Vorster], as Minister of Justice, had reached a firm conclusion about the murder and the killer without the interrogation of the murderer even having started. In this regard it is revealing that Mr P.W. Botha, former State President, said to me during a telephone conversation many years ago: "I don't want to imply anything, but a half hour after the murder a special Cabinet meeting was held and as we entered the room John [Vorster] was next to me and he said to me: 'This was one man's job.' During the course of the conversation Mr Botha also said he agreed with me that there was a conspiracy to kill Dr Verwoerd. Mr Vorster did not only share his views with Mr Botha. That same afternoon he issued an official statement to the press that on 7 September 1966 was published in *The Star* under the headline: "No sign of assassination plot. This was the work of a lone killer, says Vorster."'

The mystery deepened on 11 September 1966 when *Beeld* (then a Sunday newspaper) reported that Van den Bergh, in response to a phone call from the newspaper on the day of the assassination, had a file about Tsafendas on his desk within minutes. Vorster, a short while later, on information supposedly supplied by Van den Bergh, issued a statement to the press announcing: 'The report that the Security Police have a file on Tsafendas is devoid of all truth.' However, it is claimed by right-wing Afrikaner sources, mainly within the HNP, that the Security Police in fact had four files on Tsafendas before the assassination. Two were apparently destroyed without authorisation. A third was found in a filing section marked 'dead files' and the fourth was missing. They believe the latter was the file 'Lang Hendrik' had in front of him when telephoned by *Beeld*.

Whether or not the two former Koffiefontein inmates were actively involved in the assassination of Dr Verwoerd is a question that will probably never be answered. Van den Bergh once told a government commission investigating covert operations: 'I have enough men to commit murder if I tell them to kill. I don't care who the prey is. These are the type of men I have.' Certainly, if his network of spies was as good as he claimed and if Tsafendas was indeed a known, self-confessed communist, Van den Bergh would have kept him under close scrutiny. If that was the case, then Vorster and Van den Bergh certainly appear to have had something to do with Verwoerd's killing – even if it was just that they did nothing to prevent it.

After Vorster became Prime Minister, he and Van den Bergh moved swiftly to consolidate their power base. They set up structures to control and manipulate all intelligence operations. At that stage General Hein du Toit was Deputy Chief of Military Intelligence: 'There were a lot of problems between us and Boss,' he said. 'The problems boiled down to the areas each organisation had to cover, particularly overseas. Neither one nor the other knew anything about intelligence, so each was feeling its way. The conflict was about who had to do what.'

Van den Bergh's style was bound to upset the military men, and did so. General Magnus Malan, at the time Chief of the SADF, kept him at arm's length: 'Boss tried to get me involved once. It was at the time of the Soweto uprising. Jimmy Kruger [then Minister of Police] was given the task of sorting it out. We formed a committee consisting of representatives of the Defence Force, the Police, Boss and the Department of Education. It was chaired by "Lang Hendrik". Once or twice he invited me to join him at his private mess facilities in his building in Pretoria. He was trying to arrange closer co-operation between him and me. But I avoided him, make no mistake about that. I knew his history. He was a typical security man from the police and I didn't trust him!' Du Toit was less restrained in his opinion: 'I got to know Van den Bergh well when I was on the Central Intelligence Committee,' he said. 'He was the last man who should have been involved with intelligence. He was a sort of pathological liar. One day he'd say one thing and the next deny it. He was definitely the power behind the throne in the Vorster era.'

Du Toit did not have a very high opinion of Vorster as a statesman either: 'He never looked at what was right or wrong for the country. He looked at what suited him and his friends.' Malan's opinion of Vorster was not much better. 'In the Vorster era there was no co-operation between ministers at all. At Cabinet meetings the junior minister would take notes and when the meeting was done he'd hand them to the Prime Minister, who then locked them away in his safe. The result was, two ministers would walk out of a Cabinet meeting interpreting what had to be done in completely opposite ways. A perfect example was when the Department of Trade and Industry issued permits allowing meat to be exported to the Cubans we were fighting in Angola. There was no common strategy in Vorster's time.'

But if 'Lang Hendrik' knew he was not liked by his military counterparts in

South Africa, he refused to allow that to stand in the way of his efforts to consolidate power. In 1968 he declared that all intelligence-gathering operations would in future fall under his control. 'We sat in the Union Buildings behind green double doors,' Du Toit remembers. 'It was all very hush-hush. One day, in 1968, Van den Bergh walked in and told us he was taking over Military Intelligence. I knew Van den Bergh and definitely didn't want to work for him, so I was able to make a case that intelligence and counter-intelligence should be separated. This was done and I was appointed the Chief of Counter Intelligence with the rank of brigadier. But the situation was intolerable. You can't remove intelligence from its mother organisation.'

In April 1969 Vorster appointed the Potgieter Commission to investigate the matter. 'It wasn't an independent commission, so its findings were a foregone conclusion,' Du Toit said. 'Van den Bergh would take over intelligence – and the report was written as such. When the legislation had to be compiled we battled in every way possible to get it rectified, because Van den Bergh had some very eccentric ideas. Whenever people disagreed with him he would go into a huff and retreat to his pig farm where he sat and sulked. So when the law was compiled, much of the time he wasn't available, and so the writers came back to me.'

The legislation was structured in such a way that all intelligence had to pass through Boss, but contained clauses that allowed Military Intelligence to operate externally in the event of a war. To intelligence professionals it was a hopeless situation. If they were to be successful they needed to set up the networks long before any war broke out. 'When the coup took place in Portugal we found ourselves in a situation where the new government said it was discarding the colonies,' complained Du Toit. 'Suddenly we had no more contacts in Angola. We tried to make contact with all three liberation organisations through our military attaché in Luanda. The MPLA refused to meet him. In the meantime Boss kept telling us not to get involved in external affairs – and the quality of their people gathering information was terrible. They had no background or training. They were policemen used to working with informers. They had no idea how to deal with people overseas.'

While Military Intelligence locked horns with Van den Bergh and his henchmen, all was not well within the SADF itself. Commanders squabbled and disagreed with each other, and each arm of the service effectively went its own way. 'I wasn't the greatest of friends with General du Toit, the Chief of Staff Intelligence, at that stage,' said Magnus Malan. 'He wasn't a team man – and I believe if you're a part of the military you've got to be. You've got to operate together and there should be no secrecy amongst us. He was a loner; he was not part of the team. At the time we had no common objective within the Defence Force. Before 1961 Britain told us exactly what to do. After that we were on our own and there was a lack of leadership needed to define the objectives and say where we should go.'

But it was not only the SADF and Boss that were at loggerheads; the police and the military weren't the best of friends either. 'We [the SADF] resented it when Vorster, under pressure from Van den Bergh, used the police in Rhodesia,' said General Constand Viljoen, at that time a major general on the staff of the Chief of the SADF. 'We felt it was a military task. Then the situation arose in South West Africa and we knew the police would not have the capacity to do the job. We wanted to do it. I wanted to give my people the experience of fighting that kind of war because we all knew it was going to come South Africa's way. The problems started with the police force as long ago as the Police Brigade in World War II. They always liked the idea of military involvement because it was more exciting and adventurous. We thought they were trespassing on our terrain. I believe it was because of their involvement in Rhodesia that the police became a type of militia using crude methods not within the principles of the Geneva Convention or the principles of a just war.'

Malan also had his problems with the men in blue. 'It was very difficult when [Mike] Geldenhuys became the Commissioner of Police,' he said. 'He was really *hardegat* [hard-assed]. His feeling was: what did we [the SADF] know? We were just weekend soldiers. The police would see everything right. The situation was so bad that when P.W. Botha became Prime Minister he asked me, as Chief of the SADF, to go and see Louis le Grange, the Minister of Police, so the situation could be settled – so we could come to finality and say: "This is the responsibility of the police and this is the responsibility of the SADF." I went down to Saldanha for a week to isolate myself so I could gather my thoughts. Then I went to see Le Grange on my own. We had a three-day meeting. There I was on my own, and every day he called in five police generals. We ended up having one of the biggest fights I've ever had in my life. At the end I walked out. I reported back to P.W. Botha. I handed him a piece of paper suggesting what should be done. When he asked: "Can't you two sort it out?" I replied: "No, I'm afraid not."'

Often within the SADF itself, the left hand often did not know what the right hand was up to. At a youth congress in Outjo, Namibia, on 1 July 1975, the commander of the SADF in South West Africa, Brigadier Dirk Marais, told assembled delegates that between 2 000 and 3 000 exiles from the South West African People's Organisation (Swapo) were being trained in Angola and that 500 of them were already fully trained and ready to be deployed. His speech was picked up by a local journalist and subsequently run in the South African media. 'Though what I said was absolutely true – and was soon proved to be so – it almost cost me my job,' said Marais, who eventually ended up Deputy Chief of the Army before retiring in 1987. 'I got a harshly worded telex from the Chief of the Army, General Malan. Apparently the information I had given was news to P.W. Botha and he wanted to know why he hadn't been informed. The people in Defence Headquarters told P.W. what I'd said wasn't true.'

Marais was summoned to Pretoria to explain. 'Magnus Malan was understanding but embarrassed,' he said. 'But the Acting Chief of the Defence Force, General R.F. Armstrong, wanted to have me removed from my post.' The incident was typical of the SADF's ham-fisted handling of the media. After Marais's statements appeared in the newspapers, the SADF communications section set about trying to defuse the situation. In a report in the *Rand Daily Mail* dated 3 July 1975, the military authorities admitted it was true there were armed Swapo exiles being trained in Angola, but that it was wrong of Brigadier Marais to say so.

'Brigadier Marais said the wrong thing at the wrong time,' an unnamed Defence Force spokesman told the *Rand Daily Mail* after General Armstrong had denied that there was a significant build-up of trained terrorists in Angola. 'We don't want to say that Brigadier Marais's figures are not correct. But at the same time we don't want to be specific about numbers of this kind. We don't want to build up an alarmist psychosis, particularly at this time of détente,' said Brigadier Cyrus Smith, chief spokesman for the Defence Force. When asked by Bob Hitchcock, *Rand Daily Mail* military correspondent, if that meant Marais's figures were inaccurate, Smith replied: 'No, not at all. Though we have no knowledge they are accurate.'

A year had passed since the Portuguese coup, but South African intelligence capabilities were clearly no quicker off the mark than they had been in 1974.

In Washington things weren't much better. According to John Stockwell, former Chief of the Angola Task Force set up by the American Central Intelligence Agency (CIA), the head of the CIA station in Kinshasa sent him a note in a classified pouch advising that the agency wasn't interested in Angolan revolutionary movements. This was after Stockwell visited a training camp for the National Front for the Liberation of Angola (FNLA) in the north of the country and wrote a report detailing his observations and findings. In his book *In Search of Enemies*, he wrote that the Kinshasa chief felt 'that my visit was unfortunate because it could have been misconstrued. We didn't support the black fighters and we didn't want our Nato ally, Portugal, picking up reports that we were visiting Angolan rebel base camps.'

For years the Portuguese had claimed success in integrating their black subjects into a colonial society they claimed was free of racial barriers. The truth turned out to be somewhat different, but the CIA bought the Portuguese version without question. 'In the clandestine services of the CIA, we were inclined to accept the claims of a racially open-minded society in Angola, and it was tacitly agreed that communist agitation was largely responsible for the blacks' continued resistance to Portuguese rule,' wrote Stockwell. 'The reason was basic. Essentially a conservative organisation, the CIA maintains secret liaison with local security services wherever it operates. Its stations are universally part of the official communities of the host countries. Case officers live comfortable lives among the economic elite; even "outside" or "deep cover" case officers are part of that elite. They become conditioned to the mentality of the authoritarian figures, the police chiefs with whom they work and socialise, and eventually share their resentment of revolutionaries who threaten the status quo. They are ill at ease with democracies and popular movements who are too fickle and hard to predict.' But even if the feelings within the spy organisation had been different, Portugal held the ace in the pack – the Azores air bases, which refuelled up to 40 US Air Force transport planes per day.

'The April 1974 coup in Portugal caught the United States by surprise, without graceful policy alternatives and out of contact with the African Revolutionaries,' the Pike Committee reported to the US Congress in January 1976 in its study of CIA failures. According to Stockwell, the CIA had not had coverage inside Angola from the late 1960s until 1975. 'An official CIA station is opened only with the approval of the State Department, generally under the cover of a United States embassy or consulate. Only in rare instances is the CIA station truly unknown to the host government. Hence, in deference to Portuguese sensibilities, the subject of reopening the Luanda station was inevitably vetoed whenever it arose. Only in March 1975, when the Portuguese were finally disengaging and losing control did we finally reopen the Luanda station.'

It was against this background – underqualified intelligence services that were in disarray, interdepartmental squabbling, a defence force that lacked common objectives and a government content to muddle its way from one crisis to another – that South Africa became involved in Angola. Prior to this, South Africa had given only small-scale military aid to the Portuguese: intelligence was shared and

South African Air Force helicopters and planes were used on occasion to ferry Portuguese troops during counter-insurgency operations.

Three rebel groups fought the Portuguese in Angola. The MPLA (*Movimento Popular de Libertação de Angola*) was founded in December 1956 at a secret meeting of anti-imperialist groupings in Luanda. It believed Portuguese imperialism could not be removed without resorting to arms and a revolutionary struggle. In 1959 its first leader and the major driving force behind the organisation, Illido Macho, a postal worker, was arrested. The MPLA would have died at that stage if it had not been for a small group of well-educated exiles who continued to promote its cause overseas. One of these men, Dr Agostinho Neto, was later to become its leader.

Neto, a member of the Mbundu tribe, was born in 1922 in a village near Luanda. When he completed his schooling he worked as personal secretary to the Methodist bishop, before joining the Department of Health. A bursary from the church allowed him to study medicine at universities in Portugal, where he become involved in Marxist, anti-Salazar organisations. From 1952 to 1957 he was arrested a number of times, yet managed to complete his studies and qualify as a medical doctor in 1958, after which he and his Portuguese wife returned to Angola and opened a medical practice in Luanda. Almost immediately he began to play an important role in the leadership of the MPLA. This brought him to the attention of the authorities and resulted in his arrest in 1960. In his home village of Catete a protest calling for his release ended in bloodshed, which left 30 dead and about 200 injured.

Neto was appointed honorary president of the MPLA around this time. The Portuguese government realised they had a major problem on their hands with this political icon and sent him into exile on the Cape Verde Islands, where he spent a year before being transferred to Lisbon and locked up in solitary confinement for six months. He was then placed under house arrest. In 1962 he escaped and turned up in Kinshasa at the MPLA headquarters. In December that year he was elected president of the organisation. After an unsuccessful attempt to unite the MPLA and the FNLA in 1963, Neto and his organisation were expelled from Kinshasa and set up headquarters across the Congo River in Brazzaville. From 1961 onwards MPLA recruits received military training in Ghana, Morocco and Algeria. Weapons were supplied by a variety of Eastern European countries as well as the Soviet Union. In 1964 Neto persuaded Zambia to allow the MPLA to establish military bases in that country.

The FNLA (*Frente Nacional Libertação de Angola*) drew support from Bakongo refugees, whose number had steadily grown in Zaire. In 1960 Holden Roberto became its leader. Roberto was born in 1923 in São Salvadore, Angola. In 1925 he moved to Kinshasa and attended the Baptist mission school, from where he graduated in 1940. For eight years he worked as an accountant for the Belgian colonial authorities in the Congo. In 1951, during a visit to Angola, he watched in horror as Portuguese officials beat an old man for a minor misdemeanour. This incident galvanised him into political activism. In 1958 he was elected to represent the *União das Populações de Angola* (UPA) at the All-African People's Conference in Ghana. He had to make his way there clandestinely because blacks in the Belgian and Portuguese colonies could not obtain passports. At the conference he met many of Africa's future leaders, including Patrice Lumumba, Kenneth Kaunda and Tom Mboya. Before returning home he obtained a Guinean passport and visited the United Nations, where he was able to arrange a debate on Angola. Back home in Kinshasa, he organised Bakongo revolutionary activities and took credit for the March 1961 offensive in Angola. He succeeded in drawing in the Ovimbundu activist Jonas Savimbi as his foreign minister and cemented his relationship with Zairian strongman Mobutu Sese Seko by divorcing his wife and marrying Mobutu's sister-in-law.

Roberto steadfastly spurned Agostinho Neto's efforts to form a unified organisation of Angolan revolutionary movements. He feared that the better organised and educated MPLA would ultimately swallow the FNLA. In fact, he did all in his power to prevent the organisations from drawing closer together – by regularly having his forces capture MPLA activists in northern Angola, then transport them to Kinshasa where they were brutally killed. While Neto and the MPLA drew support from the East, Roberto turned to the West, claiming to be anti-communist. In truth, he and Neto preached the same things for Angola: national independence, land reform, democratic government, the destruction of colonial culture, etc. His organisation was far more brutal than the MPLA, but the United States, eager to develop anti-Soviet allies in Africa, supplied the FNLA with weapons and financial support.

Jonas Malheiro Savimbi was born in 1934 to a prominent Ovimbundu family in Moxico. His initial schooling was at Protestant missionary schools in the area; in 1958, as a result of a bursary from the United Church of Christ, he went to Lisbon to continue his studies. Two years later he left and went to Switzerland, where he obtained a doctorate in government sciences at the University of Lausanne. In 1961 he joined Holden Roberto, but broke from him three years later before attempting to join the MPLA, which in turn wanted nothing to do with him. This led to the formation of his own organisation, Unita (*União Nacional para a Independência Total de Angola*) in March 1966 in the Moxico district. Soon after, a small number of Unita leaders were sent to China for military training, and the organisation received a small quantity of arms from that country. President Kaunda of Zambia was friendly towards Unita and allowed it to open an office in Lusaka, which enabled Savimbi to import weapons and permitted the easy passage of recruits.

On Christmas Day 1966 Unita launched its first armed attack in Angola, when around 250 poorly armed supporters attacked the border town of Texeira de Sousa. They were easily repelled and suffered heavy losses. From that point on, Unita began moving into the south-eastern corner of Angola, an area in which the MPLA was already active. Unita was eventually expelled from Zambia when Kaunda became angered by its continual sabotaging of the Benguela railway line – a vital transport link he needed to export his country's copper. Savimbi's organisation had put Kaunda in the embarrassing position of having to route his exports through Rhodesia and South Africa at considerably inflated prices.

For a while Savimbi lived in Cairo, where he continued to foster relations with China and North Korea. On his return he took command of the Unita forces operating in south-eastern Angola, clashing violently with the MPLA. According to intelligence reports, MPLA military commanders in the area were instructed to first rid the zone of Unita, before engaging the Portuguese. The ill-trained, ill-equipped Unita forces were no match for the MPLA and were soon forced to withdraw to areas in the centre of the country. Initially Unita gave active support to Swapo guerrillas attempting to infiltrate South West Africa and even became engaged in sporadic firefights with the SADF.

Many theories have been advanced as to why South Africa sent troops to Angola. Defence Minister P.W. Botha, in a speech to Parliament more than a year after the event, said it was as a result of a situation that developed from local conditions. South Africa had to protect itself and its investments from communist aggression and attacks from Swapo guerrillas, who were concentrated in Southern Angola. (At the time the South African government was becoming increasingly concerned about terrorist infiltration into South West Africa.) Cuba's representative to the United Nations saw it differently. In a speech to the General Assembly, he said that South Africa entered Angola 'with the clear intention of preventing the independence of that country and of occupying the entire territory'. Other political observers believed South Africa saw it as an opportunity to exploit Angola's minerals and the Ruacana/Calueque hydro-electric scheme. They believed the threat of approaching communism was merely a convenient excuse.

Certainly, the South African government took a strongly anti-communist stand. The Soviet Union was arming the MPLA on a large scale, and Cuban soldiers had been brought in to participate in the conflict. In addition, South Africa wished to neutralise the Swapo concentrations in southern Angola. South Africa was concerned that, unlike in Mozambique, a government less hostile to South Africa should be established. It was vital to react before the election scheduled for 11 November 1975 so that the two pro-West liberation movements, the FNLA and Unita, could gain a favourable negotiating position against the MPLA. According to a memorandum in the military archives, the situation lent itself to a limited offensive, and a clandestine lightning strike against the MPLA could force it onto the defensive – so much so that it would welcome a political solution with its opponents, and might even be completely destroyed. There was also a fear that, with the failure of 'friendly' black states and Western countries to react quickly, the FNLA and Unita could be eliminated before Western aid arrived.

While all of the above points were considered valid by military strategists, the reason South Africa became involved in the internal affairs of Angola was a whole lot simpler: Zambia, Zaire and Unita asked for help. 'I got the impression from P.W. Botha and Vorster that they saw the request from black Africa as the sign of a breakthrough,' said General Viljoen. 'It was a very important development because, ever since we'd been involved with the Rhodesian situation, and because of the assistance we gave to the Portuguese in Mozambique and Angola, it had become clear to us in the military that the real issue for us would be to become part of Africa. The opinion-makers regarded this as a breakthrough. South Africa was starting to side with black Africa instead of the colonial powers. This was perhaps the most important reason for participating in the whole effort, apart from the idea of combating communism.'

As the white buffer countries around South Africa began to look increasingly vulnerable after the Portuguese coup, Vorster changed strategy and made friendly overtures to black Africa. In a speech to the South African Senate on 23 October 1974, he said: 'Africa has been good to us and we are prepared, as far as it is within our capabilities, to give back to Africa. If asked, South Africa is prepared to play its part in contributing to order, development and financial assistance to countries in Africa, particularly those who are prepared to stand closer to South Africa in a spirit of give and take.' Two days later, President Kaunda of

Zambia, in a speech at the University of Zambia, responded: 'This, I daresay, is the voice of reason for which Africa and the rest of the world has waited.'

In the months that followed, Vorster undertook secret visits to the Ivory Coast, Senegal and Gabon, where he consulted with the leaders of those countries. He also visited Liberia, Botswana and Malawi, and made sure his emissaries kept the Organisation of African Unity (OAU) informed. But in April 1975 his détente policies suffered a setback. At the OAU ministerial summit held in Dar es Salaam on 7 April, Zambia, Tanzania, Mozambique and Botswana were criticised for supporting South Africa's détente policies. Instead, a resolution, known as the Dar es Salaam Declaration, was adopted. It called for the establishment of majority governments in Rhodesia and South West Africa as well as the dismantling of apartheid in South Africa. It was a setback that left the South African government reeling and keen to do anything to win favour with black Africa. A few months later Vorster and Kaunda met on a train on the rail bridge near Victoria Falls. The event was well publicised but in the end proved to be little more than a public relations coup for South Africa.

When Jonas Savimbi asked for help as early as 1974, many in government were keen to assist. 'Savimbi's request for help came through Boss channels,' said General du Toit. 'But Boss chief "Lang Hendrik" van den Bergh was fiercely opposed to our giving aid to the Angolan rebel movements or being involved in the country at all. He thought it was completely wrong and never believed South Africa should become involved in any military conflict outside our borders. In my opinion he was wrong. We couldn't just ignore people across our border. We needed to influence people who were on our side and we tried to gain influence with all three Angolan organisations. But Van den Bergh opposed us strongly. He tried to sabotage everything we tried to do there. He did so by not passing on intelligence and by arranging for the enemy to get information about what we were doing.' But Vorster, largely at the urging of Minister of Defence P.W. Botha, was determined at least to explore the available options. 'I flew to Angola to see Savimbi,' said Du Toit. 'I think I was the first South African military person to meet him. We met in Silva Porto and developed a good relationship. He struck me as an extremely intelligent man. He spoke five languages – his own indigenous language, Portuguese, French, English and German. I saw him again in Europe but with great difficulty because Van den Bergh told him if he had any contact with me he would see to it Unita got no aid from South Africa.'

Savimbi told Du Toit the MPLA was supported by the communist bloc and that Holden Roberto, leader of the FNLA, while not a communist, would become a military dictator. Savimbi claimed to support democracy and said he believed Unita would win a majority in the upcoming Angolan election that was planned for 11 November 1975, but he felt sure his opponents would refuse to lay down their arms after the ballot. Savimbi felt Unita needed a well-armed and well-trained army of around 30 000 men. He also said Zambia would support South African military action in Angola – if it was kept secret. Despite Van den Bergh's protests, Military Intelligence believed the goodwill of Unita should be preserved and got P.W. Botha to use his influence with Vorster, who gave permission for a small quantity of weapons to be supplied to Savimbi's troops. On 9 October 1974, 10 × 9 mm machine carbines, 50 × 9 mm pistols and 6 000 rounds of ammunition were handed over to Unita representatives at Rundu. In December 1974 Colonel Ian Gleeson visited Luanda and returned with the recommendation that more clandestine assistance be given to Unita, particularly food and clothes.

Three months later, on 12 February 1975, General du Toit and Colonel Gleeson once again met Savimbi, this time in Luso, inside Angola. Apart from establishing the guerrilla leader's shopping list, they wanted to know more about his political ideology and his intentions as regards Angola's future relationship with South Africa. Savimbi told them he wanted whites to remain in Angola, as either Portuguese or Angolan citizens, and after vigorous questioning about his feelings towards Swapo and South Africa said he supported dialogue and peaceful existence with neighbouring states. As for Swapo, he admitted Unita had worked with them for years but didn't think co-operation with them was appropriate any longer – he wanted to concentrate all his efforts on winning the forthcoming election. It was exactly the kind of talk the South African government wanted to hear: the supply of more weapons and logistical supplies to Unita was approved. A week later 402 × 9 mm pistols, 95 000 rounds of ammunition and US$200 000 were delivered.

Though Van den Bergh opposed the policy, he was determined not to be left out of the action. On 17 and 18 April 1975 Boss representatives met Savimbi in Gaborone; on 22 April they saw him in London; and two days later they met him in Paris. At these meetings the Unita leader promised to prevent Swapo attacks. He said there were approximately 250 Swapo guerrillas near Unita bases in southern Angola but that he'd had them disarmed. He asked Boss to supply him with light weapons for 8 000 men and a radio transmitter that would be sited at Nova Lisboa (now Huambo) so he could broadcast election propaganda. He also wanted financial assistance and help in setting up a political organisation. Because of his détente programme Vorster turned down the request.

Two months earlier, on 28 February 1975, an FNLA representative had arrived at the South African embassy in London with a request for weapons. Roberto wanted the South Africans to give him 40 to 50 light artillery pieces and heavy infantry weapons. The government and the Department of Foreign Affairs investigated the appeal but did nothing about it. The FNLA, however, was already receiving assistance from the CIA. According to John Stockwell, former Chief of the CIA's Angola Task Force, US Secretary of State Henry Kissinger saw the conflict in Angola solely in terms of global politics. The United States had only recently been forced into a humiliating withdrawal from Vietnam, and Kissinger was still smarting and looking for a way to regain US credibility on the global stage. 'He was determined the Soviets should not be permitted to make a move in any remote part of the world without being confronted militarily by the US,' wrote Stockwell.

Superficially, Kissinger's opposition to the Soviet presence was being rationalised in terms of Angola's strategic location on the South Atlantic, near the shipping lanes of the giant tankers which bring oil from the Middle East around Africa to the United States. 'The argument was weak,' wrote Stockwell. 'Soviet bases in Somalia posed a greater threat. Angola was of little importance to the US beyond the small amounts of coffee it sold and the small amounts of petroleum Gulf Oil pumped in Cabinda. Kissinger, it was believed, was frustrated by the US humiliation in Vietnam and wanted to find a way to confront the Soviets. He overruled advisors who preferred to find a diplomatic solution in Angola.'

At about the same time the CIA was desperate to re-establish good ties with Zairian President Mobutu Sese Seko. Despite Western investment in Zaire to the tune of US$700 million, the country's economy was a shambles, largely as a result of the corruption of the ruling political elite and tumbling world copper prices. The conflict in Angola had closed the Benguela railway line, forcing Zairian products to be exported through Zambia, Rhodesia and South Africa. As the man in the street in Kinshasa grew increasingly discontented, Mobutu desperately sought a scapegoat. The Americans were the obvious target. In June 1975, after accusing them of fomenting a coup, he expelled the US ambassador and arrested most of the CIA's Zairian agents. They were speedily tried and held in prison under sentence of death.

The CIA found a way to please Kissinger and Mobutu and arm Angola at the same time. Officially the US observed the arms embargo that prevented weapons from being supplied to any of the Angolan factions. However, the CIA circumvented this snag by arranging for Zaire to supply armaments to the FNLA and then simply replenished Mobutu's stocks. 'It was believed we could contain diplomatic fallout that way,' wrote Stockwell, 'but we believed we would be accused of escalating the Angolan conflict if we supplied weapons to the pro-West factions.' On 27 June 1975 the first planeload of American weapons left South Carolina for Kinshasa. It was to be the first of many shipments, but it was a drop in the ocean when compared with the armaments the Soviet bloc was supplying to the MPLA.

2

OPERATION SAVANNAH

South Africa and the superpowers were primed and ready for war. For Vorster's government all that was needed was a legitimate excuse. This wasn't long in coming, although from an unlikely source: South Africa crossed the Angolan border to check aggression from Unita when it began to harass workers and personnel at the Ruacana/Calueque hydro-electric scheme.

Ruacana Falls on the Kunene River is ranked in the top ten of the world's great waterfalls. From the earliest days of South Africa's occupation of Namibia, the potential of developing a hydro-electric plant at the falls was recognised. In 1969 the governments of Portugal and South Africa signed an agreement to develop the system. It was to be a huge undertaking: by 1979 the South African government had ploughed R261 million into it. To ensure a constant water supply to the Kunene, particularly in the dry winter months, it was decided to build storage dams higher up on the river. One of them was a huge dam built at Calueque, about 20 km north-east of Ruacana, inside Angola. This would provide a constant flow of water to the pump station and an important water supply to Ovamboland in Namibia. All this construction was done in Angola, but the hydro-electric plant itself, apart from a 1 500-metre water supply tunnel, was located in Namibia.

By 1974 work on the Ruacana/Calueque scheme was in full swing, with companies and personnel from Italy, Sweden, Britain, South Africa, Turkey, Greece and Portugal. But Swapo soon identified the project as a prime military target and told workers to quit or face being killed. When Portugal withdrew its soldiers after the Lisbon coup, the construction and operational staff became nervous and were only placated when the SADF promised protection. However, as the situation in Angola deteriorated, not only Swapo but also Unita began acts of intimidation. White neighbourhoods in Calueque and Ruacana grew jittery as they increasingly believed they would be attacked. Their fears only increased when a group of MPLA soldiers visited the district.

By 1975 the pump station at Calueque was operational and pumping six cubic metres of water per second to Ovamboland through a 300 km network of canals. On 8 August 1975, Unita soldiers chased a Portuguese work crew from the area. The workers fled across the border and sought refuge with the South African Police in Namibia. At Calueque many workers refused to return to work. The pumps and the water supply to Ovamboland were switched off. The day before, 10 South African employees on their way home were held up by Unita soldiers and robbed of money and cigarettes. They too refused to return to work, unless the SADF could guarantee their safety. The remaining pump operators also downed tools.

It was the incident Vorster and his government were waiting for. After an inspection of the project and surrounding district, the SADF decided to occupy the area. On Saturday 9 August an infantry platoon, supported by two armoured cars, arrived at Calueque and put to flight all three Angolan movements in the town. Two hours later an infantry company, a Panzer car troop and medical elements joined the advance party, and the following day they set about securing the area. The occupation was kept secret from the South African press corps but was widely reported in Portugal and appeared in other publications in Europe. A few days later the Portuguese ambassador in Pretoria was briefed and P.W. Botha flew to Ruacana and Calueque. At later meetings with Portuguese government representatives, the South African government said it was prepared to withdraw if Portugal undertook to take over the protection of the scheme and would guarantee the safety of the project and its personnel after the election on 11 November 1975. It was not something Lisbon or Luanda could do and the Portuguese High Commissioner asked South Africa to continue protecting the area until 11 November and then negotiate with the election winner.

It was all the justification the South African government needed. 'Let me put that straight,' said General Viljoen, who was Director of Operations at the time. 'That was used in order to explain the presence of South Africa in Angola. It is true South African involvement in the scheme was big and it's true Ovamboland was very dependent on the water, and South West Africa on the electricity, but I must be honest, I always got the impression it was a handy way of explaining an operation that didn't have the intention of protecting Calueque and Ruacana. It was a handy explanation to use to the rest of the world.'

Shortly before the South African occupation of Ruacana, Vorster decided that haphazard aid to Unita was not suitable. He ordered the SADF to make a proper study of the assistance requirements of the pro-West movements in Angola. On 4 July 1975 Constand Viljoen and Gert Rothman of Boss flew to Kinshasa to meet with Savimbi, Roberto and Mobutu. 'I remember that visit well,' said General Malan, 'because Constand and Rothman had to sleep on a double bed together and they weren't the best of friends.' It was the first time Viljoen met Mobutu Sese Seko. 'He was a very kind person but always seemed to be extremely busy,' Viljoen said. 'When I saw him in his office he had three or four telephones, one on his lap and others on his desk. He'd be in the middle of discussing something with us when a telephone would ring so he'd stop, answer it in French then put it down and carry on with the discussions until another phone rang. I got the impression he was a great centralist who liked organising things right from his desk. And whether we liked it or not he was a key man in Zaire. During his reign – sometimes using methods that were not acceptable – he had more order and stability than there is now.'

The list of requirements from the FNLA was long. They wanted heavy weapons, armoured cars, missiles, landmines and ammunition. Unita, on the other hand, wanted rifles, pistols, uniforms, two-way radios and a 100-kilowatt radio transmitter. 'Back in Pretoria we discussed the requests,' said Viljoen. 'It was clear they felt threatened by the possibility of the MPLA joining forces with the communist bloc.' In the end Viljoen recommended that the following weapons be supplied to the two movements: rifles, machine guns, pistols, 60 mm and 81 mm mortars, rocket launchers, ammunition, landmines, hand grenades, plastic explosives, vehicles, radios, light and medium helicopters, armoured cars and a radio transmitter for Unita. He excluded Roberto's request for cannons on the grounds that they were too expensive. It was decided to try to keep the costs to under R20 million and that all weapons and supplies should be bought outside the country so as not to affect South Africa's own stocks and to maintain secrecy.

'Lang Hendrik' approved Viljoen's list, except for the helicopters, which he felt were too expensive and vulnerable to being shot down by the MPLA's SAM-7 missiles. All that was left was to get final approval from Vorster, who at the time was on a hunting trip at Klippan in the Western Transvaal. Van den Bergh, acting Chief of the Defence Force General R.F. Armstrong and Brand Fourie, Secretary of

Foreign Affairs, flew in a helicopter to the farm to see Vorster, who gave permission for R20 million to be spent. Within two days the Boss chief was overseas on a weapons-buying spree. On 17 July he sent a telegram saying he had managed to purchase all the weapons needed; that at that moment they were being packed and a ship was standing by, ready to transport them to their destination. In August the first consignments arrived at Matadi in Zaire and were quickly transported to Kinshasa, from where they were further distributed with the co-operation of the CIA. 'Contact with the CIA was always through Boss,' said General Viljoen. 'Our Defence Force was never directly involved with the CIA, except in cases when I was personally present, when American C-5A and C-141 aircraft were unloaded at the Kinshasa airbase at night. We usually had our own C-130 aircraft there. After the big aircraft discharged their cargo we delivered the weapons to bases in Angola.'

There is no doubt 'Lang Hendrik' van den Bergh had extensive contacts with the CIA. 'They manipulated him just as they liked,' said General Hein du Toit, then Chief of Staff Intelligence. 'He was thrilled to be seen by them as being so important. If his pigs got sick then two days later a plane would arrive from America with new inoculations. He bragged about that a lot. After he'd left [Boss] one of the senior people in the organisation told me he'd had a meeting with CIA representatives who said they'd always had such good relations with Van den Bergh and hoped that relationship would continue now that he'd left. "We know that," the man said, "that's why we never told him anything important."'

In October 1975 alone, 1,6 million litres of petrol was delivered to Zaire – this at a time when South Africans faced heavy fines if caught storing more than 20 litres of fuel and when petrol stations closed early in the evenings and over weekends because of fuel shortages! 'Weapons were being delivered to Unita and FNLA,' said General Viljoen, 'but it was obvious they needed to be trained how to use them. I discussed the situation with Vorster and P.W. Botha and it was decided I should go inside Angola to discuss and study the military situation in detail. I saw Savimbi in Nova Lisboa and Roberto in Ambriz. My main finding was that we were dealing with liberation movements who followed the philosophy of "fight and run away to live to fight another day". They were very experienced in guerrilla hit-and-run tactics, but it was clear they'd have to be retrained into a semi-conventional role if they were going to defend the areas they already held. What was happening was the MPLA would attack a town like Nova Lisboa, for example, and the Unita guerrillas would simply run away, because that's what they were trained to do. In this way they lost influence in their own areas. It was clear to me the MPLA and Cubans were gradually occupying the whole of Angola.' (General du Toit, however, denies that South Africa even knew Cuba was sending troops to Angola at that stage.)

P.W. Botha visited the border area and ordered that additional help be given to the FNLA to counter gains made by the MPLA forces. Plans were drawn up at Defence Headquarters, and under the code name Operation Savannah – a name that later covered all the operations in Angola – 525 machine guns, 1,1 million rounds of ammunition, 25 × 60 mm mortars with 5 000 mortar bombs were delivered to Roberto's forces. To ensure that the weapons were effectively used Commandant D.J. (Jan) Breytenbach, founder of 1 Reconnaissance Commando, was given the job of organising and setting up training for the FNLA. 'We were not told by P.W. Botha or Vorster to attack Angola,' said General Viljoen. 'The request put to us by Savimbi and Roberto was to enable them to remain forces of influence in Angola until the Organisation of African Unity meeting scheduled to take place after the elections. The goal was that, by 11 November, Unita would control their part of Angola, the MPLA would be in control of theirs and the FNLA theirs. We thought if that was the case, the OAU would have no choice but to enforce a government of national unity. Our strategy was basically the old idea of homelands. That was what was going on in the minds of the political masters. They believed, if we could assist Africa, not only would we be able to make contact with them but we'd be able to assist them in such a way that the concept of individual ethnic groupings in specific areas in a country would also be established.'

In September 1975 Savimbi caused panic in the ranks of the CIA Angola Task Force when he put out feelers to the MPLA. The CIA learned this when an article appeared in a number of newspapers in Europe and the United States. A Kinshasa CIA station officer was sent to question Savimbi – the spy organisation wanted no 'soft' allies in its fight against the MPLA. Kaunda supported Unita but his main concern was getting his copper to the sea. With the Benguela line closed, his sole alternative was through Rhodesia and South Africa, an expensive and humiliating proposition. On 10 September he gave Savimbi 60 days – until independence – to get the Benguela railway line reopened, or else he could no longer guarantee his support. This caused consternation in CIA circles. The intelligence organisation believed it needed to get the Zambian president so involved he'd never be able to defect. It planned to achieve this by an arms trans-shipment through Zambia. Kaunda had publicly supported the arms embargo against Angola, and the CIA believed that if one planeload of arms could enter Angola through

Zambia with Kaunda's permission, he'd be irreversibly committed to supporting Unita. At that stage African leaders did not know about the CIA's arms shipments, because of the Americans' policy of first supplying the weaponry to Zaire. The CIA believed Kaunda would be so embarrassed they'd be able to keep him in line. The plan, however, never got off the ground.

Preparations for the training of the FNLA began at the end of August 1975, with secrecy a top priority. As few people as humanly possible were kept in the know. It was decided not to conduct the project in the way a normal military operation would be carried out, but rather that it should be run away from headquarters through separate communications channels and liaison procedures. FNLA soldiers undergoing training would be told their instructors were mercenaries. The South Africans were to be issued with green uniforms rather than their usual 'browns' and were to remove all forms of identification. 'Things were kept so hush-hush and run by the [department of the] Chief of Staff Intelligence, that even I, as Chief of the Army, did not know about it,' said General Malan. 'I only found out when, while doing an inspection at Rundu, I came across a group of soldiers dressed in green uniforms, sitting in a hanger. When I asked them what they were doing, they said they weren't allowed to tell me. I then summoned their commanding officer and he also said he couldn't tell me, as it was "top secret". I replied: "I'm the Chief of the Army and if you don't want a transfer to some platteland commando, you'd better tell me what's going on." That was the first I knew about the SADF going into Angola,' said Malan. 'I was strongly opposed to the fact they weren't allowed to take their dog-tags or even their Bibles!'

Some of his colleagues dispute Malan's claim of not knowing. 'I don't think that would be correct,' said General du Toit, 'because it was army troops who were involved. The army was the sharp end. It wouldn't have happened without his authorisation.' General Viljoen, too, said that he would be surprised if General Malan had not known. But General Dirk Marais, who at the time was the Officer Commanding SADF forces in Angola, tells a similar story to Malan's. 'At one point large vehicle convoys were coming through and I was told to give them logistical support,' he said. 'When I wanted to know what was going on I was told not to ask any questions.'

Training of the FNLA was scheduled to begin in mid-September, but the man in charge of setting it up, Commandant Jan Breytenbach, had grave doubts that training alone would be sufficient. In a memorandum dated 3 September 1975, he wrote: 'Personally I think the success of the operation relies on good control right down to the lowest levels. In other words, white South African control and also logistical support.' The FNLA soldiers and commanders felt the same way. 'Their request,' continued Breytenbach, 'before we could even propose it, is that we should support them, not only with training but also with the physical planning and control of operations.'

The scene was increasingly being set for greater South African military involvement. On 15 September Breytenbach and four instructors began the training of the first 250 FNLA troops at Mpupa. As planned, the group was divided into a mortar platoon, a machine gun platoon and three rifle platoons. In October another training base was established at Serpa Pinto and training of another 244 soldiers began there. Instructors concentrated on infantry tactics – but after only three weeks the base commander, Major Frank Bestbier, was ordered to use his trained soldiers to launch attacks in the direction of Cuchi, Artur de Paiva and Matala. However, because of a shortage of vehicles, this could not be done and his group was airlifted to Sa da Bandeira.

In September 1975 Savimbi once again met Van den Bergh and Viljoen in Kinshasa. He was a worried man. He believed the rapid advances of the MPLA forces had created a crisis situation, and though he had enough willing volunteers, they were largely untrained and unarmed soldiers. Savimbi was also very concerned about new sophisticated weapons his men were beginning to encounter in battles with the MPLA. He told the South African military leaders of 81 mm mortars, 76 mm cannons, RPG-2, RPG-7 and 122 mm rocket launchers, and even armoured cars and tanks. It was the presence of armour that worried the two generals, and on the aircraft on their back way home they agreed that supplying weapons alone would not be sufficient. Like the FNLA, Unita needed to be trained. The fact that the MPLA possessed armour particularly perturbed Van den Bergh, who believed a small number of armoured cars would now be necessary to complete the operation. But any way they looked at it, the situation was fast becoming critical. With less than two months to independence on 11 November, and the MPLA in control of all the most important harbours in the country as well as large swathes of other territory, the outlook for South Africa's allies was grim. Pretoria believed the time had come for decisive steps to be taken.

By the end of September the South Africans had set up another training base in Capolo in southern Angola. The instruction team consisted of about 25 officers and non-commissioned officers. The highest level of secrecy was enforced: team members were all given false names and were only allowed to speak English – an instruction many of them found difficult to obey. Many of the weapons in the base were completely strange to the South Africans themselves and first had to be dis-mantled so the trainers themselves knew how to operate them. Training was no easy task: few of the recruits spoke English and the diet supplied in South African ration packs was strange to the Unita soldiers. Many had never handled a firearm before in their lives, and when they fired their first shot, they fled in terror. After medical examinations by South African doctors it was reported that 40 per cent of the local recruits were suffering from tuberculosis and the majority were mal-nourished. But training went remarkably well. By 8 November 1975, when the South Africans vacated the base, three infantry battalions would have been trained, 60 Unita soldiers selected and trained as a leader group and a further 60 trained to continue as instructors.

Elsewhere in the country the situation had deteriorated rapidly for South Africa's allies. The MPLA had succeeded in expelling Unita and the FNLA from Luanda and the Portuguese had bowed to MPLA demands calling for FNLA and Unita Cabinet ministers to be expelled from the interim government that had been set up to run Angola until independence. In various parts of the country the MPLA engaged the two other movements in bloody battles and most of the time gained the upper hand. Unita forces were driven out of Lobito, Benguela, Moçâmedes (Namibe), Sa da Bandeira (Lubango) and Luso. Thousands of white refugees fled to Portugal or crossed the border into Namibia where they were housed in temporary refugee camps. By the end of August the MPLA had cap-tured and had control of 11 of the 16 district capitals. At that point it appeared the MPLA was certain of complete victory, unless external military aid was provided immediately. The fact that it occupied Luanda and the entire coast and all the major harbours, apart from a small section north of the capital, meant it controlled the government apparatus and the country's communications network.

Unita's military structures and organisation were, as one field commander put it, at best in a shambles and at worst non-existent. Savimbi's organisation still occupied Nova Lisboa – Angola's second-largest city. But in slow but sure, con-sidered advances, the MPLA began encircling Unita-held territory. By early October South African officers in the area reported that Nova Lisboa was in grave danger of being cut off. Unita was isolated from the sea and could get no logistical support from that side of the country. Its fuel reserves had virtually run dry and increasingly the South African Air Force was having to supply them. Savimbi had heard, from what he described as reliable sources within the MPLA, that the organisation was planning to declare Angola independent on 28 October and install itself as the government, without even waiting for the election on 11 November.

Savimbi wanted to hold Nova Lisboa (Huambe) at all costs, as most of its infrastructure was still intact. It was an important city in the MPLA's military planning too, and it began advancing from Benguela. 'Lang Hendrik' was particularly concerned about the MPLA armour reported to be part of the column and Savimbi urged him to supply South African armoured cars to counter the advancing tanks and armoured cars. Unita had four armoured cars of its own, which had been supplied by Zaire at Silva Porto, but none of these was serviceable. SADF mechanics were able to use parts from two of them to get the other two running. However, almost immediately, unknown saboteurs wrecked those and rendered them permanently unserviceable. Unita was almost out of ammunition for its other weapons and was on the point of running out of fuel completely.

The South Africans then decided to move four missile launchers and their crews to Silva Porto (Bie), to try to counter the advancing MPLA armour. Panzer car instructors also worked feverishly in an attempt to train Unita personnel in the use of armour, but it was almost immediately clear to them that Unita's troops would never be ready in time for the first counter-attack. Pretoria couldn't wait any longer if the MPLA advance was to be stopped. Defence Headquarters issued the order for South African armoured car crews to man the vehicles. Then there was a further delay when it was discovered that three of the missile launchers were defective and parts had to be flown in from Pretoria. During this time the advancing enemy column progressed to Norton de Matos (Balombo), a small town 100 km west of Nova Lisboa.

Four days after the planned counter-offensive was due to begin, 19 South Africans, who were called up for 'special service', joined three Unita infantry companies and headed down the Lobito route for the first conventional battle the SADF would be involved in since the end of World War II. The South African soldiers wore borrowed Portuguese army camouflage uniforms. Each had signed a document that stated he had freely volunteered to go into Angola – the SADF and the government were absolved of any legal responsibilities or ramifications. The men were now, supposedly, officially regarded as mercenaries, despite the fact they were still on the payroll of the SADF.

The journey to the front line was painfully slow, as a result of countless roadblocks set up by Unita along the way. The battle group consisted of three missile launchers mounted on Land Rovers manned by South African crews, three armoured cars also manned by SADF members, a Land Rover with two heavy-calibre machine guns, a Toyota Landcruiser manned by Unita personnel with an anti-aircraft gun mounted on the back and a number of vegetable lorries that had either been commandeered from or abandoned by fleeing Portuguese farmers. Savimbi was there in his own Land Rover with his personal body guards in white Volkswagens, one driving in front and one behind. The Unita infantry battalion had light machine guns, mortars and a 106 mm recoilless gun.

Planning for the attack was a nightmare for the South African field commander, Major Louis Holtzhauzen. There were no topographical maps available: all he had was a somewhat outdated road map. To add to his woes it rained incessantly, then one of the armoured cars broke down and had to be abandoned. After personally reconnoitring the area, Holtzhauzen suggested the group press on before dawn on 5 October. Before long another Eland Panzer car broke down and had to be abandoned. Now the battle group had only one armoured car. As the group was approaching Norton de Matos an MPLA spotter plane suddenly appeared. Immediately the Unita crew opened fire with the anti-aircraft gun mounted on the Landcruiser, but failed to hit the plane. At that moment two flares were fired by MPLA troops dug in on high ground near the town. Then all hell broke loose. The MPLA forces rained artillery, mortar and heavy machine gun fire down on the allied troops, who were caught in an open area that was an ideal killing ground.

The very first shot fired against South African troops in Operation Savannah resulted in a direct hit. Major Holtzhausen's command vehicle was stuck and its occupants flung into the road. The most serious injury was a shrapnel wound in the cheek of one of the personnel, but 122 mm rockets, artillery shells and mortar bombs showered down on them – hand grenades were even thrown at them from the circling spotter plane. For the hastily trained Unita soldiers it was all too much. They fled panic-stricken into the bush. The tiny group of South Africans was now pretty well on its own, with only one Panzer car, some mortars and three rocket launchers that had to be fired from the road because the missiles were wire-guided and the surrounding thick bush meant they could not be launched from cover. After an hour of withering fire the South Africans pulled back. Unita scouts later reported 60 MPLA soldiers had been killed, but this could not be confirmed. Two Unita soldiers died in the battle and a number were wounded. Two of the organisation's Land Rovers were destroyed.

The battle of Norton de Matos was a rude shock and a harsh lesson for South Africa and her Angolan allies. The MPLA was stronger than they'd ever imagined, with heavy weapons that were considerably superior. In addition, they had come up against Cubans for the first time: scouts reported seeing 'light-skinned men with long hair'. It was glaringly apparent that Unita soldiers were not capable of successfully confronting the MPLA/Cuban forces without military assistance on a scale considerably larger than was presently the case. Savimbi was despondent. The MPLA's battle-readiness had improved dramatically over the past few months and based on the performance of his troops at Norton de Matos, he was no match for it. If morale was to be restored his men needed a few victories, and quickly, but that seemed increasingly unlikely. But perhaps what worried him most of all was the imminent arrival in Angola of an OAU fact-finding delegation. If Unita was to have any chance at all of being included in a government of national unity, then the OAU would have to be convinced his organisation was in a strong position.

On 8 October General Viljoen once again visited Silva Porto for consultations with Unita. 'It was obvious we were going to have to give Savimbi more help if our efforts were going to be in any way effective,' he said. 'I also realised that the South Africans involved in any battles had to be given more protection. We felt more armoured cars were needed.' This would be a dramatic military escalation, requiring approval from the government. Viljoen briefed the State Security Council and the members gave permission for more Panzer cars to be used against the MPLA forces. Between 17 and 22 October, 22 Eland (Panhard) 90 mm armoured cars were flown to Silva Porto and prepared for battle. The SADF had already set up headquarters there. Training exercises were carried out with Unita, while abandoned vehicles in the town were commandeered and those that could be, were repaired.

In the meantime the MPLA, its capabilities greatly enhanced by the addition of tanks, began a major assault from the south near Sa da Bandeira. Its plan was to link up with forces ranged along the Benguela railway line, so a final push could be made for Nova Lisboa.

In Pretoria Vorster and his advisors approved direct South African military involvement but decreed that no more than 2 500 troops and 600 vehicles could be used. South Africa was going to war. The plan was to recapture the south-western corner of Angola and retake the towns of Sa da Bandeira and Moçâmedes, then to secure the central areas of Angola, which were traditionally Unita strongholds. 'How could they expect us to do the job properly when they put those sort of troop restrictions on us?' asked General Malan. 'We were hamstrung before we even started, but as soldiers we went ahead and did the job.'

To conceal the fact that South West Africa was the springboard for the operation, it was decided not to cross the Angolan border from Ovamboland and head directly for Pereira de Eça but rather to follow the Kavango River to Caiundo and then to proceed west via Nehone to Pereira de Eça (Ongiva). On 19 October, following a series of battles along the way, the combined South African and allied forces captured Pereira de Eça. A week later Sa da Bandeira was taken after a ferocious battle around the airfield, and two days later, Moçâmedes fell.

Though press reports began appearing in Europe and America, South Africa's involvement was still being kept a closely guarded secret from the local press and communications officers steadfastly maintained a wall of denials. 'I don't know why it was kept such a secret,' said General Malan. 'You'll have to ask P.W. Botha. I suppose it was because the bulk of the South African soldiers were national servicemen and the moment their mothers get to know, you end up facing enormous pressure.' Viljoen believed that was only part of the reason. 'Savimbi and Roberto asked us to keep it secret,' he said. But this obsession with secrecy proved to be a double-edged sword. Government was afraid of the potential fallout if SADF members ended up in enemy hands, so instructions were that South African casualties should be avoided at all costs. The tactical difficulties thus caused were aggravated by commanders who were often too cautious and by less-qualified Unita/FNLA people who were placed in low-level leadership roles.

At this stage the SADF was operating on three fronts, in the east, the west and in the centre of Angola, and despite heavy opposition and an increasing Cuban presence, it continued to make gains. On 5 November Benguela was recaptured following heavy resistance and the next day Lobito, one of the best natural harbours in Africa, fell to the allies. When the South African armoured cars entered the town they were mobbed by residents who saw them as liberators. Flowers were strewn over the vehicles and pretty girls and old women clambered up to kiss and hug the soldiers, much against the wishes of the commanders, who wanted to ensure no MPLA elements were still around. It was now 44 days since P.W. Botha had submitted the plan for South African military involvement to the Cabinet. 'Our intention was never to capture Angola, nor was it the idea to put Savimbi in power,' said General Viljoen. 'We were using a limited war to apply pressure on the OAU so they'd put in place a government of national unity. Our initial intention was to withdraw before 11 November.' As it turned out, this was not to be the case.

In Angola, SADF forces came up against a weapon that would ultimately cause South Africa's arms manufacturer, Armscor, to become a major global weapons producer as the country rushed to try and counter it. The G-5 and G-6 field gun, reported to be the best of its kind in the world, was the direct result. The Soviet weapon they faced was not very sophisticated in terms of being able to deliver pinpoint accuracy – in fact, when compared with similar Nato weaponry it would probably be considered obsolete, even at that time – yet it is still a front-line artillery weapon with many armies around the world. It was officially designated the BM-21 rocket launcher by Soviet military authorities, but ground troops and those who faced it called it the 'Red Eye' because of the characteristic glow it displayed as it raced towards its target.

The BM-21, sometimes also called the Stalin Organ, was a multi-rocket system that first appeared in November 1964. It differed from previous systems in that it used a smaller calibre rocket and thus could fire a greater quantity. A pod of 40 launchers was mounted on the back of a Ural-375D truck, a vehicle with good cross-country capabilities. Each 122 mm rocket weighed 45,9 kg and had a maximum range of between 15 000 and 20 000 metres. The missiles could be fired individually, in ripple or in a salvo, and the effect at the receiving end was devastating as each rocket warhead contained 19 kg of high explosive – a battery's target could thus have 4 560 explosive kilograms land on it in 30 seconds! Soldiers who tried to describe what it was like often struggled to find adequate words, because unless you had experienced it, it was impossible to visualise. The rockets came howling out of the sky, each with a single eye that blazed in anger. They sounded like thousands of cats set on fire and when they landed it was as though all the thunderclaps in the world had been bound together and played through an amplifier. Buildings shook and crumbled, roofs collapsed, windows fell from their frames and the glass and shrapnel shards buzzed like angry hornets. Reload time was about 10 minutes (although the Czech army developed a palletised system that allowed reloads for a second salvo in about one minute). Warsaw Pact countries' artillery tactics employed multiple rocket launchers like the Red Eye to deliver a devastating concentration of fire at critical moments in a battle.

The effect on the South Africans and the allies was profound: there were many cases reported where Unita soldiers fled in blind panic and refused point blank to fight any more. The SADF had nothing in Angola (or in South Africa for that matter) that could counter the MPLA/Cuban-operated Stalin Organs. Pretoria decided to send artillery in the form of 25-pounder field guns – a poor solution, as the ageing cannons could at best fire only half as far as the Soviet rockets. Four of the old guns and their crews hastily left Potchefstroom for Waterkloof airbase, from where they were flown to Rundu in Namibia and then airlifted to the front at Benguela. But despite the Stalin Organs the South African columns swept on – their training and other equipment was superior.

Though virtually all South Africa's military objectives had been achieved, its political goals had not. But military planning to withdraw from Angola before 11 November 1975 continued. At the beginning of November both Savimbi and Roberto were informed of the SADF's plans to leave. Savimbi was devastated. He asked General Viljoen to arrange a meeting with Prime Minister Vorster. Viljoen promised to pass the request on. 'I got to know Savimbi very well,' he said, 'and still consider him a close friend. He has always been an impressive man – a colossus. His strategic insight is first class and the people loved him.' On 10 November, in the most extreme secrecy, the Unita leader was flown to Pretoria for consultations with Vorster. He asked Vorster to keep South Africa's troops in Angola and to provide more assistance to his and Roberto's movements. He told Vorster that Zambia and other moderate states wanted South Africa to remain in Angola until at least 9 December, the date of the next OAU meeting. Vorster agreed, on condition that Cuban and Russian help to the MPLA did not become so great that South Africa could not cope without outside Western military help.

In SADF High Command circles there was optimism. In both the north and the south, Unita and the FNLA were once again in control of their traditional areas of influence. Military successes by the allies had seen the Portuguese vacate Angola without placing the MPLA in government. The OAU had at that stage also not recognised it as Angola's legal authority and Pretoria believed the pendulum was beginning to swing in South Africa's favour, as increasing numbers of African states opened their eyes to the involvement of the Cubans and Russians. They believed South Africa had gained prestige and admiration for her military endeavours.

Apart from a few press reports in British, Portuguese and other European newspapers about possible South African military involvement, the government had so far managed to keep the lid on the operation in the local media. On 20 November, Defence Minister P.W. Botha briefed the South African Press Union, giving it a watered-down version of the situation in Angola. He was obviously very convincing, because all parties agreed to work together and maintain secrecy 'in the interests of the country'. On 9 December, with Vorster's permission, Botha 'fully briefed' South African editors. At the beginning of the briefing he asked anyone not prepared to maintain secrecy to leave the room. No one left. Botha urged the newsmen not to write reports that would cause panic or harm the country's international relations. They were then briefed by General Viljoen. At the end the editors were neatly wrapped up and in the government's pocket. But the lid was blown off when four South Africans were captured by the MPLA on 14 December and displayed to the world press in Lagos, Nigeria. It was a marvellous propaganda opportunity for the MPLA. Its representative at the United Nations in New York, Elcio de Figueiredo, made the most of the situation. He also claimed the CIA had given aid to Unita and the FNLA to the tune of $150 million. The result was a feeding frenzy in the American press which soon after led to the US Senate stopping aid to the pro-West Angolan movements.

In Angola, however, it appeared the tide was turning in favour of the allies. The South African column moving from the south had swept swiftly through larger Cuban and MPLA forces and by October 28 had captured Moçâmedes on the southern coast. By 7 November it had taken Benguela and Lobito and was driving north. Another column drove the Katangese, a Zairian rebel separatist group supporting the MPLA, out of Luso and moved towards Texeira de Sousa (Luau), the last railroad station held by the MPLA, on the eastern border. Mobutu had committed his elite Seventh and Fourth Commando battalions to the struggle and had flown them to Ambriz in his own C-130 transport planes. A combined force of Zairian, FNLA and Portuguese troops re-took Caxito and began moving towards Luanda itself. Outside of Luanda the MPLA now had control of only three of the 15 provinces. CIA sources reported the MPLA forces were terrified and were sending their families out of the country to safety. The Lusaka CIA Chief of Station reported to headquarters in Langley, Virginia, that the MPLA's back would be broken in a few days.

It was against this background that, just before independence, Holden Roberto, leader of the FNLA, approached South Africa to help in an attack he planned against Luanda. 'Roberto believed it would be possible to take Luanda,' said General Viljoen. 'He sent a request through Boss channels, or maybe it was even directly through the CIA itself. He said he believed he could take Luanda, but his problem was he did not have enough artillery pieces. He only had two 132 mm Chinese field guns that could shoot about 32 km.

'At the beginning of November the request reached us in the Defence Force, saying that on 9 November he planned to attack Luanda from Ambriz. He wanted us to supply him with cannons,' said Viljoen. 'I was called in by P.W. Botha and asked my opinion. I said to him: "This is rubbish. We can't do it. It's not part of our mission. We were not told to take Luanda and I doubt if Roberto will be able to do so." I explained how the approach from the north-east crosses a large swampy area about 10 km wide, and in order to get to the high ground surrounding the capital, that first has to be crossed. I said to P.W.: "This is killing ground. It'll be impossible for the FNLA troops to cross that, and in any case, we don't have any guns that can shoot far enough. Our 25-pounders can only shoot

10 km." P.W. looked at me and said: "General, are you telling me we don't have any guns that can shoot further?" I replied: "No, we have 5,5-inch guns that can shoot about 19 km. They will be able to do the job, but are so heavy we can hardly get them into an aircraft."

'That was a Friday afternoon, and he said to me: "Look here, General, if we get a request from Africa we cannot say no. It's a matter of honour. If you can't load the 5,5s intact then take them apart – but you will assist the FNLA!" That Saturday morning at about 10 o'clock we left Waterkloof Airbase in two C-130 aircraft bound for Ambriz in northern Angola. Aboard were two guns, ammunition and two reduced gun crews. To be honest, I didn't like the situation at all because I knew it couldn't work. I was with them, and when we landed in Ambriz the guns were immediately unloaded so we could begin to assemble them. Normally 10 people man a 140 mm gun, but we only sent three crew members per gun. The rest were to come from FNLA ranks and we immediately started training them. We also paid attention to their two Chinese guns. The attack was planned to start at 06h00, with a preparatory artillery bombardment commencing at 05h45. Then the infantry would go straight up the road and attack Luanda. I didn't like the idea at all, but I had my orders.'

Viljoen returned to Pretoria to direct operations from headquarters, while Roberto, the South Africans and a few CIA observers moved south from Ambriz for what was hoped would be the decisive battle of the war. In Luanda, the Portuguese High Commissioner had fled without ceremony, while Agostinho Neto was busy putting the final touches to the celebrations planned for 11 November. As MPLA leaders celebrated independence by declaring the People's Republic of Angola, 160 km south-east of Luanda a South African column advanced so rapidly the Cuban and MPLA forces had great difficulty retreating ahead of it. 'The initial bombardment signalling the start of the attack on Luanda was to be on to the high ground occupied by enemy artillery,' said Viljoen. 'At exactly 05h45 the guns opened fire and rained air-burst shells down onto the Cubans and MPLA. At the same time, three Canberra bombers began dropping 1 000 kg bombs.'

The bombing, however, was spectacularly inaccurate and ineffective. The first bomb landed in the sea, the second on the beach. The second plane dropped its first bomb south of the target and its second in the open marsh area. The third bomber, for some unknown reason, dropped none of its bombs – and the first two planes only dropped two of the three bombs they were carrying. 'Our bombardment was a complete surprise to the Angolans,' said Viljoen. 'But to take advantage of the neutralising effects of an artillery bombardment, you have to cross as soon as possible after the attack starts – while the enemy still has its head down. Unfortunately at 06h00 when the shelling stopped there were no troops – they were still having breakfast! Progress was being reported to me by radio in Pretoria and I was as mad as hell. Half an hour to an hour later the infantry attacked and were virtually through when the MPLA and Cubans recovered. By then we'd expended almost all our ammunition and could not give any more support. The enemy started shooting 122 mm rockets. That scattered the FNLA and they stampeded back.'

The CIA's John Stockwell wrote: 'The Cubans' 122 mm rockets began to land in the Quifangondo valley, not like single claps of thunder, but in salvos, 20 at a time. The first salvo went long, screaming over the heads of bewildered FNLA soldiers and shattering the valley with a horrendous ear-splitting sound. The next salvo was short, and the little army was bracketed, exposed in an open valley without cover. Soldiers' hearts burst with a clutching terror as they dived to the ground or stood helplessly mesmerised, watching the next salvo land in their midst. And the next. And the next. CIA observers on a ridge estimated that 2 000 rockets rained on the task force as it broke and fled in panic, scattering across the valley in aimless flight, abandoning weapons, vehicles and wounded comrades alike. Survivors would call it *Nshila wa Lufu* – Death Road. As for the artillery, one of the North Korean (South African reports say it was Chinese) 132 mm cannons exploded the first time it was fired, killing its Zairian crew. The second misfired, injuring its crew. Both guns were permanently out of action. The obsolete South African cannons pounded away, but their firepower was a fraction of the rocket salvos and their range scarcely over half that of the 122 mm rockets. If they did bring the truck-mounted 122 mm rocket launchers under fire, the latter quickly displaced, resuming their fire from prepared positions nearby.'

It was the beginning of the end for Roberto and the FNLA. For Viljoen, the memories still rankle. 'Militarily I realised the operation would not work, but politically I was forced to do it,' he said. 'The main complaint I have is we were not told to take Luanda. It was not part of our mission. It was never agreed that was our primary goal. Had that been the case I could have passed a great number of small pockets of resistance, gone straight for Luanda, taken it and handed it over to Savimbi and Holden Roberto. I said [to P.W. Botha]: "This is wrong: we are now deviating from the principle that was laid down right at the beginning." That was the only attack on Luanda and it was a P.W. Botha attack – there's no doubt about that.'

But Viljoen's problems were just starting. 'In the artillery there is a motto that says: "A gunner never loses his guns", but after the failed attack on Luanda I had two guns sitting in Ambriz. I knew we'd stirred up a hornet's nest. There was definitely going to be an enemy reaction and we were at grave risk of losing the guns. Eventually it was arranged with Mobutu that the guns would be towed to Zaire then shipped from Matadi back to South Africa. But I also had 26 soldiers and Brigadier Ben Roos there, and that worried me.'

As the FNLA lines crumbled before the MPLA/Cuban advances, it was obvious the South Africans could no longer play a role in Ambriz and had to get out. They couldn't be airlifted out of the town because the runway at the airfield was badly damaged. Their only option was extraction by sea. Roos and Viljoen wanted to do it secretly, at night, as they were worried the defeated FNLA soldiers would not be happy at being left behind. Orders were sent to the frigate SAS *President Steyn*, at the time patrolling along the west coat of Africa, to pick up the 26 South African personnel. It would have been madness to carry out the operation in the harbour at Ambriz. For that reason Ambrizete, some 70 km to the north, was chosen. In an attempt to avoid identification, all name boards and registration numbers were removed from the *President Steyn* and a tatty, dirty flag was hoisted.

On 27 November 1975 Roos made contact with the *President Steyn* and the retrieval operation was set for 23h00 that night. While the frigate manoeuvred into position, radio signals from aircraft flying between Cabinda and Luanda were intercepted and Russian ships picked up on radar. The ship's crew, as well as Viljoen and the others in the operations room at Defence Headquarters in Pretoria, were as tense as tightened banjo strings as they worried about the possibility of an ambush or running into a Russian warship. Late in the afternoon Roos radioed asking that the operation be postponed until 05h00 the next morning, as they were experiencing difficulties on a particularly bad road that linked Ambriz and Ambrizete. This was cutting things fine: sunrise was at 07h10, which didn't leave a lot of time to board the warship and steam out of danger.

At 04h00 Roos reported that the group had arrived at Ambrizete but that the harbour could not be used. He said they'd have to be picked up on the beach. 'I was sweating in the ops room back in Pretoria,' said Viljoen. 'It was a cloudy, dark night and the ship couldn't see where Roos and his men were, or their signalling flashes. Eventually we ordered them to turn on the lights of the vehicles so the landing party could see them.' Three inflatable rubber boats landed on the beach and after Roos radioed to say there was no danger, the ship's helicopter was dispatched to help with the extraction. Before daybreak the *President Steyn* was sailing full-steam ahead for the open ocean with 26 very relieved soldiers aboard and an even more relieved Constand Viljoen back in Pretoria: 'I can honestly say that was the most difficult night ever in my operational career,' he said. 'The guns in Ambriz were towed to Zaire, then eventually picked up by the SAS *Tafelberg* and taken to Walvis Bay.'

On all fronts the Cuban and MPLA forces were being strengthened and supplied with more and increasingly sophisticated weapons. By December 1975, intelligence reports put the number of regular Cuban soldiers serving in Angola at around 12 000 and there were claims that a squadron of MiG fighter aircraft and 100 tanks, many of them the larger T-54s, had been delivered. The Soviet Union, it appeared, was done with playing and had decided to come to the party with some serious money. CIA reports valued Soviet aid to the MPLA by as early as November 1975 at $225 million. In contrast, assistance from the United States to Unita and the FNLA totalled $31,7 million.

In December 1975 Vorster began to have doubts about the Angolan campaign as world pressure began to mount against South Africa. The government decided all SADF troops would be withdrawn by the end of the month. Savimbi was disappointed by the news. He wanted the South Africans first to take Henrique de Carvalho (Saurimo), Luso, Malanje and Texeira de Sousa, so that he'd be in a stronger position. He pleaded with the South Africans not to leave. P.W. Botha agreed and the withdrawal date was set at 3 January 1976. In America there were ominous rumblings for the anti-MPLA forces when, on 5 December, Senator Dick Clark recommended to the Senate Foreign Relations Committee that it vote to terminate the American involvement in Angola. Two weeks later the Senate accepted Clark's recommendation

On the battlefield the SADF soldiers were encountering much sterner resistance and were beginning to find themselves outclassed by the newer, more sophisticated weapons they now faced. On many fronts they came under fire from MiG fighter planes and helicopter gunships and were unable to do anything about it, as their 20 mm anti-aircraft cannons were ineffective against high-speed jets. The national servicemen gunners from 10 Anti-Aircraft Defence School grew increasingly nervous and jumpy, so much so that when they eventually managed to shoot down a chopper (on 4 January 1976), it was one of their own. Brigadier Jan Potgieter and four others died in the incident.

By mid-December the MPLA had all but defeated the FNLA in northern Angola as foreign aid to Roberto dried up. On Christmas day General Viljoen suggested to Roberto and Savimbi that their armies revert to guerrilla tactics. Vorster was a worried man. As the US Congress and Senate moved to cut off all aid to the pro-West Angolan movements, he feared being caught in a war that could easily turn out to be South Africa's Vietnam. 'There is absolutely no doubt the Americans left us in the lurch,' said Viljoen. 'One day early in November I was called back to Rundu by the Chief of Staff Intelligence. He said they had a special request from the Americans asking for my assessment of the situation in Angola. They wanted to know what I thought Unita and the FNLA's chances were, and they wanted a list of all airfields in Angola with runway lengths and the type of aircraft they could handle. They wanted to know what the ammunition and weapon requirements were and whether South Africa would be able to help with training,' he said. 'It was a long list of questions that gave me a lot of hope. I thought if the Americans were planning to come in on our side we'd really be talking business. But that was the last I ever heard. Then there was the Clark Amendment and they collapsed, the same way they did in Vietnam.'

But Vorster was getting mixed messages from America. Colonel Stange, the US military attaché in Pretoria, delivered a letter from Dr Henry Kissinger to Lieutenant General Armstrong. In it Kissinger said: 'The United States shares the concern of the RSA over the danger and provocative role of the Russians and Cubans in Angola. The United States deplores the support of the MPLA by the Russians in its rejection of a political settlement and its pursuit of military conquest. The United States will regard the imposition by force of a Soviet/Cuban/MPLA regime in Angola with great concern. The United States, however believes the FNLA and Unita has received enough and adequate arms for their own protection, including ack-ack defences. The United States believes the only solution to be a political settlement in which no one group is to dominate the others. We have made our deep concern about the Angola situation known to all concerned, including Russia.'

It was a masterpiece in political non-speak, and the South Africans had no clue how they should interpret it. General Armstrong believed it was a message urging the continuation of the military operation. Constand Viljoen saw it as exactly the opposite. He believed the Americans were pushing for a political settlement. Pik Botha, then South Africa's ambassador to the United Nations, had numerous meetings with Kissinger as well as General Brent Scowcroft, President Ford's Security Advisor. Botha seemed able to move around the US State Department as though he was employed by the Americans – a rumour that has persisted in press circles since then. 'I wouldn't know that,' said General Magnus Malan, 'but if there is one man I don't want to analyse that's Pik Botha. A politician's biggest ambition in life is to be in the spotlight and once that bug bites you don't get rid of it. A typical case is Pik Botha. There were things that happened that he wasn't aware of and that we kept from him until after the operation had started or had been completed because of the possibility he would leak it. That was the general feeling amongst certain people towards him. Whether they were right or wrong I wouldn't know.'

'I don't think he [Pik] was on the American payroll,' said former Military Intelligence Head General Hein du Toit, 'but he was a terrible attention seeker and completely untrustworthy. During Operation Savannah I was in America and went to see our military attaché, who had arranged a party for me that evening. Pik Botha was at another function, or had gone to see the Senate, but when he arrived he said to me I must report back to Pretoria and tell them the Americans say we must hold fast in Angola and that they're going to support us. At Vorster's holiday house, at Oubos, I reported this. I told them [the State Security Council] this is what Pik Botha had said and suggested Botha come out and brief them personally. I told them he said the greater majority of the Senate supported us and that he said [General] Scowcroft said we must carry on because the US will help us. When Pik Botha came along he told a completely different story. He did that every time. He's a mental case [*sielkundige geval*]! He can't stop talking. He talked all the time so everyone would see and hear him and he caused enormous harm to our foreign policy. He's a big mouth without much substance,' said Du Toit.

At a later meeting of the State Security Council at Vorster's holiday home it was confirmed that South African troops would begin withdrawing from Angola on 6 January 1976 and that by the following day they had to be south of a line between Moçâmedes and Sa da Bandeira. The decision would be conveyed to Zambia and Zaire as well as the CIA. In a document in the military archives Vorster said about his decision: 'We considered the decision about our withdrawal very thoroughly and came to the conclusion we'd be left holding the baby and if we'd have to go ahead on our own that would mean a full-scale war. Up to this point it was in truth a military adventure, but the moment the Americans and the French ran away, if we stayed it would become a full-scale war on our side.' (French aid had been limited, though some weapons were supplied to the FNLA from stocks delivered to Zaire. On the political front Paris worked behind the scenes to convince African states like Upper Volta, Burundi, Gabon, Ivory Coast, Cameroon, Rwanda, the Central African Republic, Togo and Zaire not to recognise the MPLA as sole representative of the Angolan people. But in early January France called for foreign interference in Angola to be stopped. On 17 January 1976 France became the first country in the West to officially recognise the MPLA government.)

In Namibia and Angola withdrawal plans were being put in motion and the SADF began moving back. On 5 January they were ordered to stop. The counter-order came as a result of pressure exerted by the United States and Zaire. Pik Botha was back at his post in Washington on 1 January and at midday the next day he met with General Scowcroft. Botha urged the Security Advisor to do something to fill the vacuum that would be left when South Africa pulled out. Scowcroft said they were powerless: the Clark Amendment had effectively emasculated the administration. However, he and the CIA were worried about military gains the MPLA were likely to make before the scheduled OAU summit, at which Africa would decide on the future rulers of Angola.

On 3 January Dr Hilgard Muller, Minister of Foreign Affairs, Brand Fourie, Secretary of Foreign Affairs, and General Viljoen travelled to Zaire to inform Mobutu of South Africa's position. They met at Bandolita, Mobutu's country palace. Present were five Zairian Cabinet ministers as well as Field Marshal Bokassa, President of the Central African Republic. The Zairian delegation tried to persuade the South Africans to set up a permanent mission in Kinshasa – a sort of secret embassy to co-ordinate an African grouping that would oppose Soviet and Cuban expansion in Africa. They urged South Africa not to leave Angola before the OAU meeting, but Muller steadfastly maintained it was in South Africa's best interests to leave immediately.

Mobutu refused to be swayed. He asked that one of his ministers be allowed to accompany the South African delegation home so they could put their case directly to Vorster. And so Zairian Cabinet minister Busengumana met with Vorster and urged him to delay the announced pullout until 12 January, when the OAU was scheduled to make its decision. To sweeten the pot, he said Zaire was prepared to enter into a military co-operation agreement with South Africa and would seek support from the US for such an arrangement. Vorster agreed South African forces could remain in Angola until they saw which way the OAU voted. They would simply maintain defensive positions and would not undertake any offensive actions. If the OAU decided South Africa should stay in Angola any longer, then Vorster insisted that particular decision be made public.

While Vorster and the Zairian minister were locked in meetings the SADF was already beginning to withdraw. Then came the counter-order. Savimbi and Roberto knew nothing of the South African plans and were only informed on 6 January.

In the OAU the political current had turned firmly against Pretoria. The Vorster government was widely condemned for its adventures in Angola. Pretoria's support of Unita and the FNLA probably disadvantaged the Angolan movements' cause within the organisation. Roberto and Savimbi were in fact prevented from attending one of the closed sessions. At the summit meeting held at the Addis Ababa Hilton, Brigadier Murtala Mohammed, Nigeria's military leader, proposed that the MPLA be recognised as the legitimate ruler of Angola. The suggestion provoked heated debates and when a vote was taken it was locked at 22-all. Uganda, as the country chairing the meeting, and Ethiopia, as host country, abstained from the ballot. Then some slick political manoeuvring began. A compromise proposal was submitted whereby the OAU would set up a round-table meeting between the Angolan leaders. In an attempt to influence the delegates, it was suggested that three South African prisoners of war be displayed to the Assembly. When Unita threatened to do the same with Cuban POWs that idea was scrapped – but the South Africans were paraded before the press in an adjoining hall. To cut a long tale of political two-stepping short, another vote was taken in the early hours of 12 January. Once again the assembly was split at 22–22. This time Idi Amin, the chairman of the OAU, used his casting vote and sided with the MPLA. It was all over. South Africa, the allies and the United States had lost.

On 11 February the MPLA government in Luanda was welcomed as the 47th member of the Organisation of African Unity. South Africa had failed in its gamble, and Pretoria was bitterly disappointed. P.W. Botha suggested to the Cabinet on 14 January that the SADF withdraw completely from Angola, with the exception of Ruacana and Calueque. The withdrawal should not begin before 17 January, and should be completed by at the latest 25 January, he proposed. Savimbi was not happy. At a dinner he attended with P.W. Botha at Rundu on Sunday 18 January, he told the South African Minister of Defence so. South Africa should have tried for a victory rather than a compromise, he said; they should have waited for a favourable political solution. The Unita leader was not optimistic about the future. He believed the MPLA would overrun southern Angola and that Swapo would be given a free hand by them.

On 27 January the US Congress passed the Tunney Amendment, which barred any further funds from being allocated to the war in Angola. At the same time, Kissinger did an about-turn when he told a Senate Committee: 'In early September the poorly equipped Unita forces turned in desperation to South Africa for assistance against the MPLA, which was overrunning Unita's ethnic areas in the south. South Africa responded by sending military equipment and some military personnel – without consultation with the United States.'

While the bulk of South African forces withdrew by the planned dates, some elements remained in minor support roles. On 27 March 1976 the last South African soldier crossed the border back into South West Africa. 'I heard the real pressure on South Africa came from the Russians via the British,' said General Viljoen. 'Pik Botha I don't think could handle that pressure. He brought a lot of pressure on us to withdraw because the British were pressurising him.'

During Operation Savannah, building activities at the Ruacana hydro-electric scheme had continued unabated. Experts believed the project would take another 18 months to reach completion and Pretoria was worried about the consequences of an MPLA government in Luanda. The South Africans desperately wanted to negotiate with the new Angolan government but had no way of making contact. In the meantime, the SADF continued to protect the scheme. Contact was eventually made through US Senator John Tunney's office. The Angolans were ready to do business when it came to the Ruacana/Calueque scheme, but Tunney was hamstrung by American legislation and could not act as go-between. Eventually Pik Botha discussed the situation with Britain's Ambassador to the United Nations, Ivor Richard, who agreed to approach Tanzania's ambassador and to ask him to make the necessary representations to the MPLA. After a degree of political posturing, South Africa agreed to withdraw the last of her troops and the MPLA gave assurances with which Pretoria could live.

It was the end of a phase in South Africa. Around R100 million had been spent on Operation Savannah and 35 SADF members had been killed, as were countless Angolans and Cubans. And still the situation that the South African government feared most had come to pass: South West Africa had a Marxist government on its northern border, Swapo was in a stronger position than ever, the MPLA was likely to be friendly to the South African liberation movements and all of Pretoria's efforts to woo black Africa had effectively gone down the drain.

Operation Savannah was described by many as a debacle, yet it taught South Africa valuable lessons and had ramifications that affected far more than the approximately 3 000 SADF men involved in it. 'We were let down by our politicians,' said General Malan. 'Politically the MPLA and Cubans had everything on their side and in terms of equipment they also had all the advantages. But that was one of the best things that ever happened to South Africa. It made the politicians realise they'd better spend money on the military or else, sooner or later, we were going to end up getting a hiding. Ops Savannah bought us the time we needed after we'd discovered our equipment shortcomings and established our troops were good enough. It allowed us to reorganise and begin to work as a team, and it was one of the main reasons why we brought other population groups into the military. It brought a change in political outlook too. At that stage the political situation was very conservative and we introduced something completely new when we integrated soldiers from the various population groups. We were softening up the politicians and the conservative outlook in this country. In the end, what we were doing in the Defence Force was one of the factors that led to the Conservative Party breaking away from the Nationalists.'

3

THE RISE OF THE
SECUROCRATS

While Savannah may have affected the thinking in the military profoundly, events inside South Africa at the time were also provoking great changes. A watershed in the country's history was 16 June 1976, the day pupils from Morris Isaacson High School led thousands of other Soweto youngsters in a revolt against the imposition of Afrikaans as the official medium of teaching in their schools. What started as a peaceful demonstration degenerated into a bloody confrontation when police opened fire, unleashing an orgy of violence and popular anger that quickly spread across the country. It took the government – and, if intelligence sources are to be believed, the ANC itself – completely by surprise. 'I wasn't a member of the Cabinet at that stage,' said General Malan, 'but I'm told investigations showed being taught in Afrikaans was the root cause. I don't think anyone realised how deeply students felt about this.'

There can be little doubt that Vorster's government did not see what was coming. Cabinet records from 1976 recently released by the State Archives show that the strategy used by the police in June 1976 – the use of live ammunition against the marching pupils – was not discussed beforehand by the Cabinet. The (non) policy officially left around 600 people dead. Vorster and his Cabinet had little idea about how to handle the situation, but were determined to stamp it out and prepared to use as much force as it took. 'The Minister proposes that this movement must be broken and that the police must perhaps act a bit more drastically to bring about more deaths,' Jimmy Kruger, then Minister of Justice, Police and Prisons, is recorded as having told his ministerial colleagues at a Cabinet meeting on 10 August 1976.

Though intelligence agencies are convinced that the ANC played no role in the initial uprising (despite being quick to capitalise on the situation and accept the credit), Kruger viewed the circumstances differently. 'The ANC are the central figures behind the organisation of the uprising,' he said. 'In addition the Black Consciousness movement is growing dangerously strong, but it is impossible to imprison all its leaders.' He said the government was considering negotiating with Black Consciousness leaders but that such negotiations would likely be pointless as those leaders could not 'exercise self-control'.

Vorster, as chair of the State Security Council, appointed a committee under Kruger to investigate the situation and produce recommendations. As Malan relates, 'It was held in "Lang Hendrik" van den Bergh's offices. He served on it, I was appointed onto it as Chief of the Defence Force and a member of the State Security Council, and I think Geldenhuys [not the military General Jannie Geldenhuys], who was Chief of the Police, was also on it. We had to investigate. We had a lot of people coming there and giving opinions. There were papers that had to be read. We met about once a week for umpteen months. I took it very seriously. I thought we would come up with the solution, but we never wrote a report. I can't recall that Kruger ever reported back. If he did, it was for less than five minutes. But it had taken us a hell of a long time.'

The final conclusion? The causes behind the riots? 'I wouldn't know,' said Malan. 'The feeling I had at that stage was it was basically the youth who acted spontaneously, with here and there some instigation from the ANC side. It was a rebellion against a lot of things. For instance, language was one, whether we like it or not. Whether there were really serious grievances or not can be questioned, but it was a political situation. The military wasn't really active then except on a few occasions. At one stage we had a show of power by moving a lot of troops and vehicles on the border of Soweto. It was really still a police operation. The temperature at that stage wasn't all that high, but there is no doubt a foundation was being laid for the future. From [the ANC's] side it was also a show of force, but in a different sense from ours. They were highly successful with the Soweto uprising.

'Remember at that stage Vorster was the former Minister of Police. It was police, police, police. They ran the show. We were running a sideshow, and not really inside South Africa. We were excluded. I tried from my side to communicate with the police. I doubt whether my predecessor ever had a conference with them. I started by getting Prinsloo – who was the Commissioner – and his top echelon to come and have a drink at the Army College on a Friday afternoon,' Malan said. 'We were trying to get to know each other and to get a feeling for each other, so if there was a particular requirement at least you could pick up a phone and talk to someone you knew. There wasn't really a defined area of responsibility for the one or the other. There was an understanding, yes, but it wasn't written. The understanding at that stage was that the police would be responsible internally and us externally. We said Boss can't be responsible for intelligence on the other side of the Namibian border in Angola, because they are not there. We are operating there, so we should do it. It was accepted, but not in writing. But if you look at the Truth Commission now and the people applying for amnesty you'll find that the police must have transgressed that type of understanding because they were deeply involved in operations on the other side of the border at a later stage.

'If I can be frank, I doubt if the police understood the onslaught,' said Malan. 'They didn't understand what the conflict was about. They were never trained in it. They weren't addressing the cause of the problem, because they didn't understand it. They were referring back to previous experiences of an uprising without a political cause behind it. This was something totally different.'

Though the government's heavy-handed methods seemed to cap the uprising, tensions continued to simmer in black areas and the ANC made good use of the opportunity presented to it. Large numbers of dissatisfied, politically aware black students joined the organisation, many of them leaving the country to undergo military training and join the ranks of Umkhonto we Sizwe (MK), the ANC's armed military wing. And many more left the following year, after Black Consciousness leader Steve Biko was tortured to death in police custody. (Asked to comment on Biko's death, Jimmy Kruger made international headlines when he said: 'It leaves me cold.')

But the foundations of the militant student movements had been laid years before. In early 1960 the ANC and PAC launched an anti-pass-law campaign to protest against blacks being required to carry a passbook – a sort of internal passport that severely restricted where they could work, live or travel. The response of the security forces to this campaign resulted in the Sharpeville massacre on 21 March 1960. Sixty-nine people were killed, and a further 180 wounded. The incident reverberated throughout South Africa and around the world. On 30 March 1960 the government declared a State of Emergency and enacted the Unlawful

Organisations Act; on 8 April 1960 the ANC and the PAC were banned. This forced the two organisations to set up and run underground operations: the leadership of the ANC developed a revolutionary strategy which became known as the M-Plan (named after Nelson Mandela).

The plan involved dividing black townships and areas into zones, each under control of a local revolutionary committee appointed by the regional command of the ANC. It also incorporated Operation Mayibuye, whose aim was to seize power through acts of violence and sabotage. Phase 2 of the plan set out specific rural areas from which guerrillas were to trigger a revolution. At a secret meeting in June 1961 the ANC decided to form an armed wing, and Umkhonto we Sizwe was born. A small farm called Lilliesleaf in what is today the Johannesburg suburb of Rivonia was bought, from which operations were to be launched. At the same time, Mandela visited several countries to drum up support for the campaign. The first batches of MK recruits left South Africa for military training in July 1962. But before operations could begin, the police raided Lilliesleaf on 11 July 1963 and arrested most of the ANC leadership. They were charged with high treason and Nelson Mandela, Walter Sisulu, Dennis Goldberg, Govan Mbeki, Raymond Mhlaba, Elias Motsoaledi and Andrew Mlangeni were found guilty and sentenced to life imprisonment. It was a devastating blow to the organisation.

After the Rivonia Trial the ANC, the PAC and the South African Communist Party made largely ineffectual attempts to infiltrate South Africa via Southern Rhodesia, despite financial and other material aid from the Soviet Union and other Soviet bloc countries. The government was concerned at the cosy relationship the ANC had with the Soviets and other communist states and organisations. When P.W. Botha became Minister of Defence, on 5 April 1966, a shift in defence thinking quickly became apparent. Whereas his predecessors had tended to focus on the threats they perceived South Africa faced, Botha had a much wider view. His vision of security included the East–West global ideological conflict, with South Africa forming a key component. Botha's speeches were dominated by three themes:

- the West was threatened by Soviet expansionism;
- South Africa was part of the West, and
- South Africa occupied a central role in the Soviet strategy of cutting off Europe's supply of essential raw materials; he also argued that the Cape sea route was of vital importance to the West.

Prime Minister Vorster echoed his Defence Minister's sentiments when he said: 'The ultimate aim of the communist and leftist powers is not Rhodesia and Mozambique, but what can be taken from South African soil.'

To counter this 'Soviet expansionism' the South African government entered into defence agreements with Portugal and Rhodesia. Units of the SAP were sent to Rhodesia in September 1967 in order, it was said, 'to fight against men who originally came from South Africa and were on their way back to commit terrorism in South Africa'. However, it was part of a much broader strategy that was to dominate defence and political thinking for more than a decade. The ultimate goal was to keep the defence line as far away from South Africa as possible, and Angola, Mozambique and Rhodesia formed effective buffers against direct foreign intervention.

'Vorster, under pressure from "Lang Hendrik", decided we should help the Rhodesians but that the police should do it,' General Viljoen explained. 'The police were always very keen on playing a military role. We were involved in the Portuguese provinces, assisting with the Air Force and also liaising. But the valuable aspect of that situation was that the Defence Force had long been intimately involved in studying worldwide – but especially in Africa – those kinds of wars. We were able to learn from others' experience. This had a great influence on the planning of the Defence Force and the way we executed our task,' he continued. 'It also contributed to the fact that we could carry on indefinitely against the ANC.'

In 1969 the ANC realised a new strategy was necessary. A conference was held at Morogoro, in Tanzania, at the end of which a document titled *Strategy and Tactics of the ANC* was produced. To military experts it was naïve, hopelessly optimistic and completely out of touch with the situation MK faced in South Africa. The plan was to extend the stuttering guerrilla war to a classic mobile combat phase that would ultimately lead to the collapse of the South African government. The strategy outlined three phases:

- an initial guerrilla phase, which would involve acts of armed propaganda, sabotage, land mines and car bombs;
- an equilibrium phase in which strong MK units would engage the security forces in mobile warfare; and
- a third phase planned to culminate in a general offensive that coincided with the collapse of South Africa's economy, the demoralisation of the security forces and the isolation of the government.

The arrest and imprisonment of the ANC leadership inside South Africa and the effective security force measures to minimise infiltration had created a vacuum which was filled by a group of black students who formed a student organisation called the South African Students Organisation (Saso), with Steve Biko as its first president. In July 1972 the Black People's Convention was established and together they formed the Black Consciousness movement.

The idea of playing a pivotal role in the East–West conflict became increasingly important to the government. The Cabinet believed they were already involved in a sort of indirect war. 'In the world we live in, the dividing line between war and peace is generally no longer a clear one, and the South African Defence Force must take that situation into account,' said P.W. Botha in 1968. In a speech two years later he said, 'There is a global struggle between the forces of communism on the one hand and the forces of stability, security and progress on the other.' He believed the military and economic fronts were but two of the ways in which that onslaught was being waged.

At that stage the government believed it had the situation firmly in hand and was confident that any threat posed by the ANC could easily be handled. However, the April 1974 coup in Portugal changed everything, because the two Portuguese territories in southern Africa became independent and opened their facilities to the ANC. The reason for the SADF's intervention in Angola, according to P.W. Botha, was to 'shoulder its responsibility as an ally of the free world' – but despite significant military victories in Operation Savannah, the defence buffers were greatly reduced. When South African troops withdrew from Angola in 1976 the ANC had access to vast areas in which to set up training bases and plan operations.

It was against this backdrop that Vorster launched his policy of détente. He hoped that by extending the hand of friendship and offering promises of South African aid to the countries of the region, he would be able to cut the legs from beneath the ANC, PAC and SACP. But despite many photo opportunities with some of the area's leaders, little benefit came from the policy.

In 1978 Prime Minister John Vorster was forced to resign after media investigations exposed the 'Muldergate' scandal, a government programme whereby secret funds were used to manipulate and control the press. The government, using fertiliser magnate (and later South African Rugby Football Union boss) Louis Luyt as a front man, started *The Citizen* newspaper to take on the liberal English press. In a closely fought leadership struggle, Defence Minister P.W.

Botha was elected party leader and South Africa's eighth prime minister on 28 September 1978. He retained the Defence portfolio until 1980, when General Magnus Malan, Chief of the Defence Force, was appointed Minister of Defence. According to inner Cabinet sources Malan was chosen to be Minister of Defence almost by default. 'I heard that P.W. came to him with a list of three names of serving Cabinet ministers and asked him which one the military would be prepared to accept as their boss,' said a former colleague. 'I remember one of the names on the list was that of Chris Heunis; I'm not sure who the other two were – but Malan took a look, then said he wouldn't accept any of them. P.W. replied: "If that's the case, why don't you do the job?" A few months later it was announced.' Malan would not comment on this.

With Botha's election, the concept and era of 'total onslaught' began in earnest. Botha and his advisors believed the country and his government faced threats on all conceivable fronts. For the military, his election was a relief and a breath of fresh air. 'For the first time we had the advantage in having a prime minister who come through the military and not the police,' said Magnus Malan. 'At the SSC [State Security Council] we had good discussions and I often took him up to the operational area. He was fairly involved in the military because, remember, he had the experience of Savannah and he learned the lessons that we did in Savannah and he applied them. He gave us the money, he reorganised Armscor and he kept himself to a certain extent involved in the military, which I thought was a good thing. There were times when we butted heads … oh, yes. At one stage when I was minister I made a decision and he queried it to the extent that I said I'd resign. It was about buying submarines. We didn't speak to each other for three months. He then appointed a commission of inquiry and they gave me credit for my decision.'

Malan was reluctant to discuss the details of this submarine-buying incident, but highly placed sources in the Cabinet of the time say an approach was made by a German intermediary offering brand-new submarines built for Argentina but which the South American country no longer wanted. If South Africa accepted the offer the submarines would be delivered to Durban, *voetstoots*. 'Malan would have none of it,' the source said. 'Apparently, without informing P.W. about the offer, he sent someone to Germany to tell them the conditions offered were unacceptable. When P.W. heard about it he was furious. He said he should have been informed and believed South Africa should buy the subs. Malan refused to budge and the upshot was that a commission was appointed which eventually vindicated the general.'

'He [P.W.] could be nasty,' said Malan, 'boy, there were times when he was nasty. But you had to take it. Fortunately in the military you got used to it. I think many of the politicians couldn't take it but you had to stand up and fight for your rights. It wasn't pleasant and whilst it was on, it was on, but afterwards you forgot about it, then you were friends again. What I like about P.W. Botha was if he gave you the green light you could depend on him – not like other politicians. He's a man's man, he's a hell of a good friend to have, but he's a nasty enemy. You could trust him and if he supported you you'd have no problems, but if he was against you – well then, you've got a fight. There were a lot of people who took advantage. Once in Paris we got hold of certain British missiles and we were caught out and Foreign Affairs went to P.W. and complained about it. P.W. took their side and it was a nasty thing. He wasn't always on your side, but if he was, you could depend on him.

'There's one thing I believe in and I've done so all my life. I'm a team man and I support the leader. I expect the same if I'm the leader – loyalty, and I did it for P.W. and I did it for F.W. whilst I was part of his team. If I had to disagree I did so but I always believed in covering their backs – which I did. You don't get that often amongst politicians. I took the culture and the way of thinking and management of the Defence Force to the political level. That was to my advantage and sometimes to my disadvantage,' said Malan.

In 1979 a White Paper on Defence was produced which noted 'increased political, economic and military pressure on South Africa' and expressed concern that 'the military threat against the RSA is intensifying at an alarming rate'. The idea of a total onslaught against South Africa as 'Moscow's stepping stone to world conquest' gained credence and acceptance. Today the concept of 'total onslaught' is sniggered about at dinner parties and dismissed as SADF and National Party propaganda of the time. The facts, however, present a different picture. On 4 June 1981 the Defence Force took the Cabinet to the operational area, where the Chief of the Defence Force, General Constand Viljoen, briefed them. The following are excerpts from his briefing document, which is categorised as 'secret'.

'So far there have previously been two such briefings, in March 1977 and in October 1978. In 1977 the emphasis fell upon the need for a total national strategy to be developed in order to successfully combat the total onslaught … The briefing in 1978 mainly concerned important facets regarding the total onslaught against the Republic and the SADF's responsibility in its prevention and therein the underlining of the Republic's foreign policy,' Viljoen told the Cabinet members.

'Though it was the idea to hold these briefings annually, for various reasons they did not take place in 1979 and 1980. Thus two and a half years have passed since our last meeting and in that time the general situation in South Africa has weakened considerably – so much so that the RSA, in my opinion, stands at a crossroads when it comes to national security and survival. This opinion is based upon amongst other things:

- The fall of the white power base in Rhodesia, which resulted in the failure of the solutions decided at the Lancaster House conference.
- Russian willingness, particularly after her successes in Angola, to take greater risks in direct violent actions, for example such as in Afghanistan.
- The position regarding the South West Africa question.
- The position regarding the internal situation, particularly in regard to the ANC.
- The about-turn in the attitude of the USA government towards us.
- The effect of the war of attrition [*uitmergelingsoorlog*] being waged against the SADF and the citizens [*volk*] as well as the lack of realism and understanding shown by the public with regard to the security situation.

'In truth, in my opinion,' said Viljoen, 'South Africa stands at a point that can be compared with that of the HMS *Fearless* discussions that took place between Mr Smith and Britain. Because we have to deal with a total onslaught that cannot be won solely on the battlefield, it is our intention today, and in the days to come, to present our position regarding the military aspects of the onslaught and how it can be curbed but also on other areas that affect national security. The goal of the Defence Force is to help win the struggle – not only the military part of it but the total struggle.'

'From the military's point of view, we realised the seriousness of the situation,' Viljoen explained later. 'I think the politicians in South Africa had a very unrealistic dependence on the military. They didn't realise that in this type of clash the military only represents about 20 per cent of the clash and 80 per cent is the political, psychological and economic situation. The ANC was very much more adept at using propaganda than the South Africans. Remember the Mandela–De Klerk situation. We had politicians, including De Klerk, who were absolutely clumsy in dealing with that kind of situation.

'I recall in the days when I was Chief of the Army and later Chief of the SADF at least four occasions where the Command Council of the Defence Force briefed the Cabinet on the kind of war that was going on,' said Viljoen. 'I remember being very frank with Cabinet, telling them we could carry on militarily for a very long period but eventually they would have to make some political moves to solve the problem. We told them they had to find a formula where all the people living in the country would feel involved and part of the country, which wasn't the case at the time. I remember those four times. We were very frank – we didn't exactly chastise them – but it was very good and very sound advice based on our studies. We warned the government that as every year passed their strategic options would become less and less.'

Viljoen's comments are borne out in the 1981 'secret' Cabinet briefing that took place in the operational area. 'That brings me to the essence of the problem staring us in the face,' he told the assembled politicians, 'namely the serious danger of ever-decreasing strategic options that go hand-in-hand with the passage of time in a multicultural population with a white minority where constitutional, social and economic problems are not solved in time – perhaps because of the inherent restrictions presented by the peacetime democratic process.

'The law of shrinking options is nowhere better illustrated than in the case of Zimbabwe/Rhodesia where with the passage of time and the lack of dynamic initiatives the negotiating position of the Smith government in reality became totally eroded to the point where the result of the Lancaster House conference was a foregone conclusion. In the end the situation in Rhodesia became a tragedy that stands in sharp contrast with the unbelievable optimism and confidence of the Rhodesians in the late 1960s. The Rhodesians had an unshakeable belief in a "high kill rate" and the ability of a few elite military units. The political, social and psychological aspects of the battle were left until it was too late. A basic principle in this sort of war is to make primary adjustments necessary to take the sting out of the revolution early in the battle from a position of strength rather than despair.

'I am of the opinion that when we South Africans compile our balance sheet we must be aware of this and not make the mistake of not allocating a high enough priority to the all-important time factor. The fact is, from a strategic point of view it is vitally important to use the available time optimally – politically and otherwise,' Viljoen told the Cabinet. 'The RSA is inextricably bound to the time factor of the international power game between East and West. The apparently positive and understanding position taken by the Reagan administration gives us a grace period of a couple of years but this positive development is increasingly being overshadowed by the shift of the French.

'Our interpretation is that the tolerance and pragmatism of the USA will depend upon how seriously South Africa tackles two main priorities, namely the achievement of a solution to the South West Africa question and the establishment of an internal dispensation that will accommodate the reasonable aspirations of all people and population groups and that will form a firm basis for peace and stability in the sub-continent. From a military standpoint it is imperative, while we are militarily unquestionably strong, to use the time available to us to obtain the most political advantages possible and to exploit all possibilities presented in a pro-active way to find solutions to the vital problems we face. This will only be possible if we do so in the form of a total strategy and improve the effectiveness of our interdepartmental co-ordination.'

Botha and the Cabinet listened to the military's arguments and took them to heart – not that P.W. needed convincing. The government believed that it was confronted by a total onslaught and that to counter it they had to develop their own strategy. This was identified in the White Paper for Defence, which stated: 'The process of ensuring and maintaining the sovereignty of a state's authority in a conflict situation has, through the evolution of warfare, shifted from the purely military to an integrated national action ... the resolution of conflict in the times in which we now live demands interdepartmental and co-ordinated actions in all fields – military, psychological, economic, political, sociological, technological, diplomatic, ideological and cultural, etc.'

In Parliament it was argued that the only counter-strategy that had any hope of success against a total onslaught was total resistance that could not be fragmented. Ad hoc efforts, it was argued, would be futile: the onslaught had to be resisted on a national basis in all spheres, by all national groups and inhabitants of the subcontinent. The strategy was to be based on the principles of self-determination, the protection of minority rights, Christian values, civilised norms and general welfare provided by a capitalist economy and underwritten by strong security forces.

And so the era of the securocrats was born. But the foundations had been laid some time before. The State Security Council had come into being in 1972 as a statutory Cabinet committee whose function it was to advise the government on the formulation and implementation of national policy and strategy in respect of national security, policy with regard to the combating of any specific threat facing the country, and intelligence priorities. Its members were:

- the Prime Minister (later President), who was the chairman;
- the senior Cabinet minister;
- the ministers of Foreign Affairs, Defence, Justice and Law & Order;
- the Chief of the SADF;
- the Commissioner of Police; and
- the directors-general of National Intelligence, Foreign Affairs and Justice.

Other ministers who were not statutory members were co-opted to attend specific meetings. The most notable of this group were the ministers of Constitutional Development and Planning, National Education and Finance.

The State Security Council was, many believed, a government within a government, which Cabinet sources say sometimes caused bitterness and resentment among those ministers who were left out and who felt they were not part of the 'inner circle'.

In 1978, the Joint Management System, otherwise known as the National Security Management System, was launched. Its main aim was to integrate all government departments in the day-to-day running of the country so that all facets of government would have an effect on the overall security picture. 'The Joint Management System was one of the best systems we ever had in this country,' said General Malan. 'It allowed us to address a situation like the toilets in Queenstown [in one particular case intelligence reports said a major cause of unrest in Queenstown was a lack of toilet facilities in the black residential areas] or the situation in Alexandra, which was at one stage declared a "liberated" area by the ANC. We [the SADF] approached the Public Works Department and told them they had to rectify the situation. They told us they had no money. "We don't give two hoots", we said. "Find the money and rectify the situation, it's affecting the security of the country." That was the problem. Other departments didn't realise they were involved in the security of the country. They thought of toilets, full stop. They didn't think how it affected our security.'

A series of management committees made up of representatives from all government departments was set up around the country. In almost all cases they were headed by SADF members. 'We never steamrolled any of the other departments,' said General Georg Meiring, who became Officer Commanding Wit Command in 1980 and set up the first Joint Management Centre in the country. 'In the beginning it was difficult, but later it worked very well. In years to come De Klerk made a bad mistake dismantling the system because it worked very well and was a good system. It bred some in-fighting because normally the military man was in charge because he was usually the most senior person on the committee and often the only person prepared to take on the responsibility. As the senior man he was usually elected chairman of the JMC. The department heads of all of the different departments formed part of the process. These people co-ordinated the thing on the ground and it really brought governance down to grassroots level.

'We did a lot of good things. We started a lot of hospitals and schools. We were getting people to co-ordinate these things but the blokes at the higher levels didn't like it because we were putting pressure on them. We could plan and they couldn't and it showed them up,' said Meiring. At Director General level they didn't like it all – not one bit! And specifically the ministers didn't like it. That is one of the things that put De Klerk up against P.W. – he wasn't part of the Security Management System which began in the State Security Council then progressed through the Secretariat and then to the different JMCs all over the country. He wasn't part of that system.

'Actually, for a time it really was a government within a government,' said Meiring. 'Because the military was available and had better knowledge and better know-how, they drove the system. De Klerk wasn't involved in the Security Council as a minister but his department (Education) was involved down at the bottom, and there it was getting instructions from the military. We would tell them, for example, at Schoemanskloof there must be a new school because if you build a school there you'll remove one of the major reasons for discontent and the security situation will be improved.

'I was in Wit (Command) for two years from 1979 to 1980 and the Soweto area really scared me. They weren't nice times,' Meiring explained. 'You could see things were simmering and it was going to boil over but it was difficult because the other departments didn't want to take the fire away from the pot. There was a lot of ill feeling because of departmental errors. The schools were wrong, the water was wrong, the whole system of Black Management Areas in the bigger towns like Soweto and Diepkloof didn't work. You found stupid people sitting there operating for themselves. They really didn't work for the thing as a whole. You could see the system was coming apart at its seams, so in all honesty, in the beginning, those weren't nice times.'

The management style of the military also ruffled a lot of departmental feathers. The SADF saw it as another battle that had to be won: obstacles in its path were simply rolled over. When the ANC declared Alexandra a 'liberated' area Malan decided he could not sit by idly and watch. 'Tutu was standing there and they waved the communist flag and so forth. Alex was so isolated that the police couldn't go in. I said: "Like hell, I'm going in with the military. We're going to do something about it." I did it on my own – I said to hell with the rest of the politicians. I didn't even take it to the State Security Council. Then I brought in the newspaper editors. I said to them: "You know, if I was born in Alexandra I would have been the leader of the terrorists in this country." They laughed at me. I explained the whole definition of what terrorism is, what a revolutionary war is, then flew them into Alexandra and showed them. They couldn't believe it – the filthy state of the place and the promises the government made about Alexandra that were never fulfilled. I showed them the filth and the conditions the people lived in.

'Remember, those houses were bought by the government in 1963,' Malan said. 'They paid cash of the order I would guess of about R20 000. Some of the previous owners still had the money – they never used it. There was no running water, there were no flush latrines. I went to Barend [du Plessis, Minister of Finance] and got some money from him – about R12 million. I went to the Regional Service Council and together with the Johannesburg Municipality they gave us the eastern side of the Jukskei river, approximately 140 hectares, to expand Alex. We got private enterprise in to build houses and we started cleaning up the whole area. We had a fantastic set-up there, run by a chap called Burger, he was the chairman. We changed the whole set-up of Alexandra. Unfortunately there was a chap there called, I think, Makisa – or something like that – who was initially in jail but when he came out he upset the whole public feeling there … and Alexandra is today what it used to be back in those days, except for the running water they have now.'

'But the editors, for the first time, came into Alexandra; and for the first time saw what the war was about, what the revolution was about. It was basically about getting a roof over your head, having food to eat, having education for your children, having a job to do and medical services. That was the crux of the whole thing. I doubt whether the politicians understood it. I can still recall the housing situation in South Africa. I got hold of all the contractors supplying houses and I took them to the operational area. We went to Omega base in northern Namibia and I took the Secretary of that particular department along. [Malan refused to say which department it was, but records show it was headed by Chris Heunis, Minister of Internal Affairs.] I said to them: "Gentlemen, what are your problems? Why can't you build? Why can't you progress?" They gave me umpteen reasons, but I said to them: "This is affecting national security in our country, but I can't go to a colleague with all those reasons – let's reduce them down to four or five, then I can go to a colleague and say: 'Can't we solve just these four problems? Then at least you'll make some headway.'" They gave me five reasons and one of those was that they had to get the approval of five or six departments before they could start any project, and it took ages to get those approvals. I went back and later got a letter from my colleague [almost certainly it was from Chris Heunis] telling me to keep my nose out of his business.

'That was the problem,' said Malan, 'my colleagues and certain departments

didn't know or understand what the revolution was about. They didn't understand what national security was – that they were really the people who had 80
per cent of the responsibility to supply. But they didn't supply their 80 per cent –
and that's what I testified in front of the Truth Commission. Militarily we never
lost, but politically … that's a question you should ask the politicians. That's
where they made the blunder.'

Then there was the matter of simple distrust. The military supremos were
often afraid that details of operations would be leaked, particularly by the
Department of Foreign Affairs. 'At times we had such a problem,' said General
Viljoen. 'That's maybe also the reason why we only involved Brand Fourie
[Secretary of Foreign Affairs] when they could do very little to change the whole
situation. Because it was not only the problem of leaking, but because people like
Pik couldn't keep their mouths shut. It wasn't deliberate leaking, but sometimes
they'd just talk about it and that could be most dangerous.

'Having been students of revolutionary war, we in the military realised the
importance of efficient government, of good administration, good relationships
between the blacks and the Defence Force and also the blacks and the whites in
the country. We went a long way in trying to coerce the other departments into
realising they had a very important part to play in the revolutionary war. That was
not always well received by the other departments – and I must say that a man
like P.W. Botha was very strict with the other departments. He realised that if you
caused dissatisfaction on any matter in the black community, you created a greater
potential for revolutionary reaction. P.W. Botha was very strict with the other
departments and that caused the departments to think we were the instigators
and were using him to apply pressure on them. At times that caused friction.

'I must admit the other state departments never really realised the importance
of what we were doing in countering the revolution in South Africa,' said Viljoen.
'Wherever possible we tried to brief them. Not all the specific details, but the fact
that we were going to launch an attack … yes, [Pik Botha] would know that. Let
me give you an example. There was a Swapo base in Sa da Bandeira (now called
Lubango), that for weeks we'd planned to strike using Mirage attack aircraft. We
were just waiting for the right weather conditions. Eventually when I got finality
– the weather was right and we were ready to go – I had to rush off to find Brand
Fourie, who was the then Secretary. I found him getting dressed for some diplomatic occasion. I said: "Brand, within so many hours we are going to be attacking
Lubango." At first he just looked stunned, then he smiled – I like Brand a lot, I
think he's a good chap – he smiled and said: "All right, we'll see how we deal

with this when the problem arises." So, yes – we certainly briefed them. We had to. Not on all the details of the military operation, but certainly on the fact we were going to do it.'

The Joint Management System involved the SADF in every facet of South African life. 'In February 1987 I was transferred to Pietersburg as Officer Commanding Far North Command,' said General Meiring. 'We worked there in what I called the "non-shooting war". Our strategy was not to keep the lid on but rather to take the fires away from the pot. The major emphasis was on trying to win the hearts and minds of the people. We got involved in everything. For example, we had vets and doctors all over the show. We had teachers, we repaired windmills and waterholes. We looked after sick cattle and we built roads; you name it and we did it.'

4

THE FIGHT FOR NAMIBIA

South African military involvement in Namibia began during World War I – on Christmas Day 1914, when Colonel Skinner of the Union Defence Force landed at Walvis Bay. It was the start of a campaign, ultimately led by Boer War General Louis Botha, that was to see the ill-equipped and unprepared German troops stationed in the colony quickly overrun. In 1919 the League of Nations mandated that South West Africa should fall under the control of South Africa. Once the South Africans had the country under their control they were determined not to let it go – no matter what international pressure they had to sustain or how many cases were brought before the World Court of Justice. White Afrikaner colonists were encouraged to move to the country, where they occupied huge farms on largely barren scrubland.

In effect, South West Africa, as it was called until it eventually gained independence in 1990, was South Africa's fifth province. To much of its indigenous black population this was an intolerable situation, especially as colonialism began to collapse and increasing numbers of African countries became independent. The South West African People's Organisation (Swapo), led by Sam Nujoma, grew out of this dissatisfaction.

Samuel Shafithuma Nujoma was born to a peasant family on 12 May 1929 in the remote Ongandjera region of Ovambo (Ovamboland) and spent his early years tending the family's few cattle and goats. At the age of 16 he left school to become a railway dining-car steward. After a fellow worker was discharged without compensation following a serious injury, Nujoma tried to start a trade union on the railways but was promptly fired for his attempts. Thereafter he worked as a clerk and a store assistant. In the late 1950s, together with Andreas Shipanga, he started the first Namibian trade union, the Ovamboland People's Organisation, later transformed into Swapo. In 1959 Nujoma went into exile to escape police harassment.

Swapo was founded in 1960 by Sam Nujoma, Herman Toivo ya Toivo and Jackob Kuhanga. Nujoma was elected president and spent the next six years petitioning the United Nations to force South Africa to release Namibia. After South Africa refused a UN order to withdraw from South West Africa in 1966, Swapo embarked on an armed struggle. Toivo ya Toivo was imprisoned in South Africa from 1968 to 1984. In 1973 the United Nations declared Swapo the sole representative of the people of Namibia, and in 1990 Sam Nujoma became Namibia's first democratically elected president.

Until 1973 the responsibility for security and counter-insurgency was held by the South African Police. However, as Swapo incursions increased, the SAP, though they refused to admit it, began to find it difficult to cope. 'They were still involved in Rhodesia at the time and did not have the capacity,' said General Constand Viljoen. The fact the police were committed elsewhere pleased the SADF leadership enormously. It was an opportunity to give their troops some operational experience – to blood them in a low-intensity war. 'We jumped at the opportunity when we were told to take over the security of South West Africa,' said Viljoen.

In April 1973 the SADF officially assumed responsibility for the protection of South West Africa's approximately 1 500 km northern border. But the police refused to relinquish all of the pie and remained in Namibia in the form of the notorious *Koevoet* (Crowbar) unit, which was accused of many atrocities in the country. 'Koevoet were good bush-fighters, there's no doubt about that,' said a former member. 'We probably had the highest kill-count in all of the security forces, but I suppose it is possible some of the hundreds or even thousands we racked up weren't terrs but rather civilians who found themselves in the wrong place at the wrong time. The guys in the unit weren't always too choosy. A lot of them ended up in Koevoet because it was the last step before being thrown out of the force or being put in jail. I think the brass figured they could be put to good use in South West,' he said.

Koevoet's activities and methods were the stuff bar-room war stories were made of, but they stuck in the throats of the military generals. 'I could never agree with the methods of Koevoet,' said Viljoen. 'They had a cruelty about them that certainly didn't further the hearts and minds of the people. In the SADF we made a far greater study of how to win such a war than the police ever did. They used cruel, crude methods. In whatever we did we always bore in mind the effect it would have on the general population. We realised, in a revolutionary war it is not a case of how many people you kill but rather the battle for the minds of the people.'

General Jannie Geldenhuys came to the same conclusion while commander of the military forces in South West Africa. 'They would, for example, go into an area, "clean" it up, then collect the bodies and drag them through the town behind their vehicles. Then they'd be away again, thinking they'd done a hell of a good job. Obviously this kind of action upset the local population greatly and we'd find we [the SADF] were suddenly getting no more co-operation from the locals,' Geldenhuys said. 'One of the problems was that they never had anyone stationed there permanently. If that had been the case they'd never have done operations like that because the commander would still be there tomorrow and the next week, etc. His merits would be assessed according to the security situation after he'd been there a year or two. He wouldn't be interested in dragging people through the streets. But these guys didn't care because they knew they'd soon be gone.

'The areas we're talking about were like provinces with their own chief minister and ministers. Often, as a result of intimidation by the revolutionaries it was difficult to find someone prepared to serve as the chief minister and when we eventually found someone who'd stick his neck out and finally got his co-operation, after a single incident like that he'd have no choice but to resign. It happened in the Kavango and in Ovamboland,' said Geldenhuys.

'Koevoet was not a law unto itself,' said General Georg Meiring. 'Koevoet was just *unto itself*. Their command and control system was stupid. They were controlled out of Pretoria directly whereas our system was completely different. Our commanders weren't told when to do what. They were told what to do in a broad sense but the Koevoet commander got his instructions from Pretoria. A policeman is always trained as an individual. He's the copper on the beat. He's the detective and he doesn't like anyone involved in his case because he might end up being scooped. The more successes he has, the better are his chances of promotion. He's trained from the very beginning to be an individual. The military is different. There you're trained to be part of a team. You learn from the very beginning you can't operate on your own. The military's system of command and control means a man can be held responsible for what he does. The policeman, on the other hand, is uncontrollable because he works as a loner. This means the man sitting in command back in Pretoria can never be and doesn't accept responsibility for what is being done somewhere else. It is two different ways of life, and working together is a nightmare. I hated the way they operated.'

Georg Meiring has the unique distinction of having commanded both the apartheid defence force and that of the new South Africa, but his entrance into the military was almost accidental. 'Like any little boy, I liked playing soldiers while growing up on a farm in the Orange Free State that bordered Lesotho,' he said. 'I never thought of going to war but enjoyed reading about it and followed the Korean conflict closely.' When he matriculated Meiring went to university and eventually ended up with a master's degree in physics and a position as a lecturer at the University of the Orange Free State. 'But after a difference of opinion with my professor I took a few days' leave and went to visit a friend in Pretoria who had signed on with the Permanent Force. I decided I wanted to join.' In May 1963 Meiring was told to report for duty and sent to the School of Signals, where he was appointed as an instructor with the rank of captain. Shortly thereafter he was sent to England on a 13-month-long technical officer's course and then appointed as Staff Officer of Signals, responsible for the maintenance of existing and development of new telecommunications equipment for the SADF.

'I wrote most of the equipment specifications,' said Meiring. 'When the war in Angola started we were a step or two ahead of everyone else – or at the very least we were right up there with the best in the world.' It was Meiring's expertise in electronic warfare that was to play the major role in the Defence Force's intelligence-gathering capabilities. The groundwork he did would prove crucial when, 10 years later, South Africa became involved in the biggest conventional battles it had fought since World War II. 'I became responsible for mainline communications and electronic warfare,' said Meiring. 'That involved jamming enemy frequencies, interception, code-breaking, listening in, etc. We had monitoring stations at Rundu, Katima Mulilo, a few in Rhodesia and later on also in Malawi. During the Portuguese era in Angola we also had a station at what is now called Cuito Cuanavale. We listened to everyone north of us. We helped the Rhodesians to listen to Mugabe and Nkomo. We listened to Swapo, Zambia, the MPLA, Fapla (the military wing of the MPLA) and the Cubans. It was very sophisticated. If anyone north of us opened their mouths we had it on tape somewhere. We picked up one of the Rhodesian SAS's crossings into Zambia across the Zambezi, for example. Our communications interception system was the best in the world at the time.'

'In certain aspects we were more advanced even than the Americans,' said Meiring. 'For example, they didn't have "hopper" systems (frequency hopping radios). Over 90 per cent of the intelligence we operated on during the war came from interceptions. The few other bits and pieces came mainly from aerial photography. As whites we couldn't go in amongst the blacks to infiltrate.'

But despite the sophisticated equipment there were still foul-ups that led to unnecessary deaths. 'On one occasion we got intercepts at Katima Mulilo that Swapo was laying mines and setting ambushes for the police – at that particular point in time they [the police] were patrolling the cut-line,' said Meiring. 'We went to their offices (they were next to ours at Katima Mulilo) and gave them the information. Their response was: "Fuck them! Let them carry on." Within the next hour or two they had six of their blokes dead on the cut-line!'

Electronic warfare is an exact but tiring science. 'You never really get a major interception,' said Meiring. 'Rather you get a lot of interceptions from which a pattern emerges. Out of that you build your intelligence. Thousands upon thousands of messages were intercepted.' While the South Africans were listening, so were the Cubans and the Angolans. 'There is no doubt they intercepted us,' said Meiring, 'but they were not as good as we were because our equipment at the time was much more sophisticated. The Cubans and Angolans were very good at aerial photography and could respond very quickly. In that area they had better equipment than us, as they had in-flight photo interpretation capabilities. We had to bring our material back to base for interpretation. We were also worried about satellite photography.'

Prior to Operation Savannah, Swapo's military wing, the People's Liberation Army of Namibia (Plan), posed little real threat to the SADF. Their military escapades were at best haphazard and easily handled by the South Africans. But Savannah was to be a turning point. Swapo now had a component vital for any revolutionary army: a safe haven across an international boundary. 'A military victory cannot be achieved unless the host country can be convinced, in some way or other, to withdraw its support,' General Jannie Geldenhuys wrote in his book *A General's Story*. South Africa had proved that even with obsolete weapons it could fight a conventional war, and Swapo knew it. To take the Boers on in such a way would be suicide – but a revolutionary war was another matter altogether. Geldenhuys wrote: 'The lessons I learned about revolutionary war were:

- A revolutionary war is a political war.
- The aim of both sides in a revolutionary war is to win the support of the population, their approval, sympathy and active participation.

- The government must win the political initiative by propagating a more attractive cause than that offered by the insurgents.
- The danger of complacency (refusal to acknowledge the real situation) must be avoided before and during a revolution.
- The existence of an outstanding intelligence organization is essential.
- In revolutionary warfare bureaucratic delays are as dangerous as subversion itself.

'Conventional war is influenced by exact sciences, technology and military equipment,' Geldenhuys went on. 'By concentrating fire power on the right places at the right time it is possible to cause enough destruction to win crucial battles and force a final decision. In this way a war can be ended in a short time. Insurgency warfare, however, consists of a multitude of small battles. One cannot bring such a war to a quick end through military action because the enemy does not present a geographic military target on which to concentrate fire power.'

The stage was set for a new era for the SADF. 'I have on various occasions said South Africa is not prepared to stand on behalf of the free world alone,' Defence Minister P.W. Botha told Parliament on 24 January 1976. 'Furthermore, South Africa will defend with determination its own borders and those interests and borders we are responsible for.' To many, Botha's words were little more than hot air. Politically South Africa was more isolated than ever. Vorster's gamble to win favour with black Africa had failed and South Africa's military limitations had been badly exposed. A communist, Soviet-sponsored army with an impressive arsenal of high-tech weaponry was camped on its doorstep, training Swapo and ANC guerrillas to infiltrate South Africa and Namibia. Most experts believed that Unita, South Africa's sole ally in the region, would quickly disappear following the removal of US aid. 'Savimbi has no illusions about how swiftly the end is coming. The war in Angola, beyond guerrilla fighting, is almost over,' California Democrat Senator John Tunney said in 1976. At the same time Senator Dick Clark, who was largely instrumental in getting CIA aid to Unita cut off, told the MPLA, Soviets and Cubans that 'the tide of history had turned in their favour'.

In Moscow, Havana and Luanda the Marxist leaders rubbed their hands in glee. Castro and Brezhnev, giddy with the success of their clients, began talking of an international socialist system that would sweep through Africa all the way down to Cape Town. In South Africa many believed that the country had lost to the Cubans and the MPLA and that their boys had died for nothing. 'I don't see it that way,' said General Geldenhuys. 'We need to ask whether we lost militarily, politically or strategically. In military terms we certainly did not lose. There's no doubt about that at all. The order to withdraw was not given because South Africa was having problems with the military situation.'

There is no doubt the ANC was quick to take advantage of the situation: many youngsters fled the country to be trained as guerrillas in a variety of African countries, including Angola. Swapo too had established a network of training bases in Angola and 1976 saw the beginning of a dramatic upsurge in insurgency activities by them.

'From Sam Nujoma's point of view the situation [Operation Savannah] also presented disadvantages,' said General Geldenhuys. 'Unita, which was once Swapo's ally, was now one of its bitterest enemies, and they both operated in the same areas of southern Angola. That ultimately took a lot of pressure off the SADF. Because Unita absolutely dominated in the south-east, that was one part of the border we didn't have to look at. That meant we were able to locate our forces only in those areas where Swapo could infiltrate.'

December 1976 saw a change in Swapo tactics when it began targeting traditional leaders who were sympathetic to the administration. Deputy Chief Hausiki Enkaile was murdered and the son of Chief Willipard Enkaile was abducted and taken to Angola. In February 1977 a South African base near the borders of Angola and Zambia was attacked and three soldiers wounded. Twelve insurgents died in counter-attacks before they were able to get back across the Zambian border. A month later P.W. Botha announced that during the two years since 1 April 1975, 231 insurgents had been killed in Ovambo, Kavango and the eastern Caprivi. In the same period 33 SADF members had died and Swapo had murdered 53 members of the local population.

With the end of Operation Savannah, Unita and the FNLA were left largely to fend for themselves. The South Africans told them to revert to hit-and-run guerrilla tactics, then withdrew from Angola to concentrate on their own problems. In the north the FNLA forces, which had failed in their attack on Luanda, were quickly routed by the MPLA and soon disappeared. Unita withdrew into the south-eastern corner of Angola, where it built a capital in the bush at Jamba and began regrouping and reorganising.

The MPLA–Cuban–Soviet alliance believed that with the withdrawal of the South Africans, Unita would quickly be annihilated. They could not have been more wrong. They hadn't reckoned with Jonas Savimbi. Using the lessons learned by Castro's colleague Che Guevara (with whom Savimbi had formed a friendship in the mid-1960s) during his battles with the Batista regime in the 1950s, and drawing on the teachings of Mao Zedong, at whose Nanking Military Academy he had learned to fight the Portuguese, Savimbi took his people into the bush and taught them to survive. His forces endured incredible hardships but with these they grew stronger and when it was realised that they had not simply disappeared into the mists of history, a variety of countries began supplying small amounts of direct aid. China sent small quantities of weapons which were ferried through Zaire. A number of Arab countries, as well as France, provided cash and Morocco supplied both weapons and training.

The MPLA, as the de facto government in Angola, resumed support for Swapo. Moral support quickly became active logistical and training support and the organisation was given permission to set up bases and to conduct operations from southern Angola.

Swapo activity increased. In October 1977 a skirmish involving 88 insurgents began just inside the Namibian border. In follow-up operations the SADF killed 61 Plan soldiers and destroyed two bases 20 km inside Angola. The South Africans lost six men. In February 1978 Swapo insurgents crossed into the Caprivi from Zambia and ambushed an SADF Land Rover, which they destroyed with an RPG-7 rocket, killing three occupants and seriously wounding a fourth. A month later they struck again when they murdered Chief Clemens Kapuuo, leader of the Hereros, Chairman of the Democratic Turnhalle Alliance (DTA) and a fierce critic of Swapo.

'There was a time when it was correct to say that Plan wasn't much of a factor,' said General Geldenhuys, 'but at the time I arrived in South West in 1977 they were just big enough of a factor that the political and diplomatic process had to be protected against [their] military intervention. Later, from about 1984 onwards, Plan had many commendable features as a military force. If they were in a tight spot they were good fighters. They were experts at escape and evasion. I recall many occasions where troops and junior commanders told me Swapo cadres were better fighters than Fapla and the Cubans and, if they had the choice, they'd rather engage Fapla than Plan.'

The South African government wanted some sort of political settlement at the time. 'When I was sent back to Namibia midway through 1977 it was the beginning of a new era in the country,' said Geldenhuys. 'It was the period when it was said that the South Westers must decide their own future and political and institutional steps were taken to give effect to that policy. The Administrator was replaced by an Administrator General and Namibia took over all functions of government with the exception of foreign affairs, economic affairs and defence.

An election was arranged for December 1978 to elect the leaders of the 11 ethnic groups to form a conference to write a new constitution and the government agreed to have discussions with the United Nations and the Western countries. This was a case where we [the military] couldn't say we were doing the fighting while they [the politicians] did nothing.' General Magnus Malan, as Chief of the Defence Force, gave explicit instructions to Geldenhuys, as General Officer Commanding in Namibia, that the military were to remain strictly in step with the political and constitutional developments taking place.

In 1977 the international political spotlight was focused firmly on South West Africa. Pretoria was engaged in negotiations with the United Nations and the Western Five (Great Britain, the United States, Canada, France and West Germany) about the independence of Namibia. The South African government, while not opposed in principle to the idea, had a number of reservations and wanted all Cuban soldiers first to withdraw from Angola. The last thing Pretoria needed was for Namibia to become another safe haven from which insurgents could operate against South Africa.

Internally Namibia was also undergoing profound political changes. In September 1977 Dirk Mudge led a breakaway from the ruling white National Party to form the Republican Party, which in turn formed alliances with political parties from other race groups. Swapo stalwart Andreas Shipanga returned from exile in 1978 to found the Swapo Democrats, which then became part of the Namibian National Front.

On 26 September 1977 the meeting between South Africa and the Western Five ended without any agreement being reached. In February the next year Western negotiators visited Windhoek for consultations with the leaders of Namibia's internal political parties, including the internal wing of Swapo. That same month, in New York, they met the South African Minister of Foreign Affairs, Pik Botha, and Swapo leader Sam Nujoma, but could make no progress. Nujoma said Swapo was not interested in taking part in the election, and that the aim of his struggle was to seize power in Namibia. He announced Swapo would do all it could to disrupt and wreck the process.

On 25 April 1978 the South African government formally accepted the Western proposals for a settlement in South West Africa. It was against this background that the SADF had to operate in South West Africa. 'We knew we had to prevent military adventures and violence from becoming a means to seize power or unduly influence political decisions,' said General Geldenhuys. 'The question was how we could do so.' The answer he, as the General Officer Commanding SWA, and General Viljoen, as the Chief of the Army, came up with was a new doctrine of seizing the initiative. 'The basic truth in an insurgency war is that the insurgent, potentially and often in practice, has the initiative,' said Geldenhuys. 'For example, a criminal who plans to snatch a lady's handbag is the one who selects the time, place and victim. He has the initiative. The same goes for the person who plants a bomb or sets up an ambush. In a conflict situation the one who has the initiative seldom loses and we knew we had to find the way to seize and keep the initiative. One way to do this was to act first instead of waiting, by taking the battle to the insurgents.'

On 4 May 1978, Ascension Day, the SADF put this doctrine into practice when it launched a series of semi-conventional strikes against Swapo bases in southern Angola. In an operation code-named Reindeer, the SAAF first bombed and strafed Plan's main logistics support base near Mavinga (called Moscow by Swapo), some 250 km inside Angola, then followed up with an assault by paratroopers. Simultaneously a mechanised unit attacked forward transit camps in the border area, including a large complex known as Vietnam near Chetequera, 28 km north of the border. Viljoen was in the thick of things. 'I went in with the troops,' he said. 'That afternoon we ran into trouble. The MiGs were coming from Lubango and because of the great distances our Mirages had to fly they could only stay in the target area for three or four minutes. At one stage it looked as though we wouldn't be able to withdraw by helicopter so we decided we'd have to walk out. It was the first time my people became angry with me. I was there in my capacity as Chief of the Army and many didn't think I'd done a wise thing. They were worried I'd be caught.' As it turned out, Viljoen and his party were successfully extracted by helicopter late that afternoon. 'I always said that if I had been taken prisoner I would have started negotiations in prison to end the war,' he said.

In the end the SADF lost six men in Operation Reindeer. Around 1 000 Swapo combatants died, 200 were captured and large quantities of equipment and weapons were seized or destroyed. Internationally, Swapo and its allies claimed the bases attacked were refugee camps and that hundreds of civilians had been massacred. They called it the Cassinga massacre. The claim was hotly denied by Geldenhuys. 'There is extensive evidence, reinforced by unfakeable aerial photographs showing the extensive fortifications, and the resistance offered by the defenders was so stiff and protracted that the paratroopers stayed much longer than they had planned and had to leave the garrison still holding part of the town,' he wrote in his book some 12 years later. 'It would have been impossible for 250 men to commit mass atrocities without somebody talking about it out of aversion.'

Cross-border pre-emptive strikes became a way of life for the SADF and though the government and the Minister of Defence carried the ultimate responsibility for such operations, SADF commanders on the ground enjoyed a measure of independence. The instructions from the Chief of the Defence Force changed according to the political situation and differed from country to country. The criteria when it came to crossing the Angolan border, for example, differed from those that applied to Botswana. 'The exact numbers changed,' said Magnus Malan. 'For example, the Minister of Defence would give me permission to use troops up to 200 km north of the Namibian border without first getting authority from him. I would then tell the Chief of the Army he could operate up to 150 km inside without first clearing it with me. If he wanted to go further than that I had to first give approval. He would then tell the sector commander he could go 100 km into Angola without first having to clear it, etc. When it came to some of the other countries we couldn't cross the border without first getting the approval of the Minister or the Cabinet.'

In September 1979 Angolan President Agostinho Neto died and was succeeded by José Eduardo dos Santos, who was as opposed to South Africa and Unita as his predecessor. Early in 1979 intelligence reports indicated the presence of Swapo bases inside Zambia and at a variety of places in Angola. In March 1979 two cross-border operations code-named Safraan and Rekstok were launched. Several bases around Sinjembele and the Njinje forest in Zambia were attacked and destroyed. Despite howls of protest from President Kenneth Kaunda, the Zambians, fearing more South African strikes, confidentially made it clear to Swapo that they'd be better off operating from another country. Shortly afterwards Swapo abandoned its Zambian bases.

While SADF forces attacked Swapo positions in Zambia, another force struck Swapo bases at Muongo, Oncua, Henhombe and Heque in Angola. During an air attack a Canberra bomber was hit by ground fire and crashed, killing its crew. In many quarters the two operations were considered failures: in some cases Swapo cadres had abandoned their bases by the time the SADF forces arrived. Whether or not there was a security leak is not clear. What is certain is that Swapo knew the South Africans were coming before they got there.

In Pretoria the advantages of a strong Unita had long been apparent. If Unita could be helped to dominate much of south-east Angola it would become almost impossible for Swapo to operate in Kavango or the Caprivi to any significant degree. A strong and active Unita also meant Fapla forces deployed to shield Swapo would have to be reallocated to counter Unita activities – and, as proved later to be the case, Fapla began to demand that Swapo supply manpower for its campaigns against Savimbi's forces, further reducing Swapo's ability to operate in South West Africa.

Through the office of the Chief of Staff Intelligence, in 1977 South Africa once again had begun supplying training and equipment to Unita. For the first few years following Operation Savannah, the MPLA and Cubans had tended to consider Unita as nothing more than a terrorist movement, with little or no support amongst the local people. It was a fatal mistake. Charismatic Savimbi had a large following in the areas in which his forces operated. By the time Luanda woke up, Unita had secured itself in the south-eastern corner of the country, from where it could operate with virtual impunity. By 1980 Unita was active in the central regions of the country and had captured Mavinga from Fapla. The town was to become Savimbi's main forward logistics base.

In June 1980, Operation Sceptic (better known to the troopies as Operation Smoke Shell) was launched. It was a lightning raid against a Swapo base in southern Angola and was to be the first time since Savannah that the SADF became involved in serious clashes with Fapla. It was also to be the first time the South Africans encountered mechanised Swapo units. In a number of bloody and bitterly fought clashes Swapo's forward base was destroyed and 380 Plan members died. The South Africans lost 17 men but captured hundreds of tons of equipment and supplies as well as a large number of vehicles. At the time it was the biggest South African mechanised infantry operation since World War II.

At around this time the SADF embarked on a plan to win the hearts and minds of the local population. Qualified troops were taken away from combat duties and deployed as teachers, doctors, road-builders, tractor and windmill repairers, etc. Just how successful the 'plough and plant' programmes were is open to debate. 'They tended to prevent insurgency from starting in an area but were less successful in countering it if it had already commenced,' said Geldenhuys. 'The Citizen Force men were more successful in this kind of operation than the national servicemen. A Citizen Force sergeant with a beard, proudly presenting a photograph of his wife and four kids, made a better impression on the head of a kraal than a brave and fit young lieutenant with down on his chin and a snapshot of his school girlfriend.' But there is also evidence that there were some cases where the programme backfired because local people who accepted the SADF generosity were often seen as collaborators and were singled out for retribution. Still, this was sometimes used to the advantage of the South Africans. 'If we knew there was someone politically active with Swapo, the Com-ops guy would go to him and dump a load of maize and sugar at his home,' said General Meiring. 'He'd make sure everyone heard when he yelled: "Okay, thanks for your help. See you again next month." That made the local Swapo people think he was an informer.'

The South Africans employed many other unorthodox tactics. Geldenhuys introduced a competition for SADF units, complete with a floating trophy that was presented quarterly, called the Fox Competition. 'The idea was to encourage commanders on all levels to think creatively and innovatively,' he said. 'To obtain total initiative you had to outfox your opponents all over and everywhere at the same time. The first recipients of the trophy were Commandant Deon Ferreira, then Commander of 32 Battalion, and Major Mossie Basson of the Air Force. They came up with an idea in which troops were placed at a selected location north of the border, where they stacked waste oil rags and old tyres. Smoke grenades were attached to an Alouette helicopter which would then fly high above the selected area. After a while the helicopter would dive towards the ground while the grenades released smoke. As soon as the helicopter reached the pile, it would return to base on the deck, out of sight of the enemy. In the meantime the troops would set the pile alight, sending a column of smoke into the sky. The Swapo cadres would then go to investigate the helicopter "crash" and clash with troops on terrain which they had selected and prepared.

'We encouraged the application of this technique throughout the whole operational area,' said Geldenhuys, 'and it worked. In Zambia, Commandant A.K. de Jager and his Air Force counterpart, Major Vink Hattingh, used two Impala aircraft instead of Alouettes, because they can be spotted from much further away. One of the Imps would simulate a crash by diving down to the ground and flying back home at tree-top level. The other would circle over the area of the "accident" a few times and then fly back home. It sometimes took the cadres a bit longer to reach the spot, but the result was always the same. The number of South African aircraft Zambia and Swapo reported to have shot down totalled more than the whole South African Air Force inventory!'

In Angola, Fapla and the Cubans were increasingly coming under pressure from Unita, which was making steady gains. Fapla attempted to retake Mavinga in March 1981, but was easily defeated by Savimbi's men. In May it attacked again, this time in more determined fashion, but was stopped at the Lomba River by a concerted Unita effort. When the rebels brought in four additional battalions they routed the Fapla forces, which split up and fled back to Cuito Cuanavale. A series of offensives continued against Savimbi, but all of these failed and in 1982 Unita launched its own offensive and swept north to take Lumbala and Cangonga. By the next year it controlled most of the Benguela railway line and could safely move men and supplies to launch operations further north.

In the United States the liberal Carter administration was replaced in 1981 by that of Ronald Reagan – a man with conservative, strongly anti-communist views. The Soviets and Cubans responded to the deteriorating military situation in Angola by supplying more sophisticated and expensive weaponry and equipment. The number of Cuban troops was also increased dramatically. Western intelligence reported the arrival of sophisticated MiG-23 bombers, Su-22 fighter bombers, Mi-24 'Hind' attack helicopters, T-55 and T-54 battle tanks as well as sophisticated anti-aircraft defence systems. In the meantime, the South Africans continued with a series of cross-border strikes against Plan, which moved its bases further north and dug in close to Fapla and Cuban installations for added protection. Operation Protea in 1981 saw the South African Valkyrie 127 mm rocket launcher fired in battle for the first time. It was developed after the SADF reported back about the devastating effects it had experienced at the wrong end of the Soviet BM-21 Stalin Organs during Operation Savannah. The table was being set for the final showdown in southern Africa.

At the highest levels of command there were tensions between some of the South African generals. In 1983 General Meiring took over from General Charles Lloyd as General Officer Commanding in South West Africa. 'When I left for South West Africa, General Viljoen said he wanted to give me combat command experience so I could come back and become Chief of the Army,' said Meiring. 'But while I was there they made Kat Liebenberg, who was my junior, Chief of the Army. It wasn't a problem because we were friends, but Geldenhuys didn't like me. I don't know why. There could be many reasons. I never did him any wrong. Geldenhuys is a very strange man. He's very self-centred. He likes to surround himself with people who speak the same language he does and who pay him the necessary respect. I know he says he doesn't do that but he does. He does not like to be confronted head-on by people who differ from him. He's a strong personality but not a strong commander. I worked for him as Deputy Chief of the Army when I was in Pretoria and it was very difficult because he was never there. He was writing his book at the time and he had me running the army. When I did get to see him it'd only be for five minutes before he'd say: "Time's up." I never had good communications with him.

'He had a very strong following in South West Africa and when I went there he instructed me on how to work with this person and how to work with that bloke, etc. I listened and said: "Yes, thanks for the information." When I got there I just did things naturally, the way I normally do. At some or other function in Namibia for civilians, somebody said to me: "You're the best commander we've ever had in South West Africa." Why he said that I don't know. I don't think it was true but anyway he said it. From then on, Geldenhuys, for whatever reasons, didn't like me. He had a major impact in choosing his successor when he became Chief of the SADF. It was between him and Malan. Malan said I was meddling in the politics of South West Africa, which wasn't true. I don't know why he said that but one day at an airfield he said to me: "You must stop getting mixed up in politics." My response was: "Good Lord, General, I'm not involved in politics – not even nearly!"'

At the end of 1983 South African intelligence operatives began warning that Swapo was planning a full-scale infiltration for early in 1984. To pre-empt this, Operation Askari, under the command of General Meiring, kicked off on 6 December 1983. Its aim was to disrupt Plan's logistical infrastructure and to neutralise command and control systems. The South Africans intended to achieve this through a series of air raids and ground attacks. Although the attacks were aimed at Swapo, Fapla and the Cubans soon became involved. On 3 January Fapla's 11 Brigade and two Cuban battalions clashed with SADF units when they attacked Plan's headquarters and a base 5 km from Cuvelai: 21 SADF members died in the battle, but not before the Cubans and Fapla had been driven off, leaving 324 dead. 'We annihilated a brigade of Fapla,' said Meiring. 'As a result there was a hue and cry from the Russians and Americans for us to withdraw.'

Most military analysts agree that Askari was the catalyst that pushed Luanda into negotiations with the South Africans in Lusaka later that year. The MPLA wanted to find a way to avoid clashes with an SADF that appeared militarily superior. It wanted time to consolidate so it could concentrate all its efforts on getting rid of Unita, which at that stage had virtually brought Angola to its knees. 'Although it was not the intention, the operation convinced Angola to engage in discussions with South Africa over a cessation of hostilities in southern Angola,' said General Geldenhuys. 'The talks, in which I was involved, took place in Lusaka and culminated in the signing of the Lusaka Agreement in February 1984.' It was agreed that a Joint Monitoring Committee, consisting of all parties to the agreement, would monitor the withdrawal of the South African troops from Angola. Angola undertook to ensure that no Swapo soldiers, Cuban forces or conventional weapons such as tanks or artillery pieces would be allowed in the area evacuated by the South Africans.

'Once a week General Geldenhuys, General "Joop" Joubert and I sat down with the Angolans and talked to them,' said Meiring. 'If it was jointly decided that there was not a lot of Swapo activity, we [the SADF] would withdraw to the next spot. And so we started withdrawing. Eventually we got out completely but at the same time we knew it wouldn't work so we started working clandestinely behind the lines. We monitored more than we operated. In terms of the agreement the last South African troops left Angola by mid-1985 but by the end of the year we were back again because it just didn't work. [Terrorist] incidents in Ovamboland rose dramatically. The agreement only worked for six months.'

Swapo was not part of the Lusaka Agreement and was not bound by its terms. At the same time that the SADF was doing all in its power to kill as many Plan cadres as possible, secret discussions were taking place with its leadership. 'In 1985 I went with the then Administrator General of South West Africa, Willie van Niekerk, and his secretary, Sean Cleary, to the Cape Verde Islands to speak to Sam Nujoma and his crowd,' said General Meiring. 'The meeting was set up to discuss how we could come to grips with each other politically. I think it was put together through the instigation of the Americans. Sean had a lot of contacts in the States and he put the thing together. I was brought in from the bush. I stopped just long enough to shower and change clothes before boarding the aircraft. We flew to Sal Island and were then taken to the main island where the President's guesthouse was put at our disposal. Later we were taken to a conference facility where we met the Swapo delegation. There were four or five of them. No one chaired the meeting.

'After both sides were welcomed and introduced by the president of the Cape Verde Islands we were left alone to get on with it,' said Meiring. 'It was strange when I came face to face with Nujoma for the first time. There was no hatred. I didn't feel anything at all. I had this experience later with the ANC. I wasn't fighting this guy personally. If I saw him in the bush I would have killed him, but I didn't have anything against him personally. I was more curious about what he was like as a person. How does he speak? ... What type of person is he? He's a moron, but that's beside the point. He wasn't impressive at all. He still understood Afrikaans well. At one or other stage during the discussions I said: "Nujoma, *jou gat*, man!" (Nujoma, your backside, man) and he just laughed at me.'

According to Meiring, the meeting lasted less than an hour. Swapo was in no mood to negotiate. 'We asked them to work with the Government of National Unity,' said Meiring. 'They said the GNU was just a bunch of puppets and that they wouldn't talk to them. We said we'd like you to sit down with them so we can talk about the future administration of Namibia. Their response was basically: "Bugger you!" so we got up and left amicably. It wasn't a shouting match. Nujoma's not very articulate. He didn't say very much but as we stood up to leave he said to Willie van Niekerk: "You must keep my house warm for me!"'

There is some doubt as to whether or not P.W. Botha knew about Meiring's meeting with Swapo. Many believe – bearing in mind how Botha later censured business leaders for meeting with the 'enemy' ANC – that he did not. 'I'm not sure if P.W. knew or not,' said Meiring. 'My impression is it was an initiative by Willie van Niekerk and Sean Cleary and that later they knew about it at Foreign Affairs but not while it was happening.'

5

PRETORIA VS. MOSCOW:
CUITO CUANAVALE

The Lusaka Agreement effectively hamstrung the South Africans, forcing them to curtail large-scale overt operations. The MPLA–Cuban–Soviet alliance began preparing for what they believed would be the final thrust that would destroy Unita once and for all. Troops and equipment poured into Angola at unprecedented rates. By the end of 1985 the Cuban troop presence in the country stood at 31 000 and more were on their way. They were supported by around 3 500 East Germans, and Soviets filled crucial roles in strategic planning, intelligence, training and the manning of much of the sophisticated weaponry supplied by Moscow.

In his book *The War for Africa* (Ashanti Publishing) Fred Bridgland says that according to Western intelligence reports, the MPLA received more than one billion dollars' worth of new Soviet arms between January 1984 and August 1985. Fapla's tank force was almost 500-strong, consisting of some 350 T-55/54s, 150 older T-34s and 50 amphibious PT-76s. Its Air Force had 30 advanced MiG-23 bombers, 8 advanced Su-22 fighter bombers, 50 MiG-21 fighter bombers, 16 elderly MiG-17 fighter bombers, 33 MI-24 'Hind' helicopter gunships, 27 French Alouette assault helicopters and 69 MI-8 and MI-17 transport helicopters. At the same time, the US Congress rescinded the 10-year-old Clark Amendment that prevented America from supplying weapons to Unita.

Included in the aid supplied to Savimbi were Stinger anti-aircraft missiles, the most advanced shoulder-fired anti-aircraft weapon in the world.

On 2 September 1985, to coincide with the Non-Aligned Nations Movement ministerial meeting in Luanda, the MPLA and its allies launched their largest ever offensive against Unita. Its aim was to capture the Cazombo salient and thereby retake Savimbi's main logistics base at Mavinga in the south-east. From there they could launch a final assault on Jamba, Unita's headquarters in the bush. If they could achieve their objective they would be able to cut South African support to the rebel movement and finish it off once and for all.

Fapla advanced on two fronts simultaneously, exploiting its greater conventional strength to prevent Unita from engaging first one force then the other. The northern advance towards the Cazombo salient consisted of nine infantry brigades supported by tanks and air cover. The southern force consisted of 11 infantry brigades that advanced along two axes; one towards Mavinga and the other towards the source of the Lomba River, which would then allow them to attack Mavinga from the west. Within five days both Fapla forces had reached the outer defences of their objectives.

The sheer ferocity, scale and determination of the MPLA advance took Unita by surprise and it was quickly apparent that, without South African help, it would be overrun. 'We had an unworkable situation at the time,' said General Meiring. 'In Pretoria, at Intelligence Headquarters, there was a division called Special Tasks. Their main aim in life was to support Unita and Renamo (the rebel movement in Mozambique). They had people on their staff who assisted Unita with training. We knew of them but they were not under our command, although they operated through our area. They had a depot and a base at Rundu from where they supplied Unita. The situation was unbearable in that we worked with Unita and they also worked with Unita. Special Tasks was commanded by the Chief of Staff Intelligence (CSI) – I think it was [Admiral] Putter at the time. Neels van Tonder was the staff officer controlling the whole thing but he reported to Putter. We had operations [on the go] there and were asked to assist Unita in controlling the support system at Mavinga. We operated two companies of 32 Battalion with anti-aircraft in the area.

'I came to Pretoria for some reason or other and had to say "Hello" to the Chief of the Army and the Chief of the Defence Force because they were both my bosses. I walked into the Chief of the Defence Force, General Viljoen's office. He was on the phone at the time. He put his hand over the mouthpiece and said to me: "I'm just on the phone to Neels [van Tonder]." Speaking to Van Tonder I could hear him say: "Really? Is that so? Just hold on …" He turned to me and said: "Neels says we've lost the war in Angola, we must pull out." I couldn't believe it.

I looked at him and said: "Bullshit, General!" Speaking into the telephone once again, Viljoen said: "Neels, I'll call you back." Then he turned to me and said: "Neels van Tonder said Unita is taking a hammering in the Cazombo area and we must withdraw immediately." I said: "General, that's not true. Neels and them are making a war where they don't know what to do. Put those people under my command and we'll win this war for you. We must continue because Fapla will take Jamba if we don't!" That was a Wednesday and Viljoen said to me: "Get Savimbi to Rundu by Friday. I will be there and we'll talk about this then."

'I left in a hurry, immediately flew to Rundu, contacted Savimbi and asked him to come to the meeting. On Friday evening General Viljoen was there with a large number of staff officers from Pretoria and a number of people from Military Intelligence – including Neels van Tonder and Putter – because they were controlling this part of the battle. Savimbi was there with some of his cronies and staff. As the discussions proceeded it was only Savimbi and I who maintained that we should continue fighting. Viljoen said nothing, he just listened. Eventually somebody said: "In any case, the State President will never allow us to continue with this thing!" I looked at Viljoen and said to him: "General, why don't we go and ask him?" He was quiet for a few moments then he looked at me and said: "I will!" It was 22h30 then and he got into his plane and flew directly to Cape Town. By Sunday we had the entire Air Force dropping bombs on the MPLA! I remember sitting on the airfield at Rundu on Sunday afternoon, drinking a beer with tears running down my cheeks, I was so emotional as I watched 21 Impalas take off, so heavily laden with bombs they had difficulty getting off the ground.

'Savimbi couldn't stop the MPLA, so we had to. They were using the Russian tactic of having infantry in front, followed by armoured cars then tanks. If the infantry hit something they couldn't handle, the armoured cars would come forward and if they couldn't handle it the tanks would come forward, etc. It was a rolling movement Unita couldn't stop – they just didn't have heavy enough weapons. We bombed them to a standstill. I then put in two troops of multi-rocket launchers (MRLs) and that really turned the tide. We killed many people. On one radio intercept we got the number was given as 4 719. We had two light companies there with no support or air-cover. There were a lot of MiG-21s and Su-22s flying over their heads at the time. They put down a constant bombardment but because Unita supposedly had Stingers (though I never saw one) they bombed from 20 000 feet, which wasn't all that effective. Our Air Force [operating] from Rundu could only give us five minutes of air-cover then they had to turn back: at that stage we did not have in-flight refuelling capabilities. Fapla's radar cover was good, so their planes withdrew when ours arrived on the scene.'

However, it was inevitable that the SAAF would clash with the Angolans. They shot down one MiG-21, six MI-8 helicopters and an Antonov transport plane that was carrying 10 Soviet officers to take charge at the battlefront. Savimbi denied receiving any help whatsoever from the South Africans, claiming his forces had shot down the MPLA planes and beaten back the advancing Fapla/Cuban forces. He brought foreign correspondents to visit the battlefields and showed them captured and destroyed Russian vehicles and weapons. He said Unita had stood firm at Mavinga and repulsed the offensive without South African aid – a claim that caused bitter resentment among the South African field commanders and troops who were doing duty at the sharp end.

Code-named Operation Weldmesh-Wallpaper, it was one of the forgotten secret wars. 'This battle was almost never mentioned because it wasn't supposed to have happened,' said General Meiring. 'At that time we also assisted Unita in getting its troops from Cazombo to Mavinga in what I believe was one of the best airlift operations in the world because we took off over two fires at night and landed over two fires also at night. In Angola there are hundreds of thousands of fires visible from the air and there were no GPS [global positioning system] facilities available then. We took three brigades of Unita with all their heavy equipment to Mavinga. Normally a C-130's maximum load is 90 fully kitted paratroopers. We took 173 in a C-130 with all their heavy equipment. There was not place to sit – they all had to stand. That whole night we flew with two C-160s and three C-130s. It saved the day more than the bombing did.'

By early October the Fapla offensive had ground to a halt, but fighting in the south-east continued until April 1986, when it petered out. In an effort to further harass the MPLA, Unita stepped up operations in other parts of the country. Savimbi's forces had weathered the storm at Mavinga, but not without cost. Almost 2 500 Unita soldiers had been killed or wounded.

The MPLA defeat at Mavinga stung Moscow – which by all indications was beginning to have doubts about its position in Africa and other Third World countries. As early as 1983 Soviet leader Yuri Andropov had told the Communist Party of Russia that Soviet commitment to Third World Marxist devotees would have to be reassessed. Aid to many countries was dramatically reduced as Russia began an attempt to get her economic house in order. But Angola was something of a special case. The Soviets had committed on such an enormous scale that it was decided to make one more concerted effort to rid the country of Savimbi's forces and in so doing dramatically reduce South Africa's capabilities in the area. Despite being stopped in its offensives, the MPLA was encouraged by being able to advance as far as it had. It was only after the South Africans intervened that its advance had been halted; moreover, the SADF assistance had been on a limited scale. Luanda believed that the South Africans would be reluctant or unable to provide stronger support in the future and began preparing for a new offensive against Mavinga.

In December 1985 General Konstantin Shaganovitch arrived in Angola to take charge of all forces, including the Angolan government's own troops. He was the highest-ranking Soviet officer ever to be deployed outside Europe or Afghanistan (where he had served with distinction) and was considered a counter-insurgency expert. A new Cuban commander, General Ramirez, had also arrived and Cuban troop strengths were bolstered to about 45 000. Western intelligence agencies estimated Shaganovitch had almost 1 000 fellow Soviets occupying training and command posts in Angola, including General Mikhail Petrov, first deputy on the Soviet Politburo, in charge of counter-insurgency policy. Around 2 000 East German military experts took charge of the MPLA's intelligence and communications facilities. At the same time Moscow began resupplying equipment and weapons that had been lost in the 1985 offensive. Heavy Ilyushin-76 and giant Antonov-22 transport planes flew in. From the harbours at Luanda, Lobito and Namibe they began ferrying T-55 battle tanks, PT-76 amphibious tanks and a variety of armoured personnel carriers to Menongue, Cuito Cuanavale and Luena. They replaced MI-24 helicopters and MiG 23 fighter bombers in quantities that exceeded those lost in the previous offensive. By the beginning of 1986 Western intelligence sources estimated there were 27 MI-24s, 23 MiG-23s, 70 MiG-21s and 10 Su-22s in Angola.

Unita was well aware of the new offensive planned and, as a result of the lessons learned in the 1985 offensive, changed its tactics. Rather than try to capture and hold new slices of territory, Savimbi launched a series of hit-and-run attacks against Fapla in attempts to tie down soldiers and reinforcements needed in the south-east. Shaganovitch planned to launch his offensive in 1986 but was never really able to get it going because Unita and the SADF launched a number of counter-assaults that kept the MPLA on the back foot. SADF Special Forces frogmen slipped into Namibe Harbour one night and planted explosive charges that sank a Soviet weapons-carrying cargo ship and severely damaged two others. They also destroyed two oil tanks. Luanda claimed the harbour had been attacked by SA Navy strike craft firing surface missiles. Then the SADF and Unita launched a daring attack against the airfield at Cuito Cuanavale, Shaganovitch's main staging base, destroying radars, artillery and bomb stocks. They also damaged the bridge across the Cuito River so badly that it could not be used by vehicles. This effectively brought Fapla to a grinding halt: its forces dug in and adopted defensive positions.

Then the rainy season started and Shaganovitch had no option but to sit and wait for drier ground so that his heavy armour could proceed without becoming bogged down. By April 1987 it was clear to both Unita and the South Africans that another major offensive was about to be launched by the combined Fapla/Cuban forces. Intelligence reports claimed that all the manpower at the Angolans' disposal, including 7 000 Swapo soldiers and 300 ANC cadres assigned to Fapla, was being deployed to wipe Unita from the face of the earth, once and for all. MPLA commanders on the ground were reportedly not happy with the situation. They believed their men (many of whom were little more than conscripted schoolboys) were not ready to take on the better-trained and battle-hardened Unita soldiers. They were also concerned as to what would happen if the South Africans intervened. But in Luanda pressure was mounting on the government. As the economy continued to deteriorate, so the inhabitants of the cities became increasingly dissatisfied – and these people constituted the support-base of the MPLA. The truth is, after a number of perceived humiliating defeats, the MPLA needed a victory to display to its supporters – and what better way to divert attention from local problems than to wage a war? At the same time there were signs that Moscow was growing impatient with Luanda and wanted finally to put the Unita question to bed.

But all was not well between the Soviet and Cuban high command in Angola. In his book *The War for Africa* Fred Bridgland writes: 'The relationship truly was delicate, especially between Shaganovitch and the top Cuban generals, Arnaldo Ochoa Sanchez and Rafael Del Pino Diaz. Ochoa, then aged 46, was partly of Arab descent and had had such a dazzling career that he was seen as a contender for the Cuban leadership after Fidel Castro, although the President had designated his brother, Raul, Minister of the Armed Forces as his successor. Ochoa was, by Cuban standards, an independent thinker who was well-liked by his troops. As military men go in highly authoritarian societies, he had a very sensitive personality and a tendency to bypass rules and regulations. His energy, flexibility and popularity made him a natural choice down the years for a host of difficult missions. He had fought with Castro and Che Guevara in the Sierra Maestra against

Batista. From 1966 to 1968 he was seconded to command anti-government guerrillas in Venezuela. In 1973 he fought with a Cuban unit on the Golan Heights
against Israel in the Yom Kippur War.

'Ochoa went on to command a Cuban infantry battalion against South
African forces in Angola in 1975–76. In 1977 he was appointed head of his country's
military mission in Addis Ababa and commanded the successful Cuban tank
offensive against Somalia in the Ogaden in 1978. In 1979 he commanded a
Cuban unit fighting with Polisario Front guerrillas in their successful campaign
against Mauritania. In June 1983 he was assigned to Nicaragua to reorganise the
Sandinistas into a more mobile and efficient rapid-deployment force. Under his
direction the Sandinistas destroyed the southern Contra front from Costa Rica.
By 1987 he was a deputy defence minister and a member of the Cuban
Communist Party Central Committee. Under Shaganovitch he was responsible
for the massive air transport operation in Angola.

'General Del Pino, then aged 49, was one of the most flamboyant products of
the Cuban Revolution. He too had fought against Batista as a teenager, and in
1961 he was acknowledged as the hero of the resistance to Washington's abortive
invasion at the Bay of Pigs where, as a young pilot, he shot down two B-26 war-
planes. He rose to become commander of the Cuban Air Force in Angola in
1975–76 carrying out the initial clandestine surveys for the arrival of Cuban
troops and subsequently spending years trying to kill Jonas Savimbi. By 1981 he
was deputy chief of the Cuban Air Force with direct responsibility for the war in
Angola, which he visited from Havana three or four times a year.

'Ochoa, Del Pino and Fidel Castro thought Shaganovitch's attempt to launch a
fresh offensive in 1986 was premature. They opposed the 1987 offensive also on
the grounds that it was bound to run into big trouble with the South Africans and
that too much effort was being put into a single thrust from Cuito Cuanavale
which would enable Unita and the SADF to concentrate their defensive efforts.
Shaganovitch won the 1987 argument against Castro and his generals. Ochoa
returned home temporarily to become Deputy Armed Forces Minister, but Del
Pino helped in the planning of the offensive. Castro declined to commit Cuban
brigades to what he saw as a foolhardy campaign, but out of loyalty to his Soviet
patron he agreed to attach 35 Cuban specialists to each Fapla battalion as military
advisers and artillery and armour commanders.'

On 29 May 1987, while back in Havana, General del Pino and his family
boarded a Cessna light aircraft for what looked like a routine afternoon flip. Less
than an hour later he touched down 90 miles away in Key Largo, Florida, and

asked US officials for asylum. He was the most senior Cuban official ever to defect.

Relations between Unita and the SADF had also deteriorated. Many in the rebel leadership believed that the South Africans were trying to assume command in a war the SADF thought of as its own. They wanted the SADF there but wanted them to realise they were 'guests' in their war. As a result the two sides often refused to share intelligence. 'I hold Savimbi in very high esteem,' said General Meiring, 'but he was not very well accepted by some people. General Geldenhuys did not like him at all. The two of them did not get on at all. As a politician Savimbi is better than anyone I have ever come across, but he's not very clever militarily. He was (and is) being led by the nose by his staff officers because of the African curse – you don't tell your boss things you think are bad for him. As a result we had to tell him what was going on.'

By April 1987 South African reconnaissance teams were reporting large-scale Fapla troop movements and a build-up of reinforcements at Cuito Cuanavale. It was obvious a major offensive would soon begin. South Africa was caught in a dilemma. SADF field commanders favoured sending a major battle force north-wards from Namibia to attack Cuito Cuanavale from the rear and in so doing control the road to Menongue, along which the MPLA received its logistical sup-plies. But the Pretoria government knew that the presence of such a force could not be hidden and they were worried about the local and international pressure that would come when it was learned that South African boys were once again fighting in a foreign war many South Africans believed wasn't theirs anyway. At the same time, if P.W. Botha and his generals simply sat on their hands and allowed Jamba to fall, the South Africans would face a belligerent force of some 50 000 Cubans sitting on the border of Namibia flushed with confidence from a successful battle. That too was an unthinkable situation and many warned that in such a case, Castro might just be tempted to look for a final solution to the prob-lems in both Namibia and South Africa.

In the end the South African Cabinet approved a plan for a thrust through 'Savimbiland' into an area east of the Cuito River in order to prevent Fapla from capturing Mavinga. Mavinga held no importance as a town: barely a building remained standing after a decade of conflict. But nearby, on a plateau just south of the Lomba River, was an important airfield at which heavy transport planes delivered American and South African supplies and weapons. If that were to fall, then Fapla forces would be free to advance some 250 km to Jamba, Unita's bush capital in the south-eastern corner of Angola, close to the Caprivi Strip, and they would have the benefit of a forward airbase which would make life very difficult for the South Africans.

On 14 August 1987 Shaganovitch played his opening card to start the battle that many believe ultimately changed the face of African and Soviet politics. He moved five Fapla brigades to the Lomba River and prepared to cross. The South Africans replied with bombardments from 127 mm multiple rocket launchers and 120 mm mortars. To the west Fapla's 47 Brigade began moving around the source of the Lomba River with the obvious intention of linking up and helping the other Fapla brigades (29 and 57) cross the river and establish a bridgehead. Both the Unita commanders and the SADF knew they had to stop this manoeuvre at whatever cost, or Mavinga would come under serious threat. It would prove to be no easy task. SADF field commanders were told by the brass 'not to lose any men or equipment' while at the same time they faced an army that had learned many lessons from previous confrontations with the South Africans.

At Cuito Cuanavale, Fapla and its allies installed a wide range of the most sophisticated Soviet radars and ground-to-air missiles. Every day between eight and ten giant Ilyushin-76 transport aircraft flew into Menongue bringing food, weapons, fuel and other supplies. Convoys with hundreds of vehicles, and escorted by two infantry brigades, travelled regularly from Menongue to Cuito Cuanavale. The sheer scale of the operation took the South Africans and their allies by surprise. Despite their best efforts, 47 Brigade, supported by large contingents of armour, rolled on towards the source of the Lomba River. The generals in Pretoria realised the seriousness of the situation and agreed to dramatically increased measures. Permission was given for a battery of G-5 field guns to be deployed. This cannon is reputed to be the best of its kind in the world, capable of firing 43,5 kg shells with computer-controlled pinpoint accuracy at ranges up to 42 km or as little as 3 km. It was developed after Operation Savannah when, in terms of artillery power, the South Africans found themselves completely outgunned.

While 61 Mechanised Battalion was placed on standby, SAAF Mirages and Canberras bombed 47 Brigade unmercifully as it rounded the source of the Lomba River and headed towards Mavinga. To counter Fapla's radar, anti-aircraft defence systems and superior aircraft, the SAAF pilots developed a procedure they called 'toss bombing'. The technique was to come in towards the target at tree-top level then, as they got there, to climb steeply over the target so the bomb got 'tossed' onto it, then once the bomb was gone, to get back down to an altitude of about 30 metres and out of harm's way as quickly as possible. It meant they came in under the Fapla radar cover, were only exposed to it for a few moments when they climbed to release their bombs and then were back under it again and on their way home.

On Wednesday 2 September 1987 a South African Bosbok spotter plane was shot down by SAM-8 missiles. It took the South Africans completely by surprise and shook the SADF hierarchy, who had assumed Moscow's most sophisticated surface-to-air missile would not be deployed at the front line but rather be placed around strategic points further back. It was a harsh wake-up call to the quality of the Soviet equipment: the fact that it could survive being transported over some of the roughest terrain in the world was ample proof of that. The SAAF ordered the immediate withdrawal of the ponderous Canberra bombers, which would be like sitting ducks to the SAM-8 operators, but increased the number of 'toss-bombing' raids of the Mirages. From a range of around 21 km the South African G-5s pounded 47 and 21 Brigade while the multiple rocket launchers rained down missiles.

Late on the afternoon of Wednesday 9 September two 450-man infantry battalions from 21 Brigade managed to cross the Lomba River and set up a bridgehead in the tree-line about 3 km south of the river. At first light next day the SADF counter-attacked with two companies from 101 Battalion and a troop of four Ratel-90 armoured vehicles, each armed with a 90 mm gun. Further down the river the South Africans came across a Fapla unit putting the finishing touches to a mobile bridge and destroyed a Soviet armoured car and a giant GAZ truck with a ZT-3 anti-tank missile that until that day had not been tested in battle. It was fresh off Armscor's production line, and the arms manufacturer claimed it had a longer range (3,5 km) than any other modern anti-tank weapon. The ZT-3 was launched from specially modified Ratel-90s, designated Ratel-ZT-3s. Moments later the South Africans engaged five T-54 tanks with the ZT-3s and conventional Ratel-90s, knocking out three before the other two escaped back across the river. In the meantime, other SADF elements pounded 21 Brigade with G-5s, MRLs and 120 mm mortars in a battle that continued for two days until one Fapla battalion was almost completely annihilated and the other retreated back across the river to regroup. Overhead MiGs and Su-22s flew continually, trying to locate the G-5s, but the South African gunners received adequate advance warning of when the planes took off from recce teams hidden in deep cover by the airfield. Consequently they were able to camouflage the guns, which were never seen from the air.

On 22 September SADF electronic warfare experts picked up radio transmissions from Russian commanders giving Fapla permission to use gas against the South Africans. It was not a total surprise, as Shaganovitch was a known chemical warfare specialist, but it forced the South Africans to retreat some 15 km at a time when they had 21 Brigade pinned down and at a severe military disadvantage. At the time the forced withdrawal caused bitter disappointment, but the gods of war were smiling on the South Africans that day. They'd no sooner vacated the area than Fapla launched a huge, co-ordinated artillery and aerial bombardment on the very land they had just occupied. Fapla believed it had inflicted heavy casualties on the South Africans and that they had been forced to withdraw and lick their wounds. Then the SADF electronic warfare engineers intercepted radio messages that 21 Brigade was preparing to move all its remaining forces back across the Lomba River. The South Africans manoeuvred back into position and watched in amazement as 21 Brigade formed up on the northern bank and began crossing the river on a mobile bridge. Their mouths watered at the sight of two battalions of infantry with tanks interspersed between them moving slowly in single file.

When the Angolan infantry was across the river and strung out in the open in a flood plain, the SADF forces opened up with everything they had. G-5s, rockets and 120 mm mortars rained down on the infantrymen while ZT-3 missiles streaked into the tanks, killing all trapped inside them. Those Fapla troops not killed or injured in the barrage fled back towards the river and marshes in blind panic, only to be cut down by the 30 Casspirs of 101 Battalion and the Ratels of 32 Battalion, which picked them off with withering .50 calibre and 7.62 machine gun fire. It was described by the SADF troops as 'a slaughter'. At the end of the battle more than 300 bodies were counted. Only one South African was slightly wounded by shrapnel. The mobile bridge was destroyed by the G-5s.

For much of the rest of the month 21 Brigade made further attempts to cross the Lomba at the same place, but was easily repulsed. Further up the river, elements of Fapla's 59 Brigade succeeded in crossing and establishing a bridgehead. They were soon attacked by a small force of Ratels which ran into a strong force of T-54 and T-55 tanks. Despite suffering casualties from the much more heavily armed tanks (eight SADF members were killed and one Ratel and two Casspirs were destroyed) the Ratels acquitted themselves well by using their superior speed, mobility and shoot-and-scoot tactics. The South Africans had effectively stopped 21 Brigade from crossing the Lomba and had successfully prevented 47 and 59 Brigades from linking up. Once again, they had saved Unita. Though the field commanders wanted to chase Fapla, Pretoria forbade the South Africans to cross the river, so they settled into a routine of relentlessly bombarding Fapla with G-5s and 127 mm rockets while the SAAF rained destruction from the air. Sitting in specially designed electronic warfare (EW) vehicles, EW experts monitored Fapla constantly. When the MPLA thought that an area was clear and was going to move into it the South Africans simply got into position and waited until it got there before opening fire with the G-5s from as far away as 42 km. The Angolans suffered terrible devastation and destruction from the big guns. As the campaign progressed the SADF gunners, with the help of forward observers, were able to fire so accurately they could take out individual targets. A number of SAM-8 launchers and fire controllers were knocked out this way, as were Mi-8 and Mi-24 helicopters.

By the end of September Fapla's 21 Brigade, down to about a third of its original strength, had begun to withdraw. The South Africans and Unita, who'd been employed primarily in an infantry role, had won the first phase of the war. In the meantime, the SADF concentrated on the destruction of 47 Brigade, which had come round the source of the Lomba. Recce commandos monitoring its progress constantly sent co-ordinates back to the fire control officers of the MRLs and G-5s and their crews who then launched constant salvos. Two psychologists from Defence HQ, with special knowledge of the African psyche in warfare, were sent to join in the battle against 47 Brigade. At night loudspeakers blared propaganda at the Angolans in an effort to demoralise them and, more practically, to keep them awake. Helium-filled balloons with strips of aluminium foil were floated towards Fapla, who picked them up on radar and fired expensive missiles at them. On at least two occasions, as a result of the balloons, the MPLA scrambled their fighter planes, believing they were being attacked by the SAAF. Bombs with time-delayed fuses designed to explode between one hour and 48 hours after they had plunged into the sandy earth were dropped in abundance. They made Fapla movement in the area difficult and made life a living hell for the troopers when they exploded in the early hours of the morning.

Fapla's 47 Brigade's advance had been stopped. From radio intercepts the SADF commanders knew the Angolans were in serious trouble and were digging in. The South African commanders realised that in order to defeat 47 Brigade once and for all, they would have to commit their own armour. They were also worried that 59 and 21 Brigades would make another determined effort to cross the Lomba in the east. On 1 October SADF electronic warfare monitors picked up a radio message sent from Cuito Cuanavale to the Commander of 47 Brigade, Commander Silva, ordering him to withdraw and to 'ensure that the Russians were not captured'. The next day SADF recces reported Fapla was busy building wooden roads and temporary bridges across the marshes. As 47 Brigade began gathering and attempting to cross the newly made bridges the South Africans kept up regular shelling with the G-5s. When a SAM-9 tried to cross the bridge it was hit by a G-5 shell and ended up blocking access for other vehicles.

At dawn on 3 October 1987, South Africa's 61 Mechanised Battalion, together with Unita, attacked 47 Brigade with more than 50 Ratels. Included in that number were the specially equipped EW vehicles whose function it was to monitor and relay all enemy radio transmissions and in addition to jam Fapla communications so that tank commanders in particular could not issue orders to their troops. At ranges of sometimes as little as 15 metres, the SADF armoured vehicles slugged it out with T-54 and T-55 Fapla tanks, using their greater manoeuvrability to offset the tanks' heavier firepower. By 5 pm 47 Brigade was in retreat, 127 of its vehicles, including all its tanks on the southern bank, either abandoned or destroyed. The South Africans had just won the biggest battle they'd fought since World War II.

It was here that the SADF took possession of a complete and undamaged SAM-8 missile system. No western country had yet got its hands on this top-of-the-line Soviet anti-aircraft weapon – first seen in Moscow in the mid-1970s. The fired missiles travelled at double the speed of sound, with a range of 13 km, and could knock fighter planes out of the sky at a height of 12 000 metres (40 000 feet). Each SAM-8 missile system consisted of three separate vehicles. The launcher was built on the chassis of a six-wheeled amphibious vehicle and contained six launcher tubes. Eight more missiles were stored on the launcher and 36 additional projectiles were carried in the logistics support vehicle. The launch vehicle had surveillance radar mounted at the rear while in front it bristled with an array of radars and transmitters for guiding the missile on to its target. The third element of the system was the fire control vehicle. For the South Africans, the capture of the SAM-8 system was an enormous prize and despite vehement protests from Savimbi, who wanted to hand the weapon to the Americans, it was taken back to Pretoria to be picked apart by Armscor engineers.

The Fapla–Cuban resolve had been broken and their brigades began limping back to Cuito Cuanavale. The scoresheet left no doubt as to the result of the battle. One SADF man was killed and one Ratel destroyed, as opposed to around 600 Fapla 47 Brigade members either killed, wounded or captured. According to SADF figures, the following 47 Brigade equipment was either destroyed or captured:

- T-54 and T-55 tanks – 21 (4 T-54s were captured and handed over to Unita)
- SAM-8 missile launcher vehicles – 4 (1 captured intact)
- BTR-60 SAM-8 logistics vehicle – 1 (captured intact)
- BTR-60PU SAM-8 command vehicles – 1 (captured intact)
- BTR-60 armoured personnel carriers – 22 (11 captured)
- Truck-mounted BM-21 multiple rocket systems – 4 (2 captured)
- BMP-1 mechanised infantry combat vehicles – 3 (2 captured)
- Logistics trucks – 83 (45 captured)
- BTS-4 armoured recovery vehicles – 2 (1 captured)
- BRDM-2 amphibious scout cars – 26
- TMM mobile bridges – 2
- Flat-face air defence radars – 1 (captured)
- 23 mm ZU-23 anti-aircraft guns – 6 (4 captured)
- 122 mm D-30 Howitzer long-range guns – 3 (2 captured)

As Shaganovitch's forces moved back in the direction of Cuito Cuanavale, Pretoria ordered that they be chased and that maximum casualties be inflicted to prevent their regrouping and counter-attacking. But for that the field commanders needed heavier armament. As the remaining Fapla brigades consolidated, the South Africans, with a force of only 1 500 men, would be facing some 15 000 enemy soldiers and a formidable arsenal of tanks and heavy weapons. While the Ratels had performed miracles using 'guerrilla' tactics against the Soviet tanks, what was now needed were the big guns. Defence HQ gave permission for a squadron of 13 Olifant tanks, an additional battery of eight G-5s and a troop of three G-6 guns (the self-propelled version of the G-5) to be sent from South Africa. In the meantime the SADF gunners brought Cuito Cuanavale and the airfield under heavy bombardment so that Fapla would have to fly sorties from Menongue, some 175 km to the west. By Wednesday 28 October the airfield was so badly damaged it could no longer be used by Fapla jets or heavy transport planes. On 9 November 1987 South African tanks entered battle for the first time in over 40 years. Within nine minutes of being given the order to engage, two T-55s had been shot out by the Olifants.

By late November the military tide had turned against the Fapla–Cuban alliance as all their forces continued to withdraw towards Cuito Cuanavale. By Christmas, Fidel Castro was starting to feel the heat. Fearing a military catastrophe, he ordered Cuban diplomats and MPLA officials at the United Nations to contact the South African UN mission in New York to explore the possibility of a negotiated settlement in Angola. He suggested that such an agreement should be linked to a settlement in Namibia – exactly what the South Africans had been calling for for years. Moscow was also putting the squeeze on Castro economically. There were clear signs Gorbachev was rapidly growing disenchanted with developments in Angola. At the front line, however, the SADF field commanders were concerned with more mundane matters. They wanted to launch a final, decisive attack on Cuito Cuanavale from the west, cut the town off from its supply lines to Menongue and destroy the Fapla–Cuban alliance once and for all.

The South African generals, however, were under pressure from Foreign Affairs to allow the Cubans to find a face-saving way of withdrawing from the conflict, and were afraid an all-out assault would end up scuttling the diplomatic initiatives. It was decided the SADF should rather launch an attack from the east to try to drive Fapla back across the Cuito River. It was believed that if such a plan was successful it would exert just enough pressure to speed the negotiation process up. But this was not going to be easy. It was by far the harder option. The SADF commanders knew they did not have enough men at their disposal to drive Fapla back across the river, particularly as Fapla had dug in and set up elaborate defensive positions. The Tumpo Triangle into which Fapla and the Cubans were being forced was ideal defensive terrain. The only plan that made military sense was to attack Cuito Cuanavale from the west, but Pretoria would have none of that. In the meantime, Fapla convoys 300-strong regularly arrived at Cuito Cuanavale from Menongue, and despite regular harassment by SAAF bombing attacks and marauding bands of Unita and 32 Battalion members, supplies continued to get through to the Fapla positions

International pressure began to mount on South Africa. On 13 December the United Nations Security Council unanimously demanded that South Africa withdraw all its military forces from Angola. Pik Botha rejected the demand out of hand, saying South Africa would only withdraw when her security interests were no longer directly affected by the Soviet and Cuban presence in Angola. In the Tumpo Triangle SADF mechanised units attacked 21 Brigade with tanks and artillery but, despite inflicting heavy casualties, were unable to dislodge or destroy Fapla: 21 Brigade dug in further. More MPLA reinforcements and tanks were sent so that by February there were around 50 T-54 and T-55 tanks on the east bank of the Cuito River. To add to the South African problems, units from Fidel Castro's elite 50 Division, normally assigned to guarding Havana, began arriving in Cuito Cuanavale.

Castro was preparing to make a last stand. He asked for and got permission from Angolan President José Eduardo dos Santos for Cuba to take over the responsibility for defending Cuito Cuanavale and even began to direct some of the operations from Havana. General Ochoa Sanchez was dismayed. He believed he was being asked to oversee a retreat that Castro had already decided upon and that he would eventually be blamed for Cuba's failure.

On 14 February 1988, in a bitterly fought armour battle, the SADF and Unita effectively destroyed Fapla's 59 Brigade, which was heavily supported by Cuban contingents. As a result, most of Fapla's forces were pinned down in a 30 km square just across the Cuito River from Cuito Cuanavale. The main objective now was to drive them from this area and to destroy their supply and logistics facilities, then to hand over the bridgehead positions to Unita so Fapla could not launch another attack against Mavinga. Also in February, the SADF launched two more assaults on the Fapla/Cuban brigades in the Tumpo Triangle, but was beaten back again.

Despite the failure of the South Africans to dislodge Fapla, there appeared to be light at the end of the diplomatic tunnel. Angola and Cuba told the Americans they accepted the fact that all 50 000 Cubans needed to be withdrawn from Angola if a settlement was to be reached. The Russians, according to the Americans and the West Germans, also wanted the Cubans out of Angola. That month, the Minister of Foreign Affairs, Pik Botha, Neil van Heerden, the Director General of Foreign Affairs and General Jannie Geldenhuys, Chief of the SADF, met with US chief negotiator Dr Chester Crocker, Angolan Foreign Minister Alfonso van Dunem and Cuban Politburo member Jorge Risquet. On 23 March 1988, while the diplomatic initiatives continued, the SADF launched what was to be its final attack on the Cuban/Fapla positions in the Tumpo Triangle. This too failed to change the situation.

The war was effectively over, and it had changed the course of history. In a far corner of Africa, with virtually no outside help, the SADF had effectively stopped the march of Soviet imperialism, despite the presence of an estimated 52 000 Cubans. Soviet imperialism is something easily dismissed by some factions today, yet it was a publicly stated goal of the Kremlin. The Russians, after Angola, were tired of war. Following this failed adventure, they dramatically reduced support to Cuba, whose international role has since diminished dramatically. The SADF's endeavours in Angola allowed a peaceful, democratic election to take place in Namibia, in many ways setting the tone for democratic election to be held in South Africa later. If the MPLA/Cuban forces had succeeded in driving the SADF out of Angola there is little doubt they would have pushed on into Namibia.

Moscow would have been sufficiently encouraged to continue; the anti-Pretoria movements, smelling blood, would have seen little reason to sit around a negotiation table – if they had, South Africans would most certainly not have enjoyed the constitution or freedoms they now have. As Richard Nixon is reported to have said: 'If you've got them by the balls, their hearts and minds will follow.'

The Cuban propaganda machine immediately fired up in full force. Castro and his spin doctors claimed they'd thrashed the South Africans and repelled every attack the Boers launched against Cuito Cuanavale, dressing up the fact that the Cubans were still in the Tumpo Triangle as a glorious victory. The hard facts tell another story. On the Cuban/Angolan side 4 785 men were confirmed killed in action. That does not include those wounded or deserters. The South Africans lost 31 men and a further six died as a result of cerebral malaria. Fapla and the Cubans were right back where they started from before they launched their 1985 offensive. Unita was in a stronger position than ever as a result of the massive stocks of captured weapons the South Africans had handed over. The 'scoresheet' also tells the tale:

FAPLA/Cuban vehicles and aircraft destroyed or captured by SADF/Unita forces:
- Tanks – 94
- Armoured troop and combat vehicles – 100
- BM-21/BM-14 MRLs – 34
- D-30/M-46 field guns – 9
- TMM mobile bridges – 7
- Logistics vehicles – 389
- MiG-23/21 fighter aircraft – 9
- Helicopters – 9

SADF equipment destroyed or captured by FAPLA/Cuban forces:
- Tanks – 3 (captured during the last Tumpo Triangle assault)
- Ratel infantry fighting vehicles – 5
- Casspir infantry fighting vehicles – 3
- Rinkhals transport vehicles – 1
- Withings transport vehicles – 1
- Kwêvoël trucks – 1
- Mirage F-1 fighter aircraft – 2 (1 as a result of enemy action, 1 as a result of an accident)
- Bosbok light reconnaissance aircraft – 1

On 22 December 1988 South Africa, Cuba and Angola signed a tripartite agreement in New York and the war was officially over – but in the meantime, during the 'talks about talks' phase, Fidel Castro had taken one last roll of the dice. The Cuban leader realised that the defeat of the MPLA would be seen as a defeat of Cuba's efforts to further its revolution in southern Africa. 'We could not allow a military and political catastrophe to occur,' he told the Council of State in Havana on 9 July 1989.

From January 1988 increased numbers of Cuban troops had begun to be moved westwards towards the Namibian border, opposite Ovamboland. By the end of that month the Cubans had over 3 500 troops deployed there. It was a situation that began to concern the South Africans. The Lusaka Agreement of 1984 stipulated that only the MPLA should occupy that area and that Plan and the Cubans should not cross a point approximately 300 km north of the Namibian border. In practice this was not the case. Swapo returned and the SADF launched regular raids against its bases. The Cubans largely kept out of the way and avoided contact with the SADF – until 1987. In one incident in April an SADF major was killed when a Cuban unit intervened in a Swapo/SADF skirmish. Later the body of a South African medical orderly, Corporal du Toit, was found in a shallow grave. On 4 May 1988, while peace talks were taking place in London, a Cuban force attacked an SADF unit from 101 Battalion that was on a reconnaissance mission some 50 km inside Angola. One South African soldier died and another, Private Johan Papenfus, was captured and later displayed to the media in Havana.

Intelligence reports at the time led the SADF hierarchy to believe Fapla and the Cubans might have been planning to open a new front in the west in order to weaken South Africa's military capabilities on the eastern front. The air bases at Xangongo and Cahama had been upgraded and MiG-23s and MiG-21s were flying across the border of Namibia to within 20 km of Oshakati and Ondangwa. They did not attack but were obviously trying to gauge the SAAF's reaction. The SAAF did not want to show its hand – it had no fighters based there that were capable of intercepting the MiGs and the Cuban pilots kept out of range of the South Africa anti-aircraft missiles – so it did nothing. In the meantime a combined Cuban/Swapo force began building up to alarming proportions in an area around Techipa, a small village about 30 km north east of Ruacana on the Namibian border, within 20 km of the Calueque Dam. By early June more than 11 000 Cuban troops were stationed in the area, backed by more than 100 T-55 and more advanced T-62 Soviet tanks. The area bristled with anti-aircraft radars and missiles, including SAM-8s.

The fact that Castro and the Cuban generals had taken over command in January worried the SADF military commanders. They figured the Cuban leader might just be crazy enough to launch an attack into Namibia. 'There was a possibility that [the Cubans] had accepted their defeat at the Lomba as a historical fact and were now searching for victory at another place, even if it were inside South West,' said General Geldenhuys. 'Information from overseas tended to support this hypothesis. It indicated that the least of South African offensive actions would be used by the Cubans as provocation to attack targets on South West African soil. Swapo could then capitalise on these attacks with Cuban support.

Minister of Defence General Magnus Malan and State President P.W. Botha ordered the SADF to remain prepared but to exercise restraint and to do nothing that would escalate the situation. 'But,' said Geldenhuys, 'Mr Botha also said: "If they put one foot across the border hit them with everything you've got. If that happens then Ovamboland becomes the new battlefield."' The situation was teetering on a knife-edge: if not managed properly it could see South Africa in a full-scale war. Preparations were made to call up 140 000 Citizen Force members if the need arose. But at the same time the SADF couldn't simply sit on its hands and do nothing about the hostile build-up at Techipa. Initial attempts were made to rough up the Fapla/Plan/Cuban forces through air strikes but when the South African Impalas had SAM-6s (a missile effective at ranges up to 60 km) fired at them, that plan was abandoned.

Geldenhuys decided that 61 Mechanised Battalion should cross the Cunene River at Calueque and move towards Techipa. The plan was to lure the Cubans away from Techipa into the open where they could be attacked and stopped in their advance towards Calueque. On Sunday 26 June the proceedings were opened by a six-hour SADF artillery bombardment on Techipa. The Cuban HQ in the village took a terrible pounding and their communications network was destroyed. But despite this, the Cubans continued to advance towards Calueque. Just north of the dam, Cubans and South African armoured forces clashed in a fierce battle that saw two Cuban T-54 tanks, two ZU-23 guns and a number of Cuban vehicles destroyed. Two SADF Ratels were destroyed and 19-year-old Second Lieutenant Muller Meiring was killed. Then the Cuban advance stopped and they started moving back towards Techipa. Minutes later eight MiG-23s streaked towards the Calueque dam. Each plane dropped two 250 kg parachute-retarded bombs on each pass. Six bombs hit the dam wall and the ramps leading up to it. On their second run one of the bombs landed between a group of vehicles and instantly killed 11 SADF troopies. The deaths of the 12 South African soldiers that day caused waves of anger in the Republic. The fact that the oldest of the victims was only 23 made it seem even worse.

And then it was over, almost as suddenly as it began. Just before midnight on 27 June 1988 the field commanders inside Angola were told to withdraw immediately and, as field commanders were reportedly told by their senior officers, 'from that night onwards a toe was not to be put across the border into Angola'. It was the closest South Africa had ever come to becoming embroiled in a full-scale war on her own territory. By November 1989 the last SADF troops had left Namibia, and the country became independent in March 1990 in a multi-party election supervised by the United Nations. The last Cuban soldier had left Angola by 1 July 1991.

So who won the war? If the numbers are totalled, then South Africa did. But Fidel Castro saw it differently. His propaganda machine claimed South Africa eventually overstretched itself, then came up against superior forces and was forced to enter into negotiations. His story was repeated so often that much of the Western press began to believe it was the truth. However, in speeches to the Cuban Communist Party later that year, he admitted that a critical situation arose at Cuito Cuanavale and that South Africa had dealt Fapla a number of military blows at the Lomba River. He also severely criticised the Russian military advisers in Angola. But perhaps the greatest proof of how Cuba really fared was the fact that General Arnaldo Ochoa Sanchez, the man Castro sent to Cuito Cuanavale to save the situation, was executed by firing squad after being found guilty on trumped-up drug-smuggling charges, barely a year after the South Africans and Cubans had fought their last battle.

The South African generals have little doubt as to who won. 'There is absolutely no doubt we won the military war,' said General Viljoen. 'We never lost a major battle. Our victory in Angola had a direct bearing on the collapse of the Soviet Union. The USSR collapsed in 1989. There is no doubt economic attrition had something to do with that, but militarily they lost on three major fronts. One was the Middle East, where Israel played an important part. The other was Afghanistan, and the third was southern Africa, where we played the major role. Those three military theatres actually caused the downfall of the USSR.'

General Geldenhuys is equally adamant. 'There are people who say nothing was achieved by the war,' he said. 'Naturally I will be inclined to correct the distorted picture as I see it. It was meaningful that we kept the security situation stable until 1988. We won time to create a favourable situation for a political solution. Swapo won the elections [in Namibia], that is true. But Namibia is a multi-party democracy with a sound constitution that only needs to be maintained. If a settlement had been negotiated under military pressure during the middle 1980s you can imagine how one-sided and excessive the revolutionaries' demands would have been. Namibia would have become a totalitarian state like Angola. I do not believe that the result of the war caused the end of the Cold War. However, I do believe that the Soviet Union's involvement in the war as a whole, together with its involvement with armed conflict elsewhere in the world, decidedly contributed to its crumbling. Winners? South Africa and Unita won the war. The MPLA and Unita continue to fight, but the people of Namibia got peace, peacefulness and democracy – a rare phenomenon on this subcontinent.'

6

MOZAMBIQUE

In 1951 the East African area became an overseas province of Portugal, which unlike most other colonial authorities of the time categorically stated it would never decolonise. (The words *Aqui e Portugal* – Here is Portugal – were set in black-and-white mosaic in the pavement outside the city hall of Lourenço Marques.) Like other countries in the region, Mozambique was segregated along racial lines, and strict education criteria made sure that less than 1 per cent of black Mozambicans became full citizens. It was a situation guaranteed to cause resentment, and in 1962 Eduardo Mondlane united various nationalist movements in Dar es Salaam to form the Mozambique Liberation Front (Frelimo). With aid from radical African, Arab and Eastern European states, as well as China, they began an armed struggle in northern Mozambique in 1964 in an attempt to achieve independence from Portugal.

The movement suffered considerable political infighting and underwent a number of violent purges until in 1969 Mondlane was killed when he opened a parcel bomb believed to have been sent by Frelimo dissidents and the Portuguese Secret Service. Following an intense power struggle, Samora Machel consolidated his control within Frelimo, and the organisation's military fortunes gradually began to change. Frelimo's expansion into the north-western province of Tete from its strongholds near the Tanzanian border in the late 1960s was a huge psychological blow to the Portuguese. They responded by launching Operation Gordian Knot in 1970, their biggest counter-offensive ever, complete with napalm and scorched earth tactics. Rural villagers were forcibly moved to con-trolled settlements called *aldeamentos*. But the coup in Portugal led to 60 000 Portuguese troops being withdrawn and riots breaking out in the Mozambican capital.

On 7 September 1974 the Lusaka Accord was signed and Portugal handed power to a surprised and politically inept Frelimo-dominated transitional gov-ernment – the organisation had precious few military successes to show and some of its leaders had only recently predicted 10 more years of armed struggle before independence could be achieved. On 25 June 1975 Samora Machel became presi-dent of the People's Republic of Mozambique, a country from which most of the Portuguese professional class had fled, where 90 per cent of the population was illiterate and where the administration of the state and the economy was now in the hands of inexperienced Frelimo cadres.

Those white colonialists who remained were embittered, and many sabotaged the country's efforts to rebuild – not that rebuilding featured high on Machel's list of priorities. He was more concerned with consolidating his own and Frelimo's position and with getting rid of any potential opposition. One-party rule and a range of other measures were implemented to limit opposition and curb resist-ance by the population. Opposition leaders and Frelimo dissidents were arrested and sent to 're-education camps' in the north of the country. There were reports of torture and executions. Dynamising committees were set up with extensive powers to supplant traditional authorities in the rural areas and to send 'unpro-ductive' urban residents for re-education. The National Service for Public Security, a secret police service, was established with sweeping powers to detain anyone suspected of anti-state sentiments or activities. Churches, especially the Roman Catholic Church, which Frelimo said had allied itself with the colonial regime, were targeted for re-education. Reports claim that as many as 10 000 Jehovah's Witnesses were sent to re-education camps.

At Frelimo's third party congress, in February 1977, Frelimo declared itself a Marxist–Leninist vanguard party, with a mission to 'lead, organise, orientate and educate the masses, thus transforming the popular mass movement into a powerful instrument for the destruction of capitalism and the construction of socialism'. Privately owned schools, hospitals, businesses and property were nationalised by the new government. 'Mass democratic organisations' were set up to mobilise and ensure Frelimo control of workers, women and the press. Links were solidified with the Soviet Union and other Eastern bloc countries that provided political and military support. But despite all the rhetoric, the party political elite and its allies were given preferential treatment and enjoyed the spoils of victory. State farms, mainly large agricultural estates abandoned by the Portuguese, enjoyed government investment while peasant farmers received little or nothing and saw their markets decline. The political 'chosen' got richer while the poor got poorer and could say and do nothing about it.

Developments in Mozambique were of concern to the South African government. As part of the 'total response' strategy, support was given to nationalist movements that opposed governments hostile to South Africa, primarily through the offices of Military Intelligence. Apart from Unita in Angola, internal anti-Swapo factions in South West Africa (before the election took place in that country) and the Basuto Liberation Army in Lesotho, support was given to the Mozambique National Resistance (Renamo).

Renamo was established in 1977 by the Rhodesian Central Intelligence Organisation. This was done to counter Mozambican President Samora Machel's growing support for the Zimbabwean National Liberation Army (Zanla) – one of two guerrilla movements engaged in a bitter struggle with the Rhodesian government – and in retaliation for his enforcement of United Nations sanctions against Rhodesia. In its early years Renamo comprised soldiers who had fought with the Portuguese, as well as Frelimo dissidents. Its primary functions were to disrupt and destabilise the Machel government and to provide intelligence on Zanla guerrillas operating within Mozambique's borders. 'Our aim was simple,' said a former Rhodesia SAS member who was involved in the training and supply of logistics to Renamo. 'We wanted them to keep Machel and Frelimo so busy they couldn't devote time or attention to supporting Zanla.'

The Rhodesians' plan was only partially successful. Renamo initially enjoyed limited grassroots support but did not pose a serious military threat to the Mozambican authorities. But that changed after 1980. With Zimbabwe's transition to majority rule, many of the former Rhodesian Defence Force intelligence operatives and military specialists trekked south across the Limpopo and joined the SADF; and Renamo, like a ripe plum, fell into the lap of the SADF Military Intelligence Directorate, who were only too eager to pick up where the Rhodesians had left off. For a year or so nothing much seemed to happen, but behind the scenes the South Africans were reviewing and reorientating the organisation. Special Forces experts began intensive training of the rebel soldiers. In March 1980, to protect Renamo members from retaliatory actions, approximately 200 members of the organisation were transported to South Africa and housed in a military base near Phalaborwa. As with Unita, the Chief of Staff Intelligence

(CSI) was responsible for the co-ordination of support to Renamo. CSI was in turn responsible to the Chief of the SADF.

'We might have trained them [Renamo in general] a little bit,' said General Malan. 'I'm not sure about that. We trained them initially – Cor van Niekerk did a marvellous job as far as Renamo was concerned. He brought Mozambique to the situation where we could talk to them, whereas in Angola we couldn't get Dos Santos and Savimbi to talk to each other. He was the cornerstone of Renamo.'

Renamo's strength quickly increased from 500 to 8 000 fighters; by 1982 it conducted operations throughout most of Mozambique and posed a serious military threat to the Maputo regime. The strategy was to prove remarkably successful. On 16 March 1984, at the border town of Komatipoort, South Africa signed an agreement known as the Nkomati Accord, in which it agreed to stop supporting Renamo, and Frelimo agreed to shut down ANC training and support facilities.

According to an editorial in the third quarter edition of the 1984 *African Communist*, 'The ANC presence in Mozambique has been reduced from a substantial working cadre to a "diplomatic mission" [of] only 10 approved members, with the President and one or two others having the right of entry. All other ANC cadres are being deported, or restricted to refugee camps to which the ANC leadership will be denied access. And at the frontiers, Mozambique's troops "exercise … rigorous control over elements proposing to carry out or plan hostile actions against the apartheid state."' Further on, the writer of the article says: 'And just because we and our revolutionary movement are at the centre of the Nkomati Accord, it is our movement and our people who are most directly affected by it, and who feel its most immediate consequences. No one could possibly pretend that the Accord has not adversely affected our freedom to operate. Of all the valuable acts of international aid our movement has received from many countries, the facilities accorded to us by Mozambique in the past have been amongst the most important. Now these facilities have been severely restricted, [and] in some spheres totally withdrawn … [S]uch an agreement may seriously handicap the South African Freedom struggle.'

It was a strategic triumph for the South African government and military – but though they had achieved what they set out to, they weren't taking any chances. Support to Renamo continued, in a different form. When Casa Banana in Mozambique's Gorongoza province was captured from the rebels by Frelimo, documents and a diary were found outlining SADF military assistance to the MNR (Mozambique National Resistance), Renamo's military wing. South African officials attempted to explain their existence and contents by saying the details revealed were only about incidents that took place before the signing of the Accord. But General Malan confirmed aid had continued after Nkomati. 'Ja, we did,' he said. 'We did it with the approval of Samora Machel. I gave the approval. But what I did for the one side I did for the other. They [Renamo] needed a lot of medical supplies. But you need to define support. We didn't supply ammunition and weapons. But we did give medical assistance. I said to the chaps: "What you do for the one do for the other. In other words if they need a lot of medicine, band- ages and things to that effect and petrol and radio communications – because Pik said he wants to talk to Renamo – give it them but give it to the other side too."

'Samora Machel definitely knew about it. He gave me the approval to do it. And Pik knew about it, because he requested the radios – but now he can't recall it because he didn't understand that putting radios on that side you [had to] define as support. But how do you speak to people [without radios]? I mean if we can't talk to them how the blazes can you get the two parties together? Because right from the beginning we said it's about reconciliation – let's get the two parties together.'

But there are others who believe more strongly that the terms of the Nkomati Accord were not breached by South Africa. 'No. I'm very firm on that point,' said General Chris Thirion, former Deputy Chief of Staff Intelligence. 'I don't believe there was real support. There were problems of interpretation of what happened. Support in terms of supplying anything in the form of logistics, being arms or ammo, I say "no". And there was never proof of that. Yes, there was contact after the Nkomati Accord. It was about taking people into Mozambique to talk to [Renamo leader Alfonso] Dhlakama, for instance, and to try to convince him Renamo should go for a political solution. For that the presence of senior politi- cians was needed. On one occasion some senior officers took Louis Nel, Deputy Minister of Foreign Affairs, into Mozambique after the Agreement, which was seen as a breach. It wasn't, it was contact with Dhlakama in trying to convince him to go for a political solution. Cor van Niekerk's diary that was found dated back to before Nkomati but the propaganda made it sound as though it happened after Nkomati.'

Military Intelligence sources admit that aid continued after 16 March 1984, which fell outside the letter of the agreement. However, they are adamant it was mainly of a non-military nature, was primarily aimed at getting Renamo to the negotiating table and was done either at the request of or with the support of the Department of Foreign Affairs – a claim denied by former Minister of Foreign Affairs Pik Botha. In his submission to the TRC on 14 October 1997 Botha said: 'I exerted myself to negotiate an agreement with the Government of Mozambique to achieve peaceful co-operation between the two countries. My efforts resulted in the signing of the Nkomati Accord by the Prime Minister of South Africa and the President of Mozambique on 16 March 1984. News of this event reverberated throughout the world and was acclaimed by major governments. The Nkomati Accord did not come about overnight. I personally initiated the idea early in 1982 in meetings with members of the Mozambique government …

'In terms of the Accord, a Joint Security Commission (JSC) was established to ensure that the objectives of the Accord were respected by both countries and to monitor security violations by either party. The JSC met several times before Mozambique unilaterally withdrew from its activities on the "discovery of the Gorongoza documents" in 1985. I was invited by President Samora Machel to meet with him in Maputo on 16 September 1985 to discuss the matter. President Machel started the meeting with complimentary remarks about the role I had played in the peace process between Mozambique and South Africa. However, he informed me that he was perturbed by information contained in documents seized during a recent attack on Renamo's bases in Gorongoza. The documents revealed open violations of the Nkomati Accord. He said the documents showed that South Africans had trained, equipped and supported the "bandits" (i.e., Renamo rebels) in various ways. Advisors continued to be sent to train the bandits. At this point I asked President Machel whether he was saying that this was happening at that very moment. The President replied in the affirmative.

'It was arranged that my delegation and I would immediately meet with officials designated by President Machel. I thanked the President for conveying the information to me and assured him that we would thoroughly peruse the documents and investigate the allegations. I regarded the matter as critically serious and telephoned the State President's office to arrange a meeting with the State President that same evening on my return from Maputo. I gave an indication of the nature of the charges against us and suggested that the Minister of Defence and the Chief of the Defence Force should be invited to attend the meeting with the State President.

'My delegation and I then spent some hours with the Mozambique ministers showing us inter alia the original diary kept by a Mr Vaz, Secretary to the President of Renamo, in which it was clear, on the face of it, Renamo was receiving support from the South African Defence Force in violation of the agreement on non-aggression and good neighbourliness signed by the two countries on 16 March 1984. According to the diary, frequent meetings took place between

Renamo and officers of the Defence Force in Gorongoza to arrange for the delivery of equipment. A number of entries contained derogatory remarks made to Renamo about Pik Botha by officers of the South African Defence Force. I was dismayed because the diary appeared to be a genuine entry book.

'On my arrival that evening at the State President's residence the Minister of Defence and the Chief of the Defence Force were present. I was accompanied by two officials of the Department of Foreign Affairs. At first the State President was not impressed by my report. He thought that the diary could be a fake. I disagreed most strongly. The conversation developed into a heated exchange at the end of which the State President agreed that a committee could be appointed to investigate the whole matter. I suggested a judicial commission. The State President turned my proposal down. A Committee of Enquiry was appointed the next day consisting of Lieutenant General R. Rogers, retired Chief of the Air Force, and Dr J. Gilliland, an expert in civil aviation.

'The committee set to work immediately and completed its report in less than two days. The committee found that the allegations contained in the diary were in general correct, but that the alleged violations of the Nkomati Accord had arisen from the efforts on the part of the South African Government to bring about negotiations on a cease-fire agreement between the Government of Mozambique and Renamo. The Committee's finding was: "According to the provisions of the Nkomati Accord violations did occur. We are however convinced that the overriding motive for these violations was to bring about negotiations between Frelimo and Renamo."'

While compiling this book I interviewed dozens of former SADF members of all ranks as well as politicians and former senior civil servants. Some were understandably reluctant to speak to me; others did so on condition they were not identified. There were even times when I spoke with people whose identities I never uncovered. One day I opened my post box to find a plain, white envelope, postmarked Pretoria. Inside was a photocopy of a typewritten document titled *SADF Support to Renamo* (*SAW Steun aan Renamo*). No author was listed and it had no security classification stamped on it, but it certainly looked like an SADF document, and I have examined thousands. The layout and style of writing was certainly consistent with that of the SADF. It appeared to be a report to a senior officer or answers to questions about support to the Mozambican guerrillas. I do not know who sent the document; it could have been any one of dozens of people, it could even have been someone I never met or interviewed. I cannot say if everything contained in it is accurate or true, but what I can say is that impeccable Military Intelligence sources have confirmed that many of the outlined incidents did in fact take place. With that proviso in mind I have included extracts (translated from Afrikaans) from the document.

Paragraph 2 reads as follows: 'After the Nkomati Accord the SADF gave limited support to Renamo. Despite the fact that it was contrary to the letter of the agreement it ensured Renamo's involvement and later support [for the Agreement]. This support was given at the request of or with the knowledge of the Department of Foreign Affairs. It was primarily of a non-military nature. No documentation regarding this support could be found. Rather management personnel of the time put together a chronological list from memory which is attached to this document. It must be accepted that this list is incomplete and perhaps has mistakes in the dates ... ' The chronological list of support to Renamo reads as follows:

'02 AUGUST 1984. Two C-130 aircraft deploy Evo Fernandes and two SADF members with approximately 16 tons of cargo in the Sofala province. The cargo consisted mainly of ammunition for one platoon, blankets, clothes, radio equipment, medicine and seed. [Evo Fernandes was Renamo's Secretary General. He replaced the organisation's first Secretary General, Orlando Cristina, who was murdered at a Renamo base in 1983. In the Wouter Basson trial, under way at the time of writing of this book, claims have been made that the CCB and members of the SAP obstructed justice concealing the true facts about the incident.]

09 AUGUST 1984. Evo Fernandes and two SADF members are withdrawn from the coast north of Beira by a (Navy) Strike Craft. At the same time six Renamo members who were in hospital at the time of the Nkomati Accord were put ashore.

21 AUGUST 1984. Two SADF members were deployed from a DC-3 aircraft in Gorongoza to prepare an aircraft landing strip. Ammunition for one platoon was delivered to Renamo.

31 AUGUST 1984. The two SADF members are withdrawn from Gorongoza by DC-3 aircraft.

17 SEPTEMBER 1984. Renamo's Inhambane commander was withdrawn from the Inhambane coast by submarine and taken to South Africa to form part of Renamo's negotiating team.

18 SEPTEMBER 1984. Renamo's Gaza commander is withdrawn on foot to South Africa via the Kruger National Park border to form part of

Renamo's negotiating team. This was done in the presence of a Parks Board Official.

20 SEPTEMBER 1984. Renamo's Inhambane and Gaza commanders, together with 12 tons of cargo in two C-130 aircraft, are returned to Gorongoza. The cargo consisted of radio equipment and humanitarian goods.

25 SEPTEMBER 1984. Withdraw Alfonso Dhlakama in a DC-3 aircraft from Gorongoza to South Africa.

01 OCTOBER 1984. Take Alfonso Dhlakama back to Gorongoza in a DC-3 aircraft.

12 OCTOBER 1984. Two SADF members deployed at Gorongoza from a DC-3 with ammunition for a platoon.

13 OCTOBER 1984. A military doctor lands at Gorongoza to treat Alfonso Dhlakama after an accident. He returns to the RSA the same day.

21 OCTOBER 1984. The two SADF members as well as 10 Renamo leaders are withdrawn from Gorongoza to South Africa by DC-3 aircraft.

18–24 JANUARY 1985. Evo Fernandes visits the RSA from Europe for discussions with Minister R.F. Botha and his Deputy Louis Nel.

26 MAY 1985. Four SADF members, two of them doctors, land at Gorongoza in a DC-3 with ammunition for two platoons and medicine.

07 JUNE 1985. Deputy Minister Louis Nel and two SADF members visit Gorongoza by DC-3 aircraft to negotiate with Renamo.

08 JUNE 1985. Deputy Minister Louis Nel and six SADF members are withdrawn from Gorongoza by DC-3 aircraft.

JULY/AUGUST 1985. Four SADF members, two of them doctors, are deployed by DC-3 aircraft at Gorongoza with ammunition for two platoons, scrambler motorcycles and medicine.

AUGUST 1985. Deputy Minister Louis Nel and one SADF member visit Gorongoza by DC-3 aircraft to negotiate with Renamo.

AUGUST 1985. Deputy Minister Louis Nel and five SADF members leave Gorongoza by DC-3 aircraft.

JULY 1986. Evo Fernandes and three SADF members, one of whom is a doctor, are deployed by King Air aircraft at Maringue.

JULY 1986. Two C-130 aircraft deliver 12 tons of cargo to Maringue. This consists of ammunition for one platoon and medicine.

JULY 1986. Evo Fernandes and three SADF members as well as two female Renamo soldiers are taken from Maringue to South Africa by King Air aircraft.

02 SEPTEMBER 1986. Three SADF members including a doctor are deployed at Maringue by King Air aircraft.

04 SEPTEMBER 1986. Two C-130 aircraft deliver 12 tons of cargo to Maringue. The cargo consists of ammunition for one platoon, medicines and other humanitarian supplies.

06 SEPTEMBER 1986. The three SADF members are withdrawn from Maringue by King Air aircraft.

30 NOVEMBER 1986. Three SADF members including one doctor are deployed by King Air at Caia.

05 DECEMBER 1986. The three SADF members are withdrawn by King Air from Maringue.

1987. Approximately three SADF members and two anti-aircraft crews from Renamo are deployed from a C-130 aircraft together with six tons of cargo east of Inhaminga. The cargo consisted of ammunition for one platoon, two 20 mm aircraft cannons, 20 mm ammunition and humanitarian supplies. Remark: It is not certain if the 20 mm aircraft cannons and ammunition were delivered or not. It is not clear how and where the two crews were first withdrawn (for training) to the RSA.

1987. Approximately three SADF members are withdrawn from east of Inhaminga by DC-3 aircraft. The purpose of the visit was to prepare a landing strip for the DC-3.

1987. Two C-130 aircraft deliver 12 tons of radio equipment, ammunition and humanitarian supplies to Inhambane province.

1987. Alfonso Dhlakama is escorted over the border through the Kruger National Park with approximately 16 tons of cargo. The cargo consisted of ammunition for one company, radio equipment, scrambler motorcycles and humanitarian aid. This was done in the presence of a Parks Board official.

1987. Fetch and bring Alfonso Dhlakama across the border through the Kruger National Park. This was done in the presence of a Parks Board official.

1988. Two SADF members meet Alfonso Dhlakama in Malawi for discussions.

1988. One SADF member meets Alfonso Dhlakama in the Tete province beside the Malawi border for discussions.

1984–1988. Accommodate Alfonso Dhlakama's family in the RSA.

1984–1989. Maintain radio communications with Renamo.

1984–1989. Various instances of financial support for travel and accommodation costs to Renamo for travel to and from Europe are supplied.'

Paragraph 3 states: 'The military support given to Renamo after the Nkomati Accord formed part of the above mentioned initiative and can be explained as follows:

A. Where members of the SADF and/or Department of Foreign Affairs visited Mozambique sufficient ammunition was supplied to Renamo to ensure their protection.

B. Where the SADF convinced Alfonso Dhlakama to visit the southern regions of Mozambique to promote the peace initiative sufficient ammunition was supplied to equip a protection force.

C. To further the peace initiative relatively large quantities of communications equipment were supplied to Renamo so that it could effectively communicate with all its regions particularly with regard to a cease-fire.

D. In two instances ammunition was supplied to Renamo to:
   I. ensure the safety of hostages; and
   II. as a means of persuasion to free the hostages and to make concessions in the negotiations.

E. Two Renamo anti-aircraft crews were trained and deployed in Mozambique with obsolete aircraft cannons to protect Renamo's headquarters from Frelimo air attacks so that Renamo would continue with the negotiations and not withdraw as it had threatened to do.

F. Remark: Some of the management personnel are of the opinion that the (anti-aircraft) crews were trained but that the weapons and ammunition were not delivered as a result of technical problems.'

Paragraph 4: 'The SADF support to Renamo was co-ordinated by the Intelligence Division (*Afdeling Inligting*). Execution was carried out by the various arms of service.'

Paragraph 5: 'The SADF is convinced that its involvement in contact and support for Renamo after the Nkomati Accord made a large contribution to maintaining Renamo's participation in the peace process in Mozambique, even though from 1988 it was with the facilitation of the Italian Government and the church, and eventually peacefully took part in democratic elections and accepted the results thereof.'

The document also claims that Dhlakama's family was housed in South Africa for over a year to ensure their safety.

Pik Botha continues to maintain that he knew nothing about his Deputy Minister's visits to Renamo. In his submission to the TRC he said: 'I also dealt with Deputy Minister Nel's unauthorised visit to Renamo in Mozambique. I said that he explained to me, when I asked him about the visit, that he did not seek my approval because I probably would have disapproved of the visit for fear of Mr Nel's personal safety. In view, however, of my instruction in March 1985, that Mr Nel should continue his efforts to achieve reconciliation in Mozambique, he should not be blamed for meeting with Renamo … There was also a request from the Soviet Union to assist in tracing two Russians who had disappeared in Mozambique and were thought to be taken prisoner by Renamo. I authorised Mr Nel to offer Mr Dhlakama, leader of Renamo, R100 000 in exchange for the two Russians.'

'It seems strange,' said a senior field officer, 'that on the one hand Botha can claim neither he nor his department knew about violations or his Deputy's visits to Renamo, and on the other, authorise the payment of a large sum of money to the very leader of the organisation he claims to have no dealings with. It looks like yet another case of the former Minister covering his arse at the expense of the SADF!'

On 20 October 1986 General Malan, then Minister of Defence, was woken by the telephone at his Waterkloof home, around 06h00 in the morning. When he picked up the phone the voice on the other end said: 'What the hell did you guys do?' It was Louis le Grange, Minister of Police. 'What do you mean?' Malan asked. 'Samora Machel has crashed in South Africa and he's dead,' said Le Grange.

The day before, at 21h21:39, the Mozambican presidential aircraft, a Tupolev TU 134A-3, had ploughed into a hill near the village of Mbunzini near Komatipoort in Mpumalanga. The plane was on a return flight from Zambia, where, according to press reports, Machel had criticised Malawian President Hastings Banda for doing nothing to stop Renamo rebels from launching attacks from his territory. Thirty-four people died in the crash.

The case is full of claims and counter-claims. On one side, the then South African government, the SADF and the commission of inquiry appointed to investigate the crash say it was as a result of human error – the crew mistakenly locked on to a radio navigation beacon at Matsapa in Swaziland and simply flew into the mountains. On the other side is a large range of people, including well-known investigative journalists and the Soviet investigators of the time, who believe SADF Special Forces placed a decoy beacon to lure the plane into the death zone. They believe there may have been a conspiracy involving disgruntled Frelimo generals whom Machel supposedly threatened to fire shortly before his death.

'We didn't do it,' said General Malan. 'Firstly, we couldn't, we didn't have the technology, and secondly, we'd have nothing to gain by doing so.' His sentiments were echoed by General Thirion, former Deputy Chief of Staff Intelligence. 'That plane crash was an accident,' he said. 'I spoke to many Air Force ops people at the time asking whether it could have been done. Could one put up a mast and send out false signals? I got confirmation from top Air Force ops guys who said that particular flight wasn't even known to us. They wouldn't have said it at the time, but they said we never realised the aircraft had crossed the border. This says it was flying so low when it crossed the border that the early warning systems did not pick it up. To be honest … it was good news in some circles that Samora Machel was gone – it was good news for a lot of people. I think there were a lot of people who would have liked to believe we were so good we could have lured that big Russian plane with all its instruments over the border and got rid of it. But it would have served no purpose. It didn't change the situation one bit,' said Thirion.

Not so, say others. Dutch researcher Klaas de Jonge, in his report on the plane crash, rehashed a number of old statements made by a variety of people. Though he produced precious little evidence, he concluded, in the space allocated for the name of the perpetrators (admittedly between two sets of question marks) that it was South African covert forces. De Jonge reported: 'President Samora Machel was "a major target" of SA … and [was] accused, 2 weeks before the crash, of renewing support for ANC rebels. Pretoria banned the new migration of Mozambican workers into SA. In the weeks before the crash the SA government had conducted a prodigious destabilisation campaign against Mozambique. On 7 October Defence Minister Gen. Magnus Malan threatened the Mozambican leader personally. The unusually vitriolic tone of SA criticism of Mozambique and of Machel, especially by military spokesmen, gives credence to theories that the SA government got tired of Machel and … wanted him gone.'

Speaking after a landmine blast in the Mbunzini area on 6 October 1986 which injured six SADF members on patrol and which was alleged to have been laid by ANC cadres who came from Mozambique, Malan had said: 'If President Machel chooses landmines, South Africa will react accordingly. If he allows a Moscow-inspired revolutionary war against South Africa, he must also be prepared to take responsibility. If he chooses terrorism and revolution, he will clash head on with South Africa.' After the plane crash the media and Mozambican officials claimed the South African Defence Minister had threatened Machel's life personally. It is a claim he has vigorously denied.

'Mozambique was at a critical moment in the struggle: Renamo had started a huge offensive and threatened to cut Mozambique in two parts. The SA leadership believed that the Mozambican government was on the verge of collapse ... ' De Jonge wrote. 'According to former Mozambican Minister Cabaço ... there is no sufficient proof that SA murdered President Samora Machel, but personally he believes that they were responsible for his death and well [sic] for the following reasons:

1   on the Wednesday before the death of Samora Machel, Carlos Cardosa director of AIM agency received a message that the President had died.

2   before leaving for Lusaka Samora Machel organised a meeting with journalists, the party leadership and the military. He told them that he had received information that the SA wanted to kill him. He gave clear instructions what to do if he wouldn't come back.

3   SA wanted to get rid of Samora Machel for the following reason: Under pressure of some presidents of the frontline states, President Banda was forced to expel the Renamo soldiers who used Malawi as a springboard for attacks on Mozambique. Banda complied with the demands of the frontline states' leaders, but allowed Renamo to cross into Tete and Zambezia province. Renamo mounted a huge offensive in Zambezia (where Frelimo had few troops at his disposal), and approached the city of Quilimane, trying to split Mozambique in two parts and to provide Malawi with an outlet to the sea. The South Africans expected that the death of Samora Machel would cause a power struggle in Maputo and that no Mozambican troops would be sent to counter the Renamo offensive, until the leadership crisis would be over.'

Investigative journalist Debora Patta produces a more convincing argument about a South African conspiracy. Her argument is contained in an article that appeared in the *Electronic Mail & Guardian* of 14 July 1998. In it she raises the possibility of the black-box flight recorder having been tampered with by police forensic experts. The reason behind this claim is a statement by Civil Aviation Investigator Piet de Klerk, who said: 'he put [the boxes] in black plastic bags and sealed them and they were muddy and dirty and whatever – and the day that we arrived here they were spotless. There are little holes and things that are plugged with wax, and the wax was gone. We did not know whether they'd been opened or X-rayed and the more questions we put to the police the more obtuse they became. So we left here just hoping they would work and … everything we got from the boxes was excellent.'

Then Patta introduces a spy hiding out in Italy who was one of Machel's most trusted agents but also a double agent working for the South Africans and feeding information back to the Mozambican president. 'One of his regular contacts was a female MI agent whom he has identified but asked that we call simply "Maureen". It was during a routine meeting with Maureen that Casadei stumbled on the information that South African and Mozambican agents were plotting to kill Machel,' Patta wrote. 'He described how "she asked me if the South Africans could trust the Mozambicans. Because they had asked the South Africans: if they assisted in killing Samora, what would the South Africans do to help those who'd assisted in the murder to take over power in Maputo?"'

'Now that he knew the identities of the Mozambican officials planning on betraying their leader, Casadei went straight to Machel and begged him to let him kill the two generals. "Samora now knew who was plotting against him, but he refused [to let] me kill them, he did not give me the permit to kill them. And so he gave them time to kill him. This was the big problem," said Casadei, shaking his head regretfully. It was not long after this that the crash occurred.' Patta's article claims: 'There is a foreign intelligence document from a neighbouring country in the possession of Radio 702. The document names the Malawian, Mozambican and South African agents who conspired in the plot to kill Machel. The Mozambicans named in the report are the very same ones who sent assassins to kill Casadei. The document states that South Africa was charged with the responsibility of overseeing the technical aspects of the crash. Senior South African generals and a Cabinet minister are named in the report.'

And lots of other things are mentioned: an airport official being paid R1,5 million to switch off the Maputo radar system or the navigation beacon (the dates and names of the institution into which the money was supposedly paid are known but there is no paperwork); an unnamed 32 Batallion member who claimed to be a member of Special Forces (though 32 Batallion was a unit on its own and not a member of the Special Forces); a military radio blackout that the unnamed 32 Batallion Special Forces member said meant only one thing – 'a black op, a highly secret operation, the details of which would only be known at a presidential and senior general level'; a national serviceman who had to serve refreshments to the SADF top brass, including Magnus Malan, Kat Liebenberg and "Joop" Joubert, at Military Headquarters in Pretoria on the night of the crash. His contribution to the solution of the mystery was this: 'These guys were hungry. They had an appetite.' They must have been – the next day and the day before they were reported to be braaing near the site of the crash.

The TRC reports that 'Ben', a former Military Intelligence operative who had been based at Skwamans – a secret security police base shared with MI operatives half-way between Mbuzini and Komatipoort – at the time of the incident tesitified that 'a number of high-ranking security force officials converged on Skwamans for a meeting and a braai the day before the crash. They left late that night in a small plane and some returned after the crash had taken place. In a sworn statement, he provided the names of General Kat Liebenberg, Foreign Minister Pik Botha, General van der Westhuizen of Military Intelligence and about 15 others, mostly from Eastern Transvaal Command and Group 33.

'Also there that night [at Defence HQ],' wrote Patta, 'was former electronic warfare head Lieutenant Colonel Mossie Basson. He has confirmed the presence of Joubert, and says by some strange coincidence there was a secret operation under way that night. However, he says it had nothing to do with the Machel plane crash.'

The claims have all the elements needed to produce a best-selling spy novel. But there are many who strongly reject the false beacon, South African/Mozambican/Malawian/Renamo conspiracy theory. The question is, if this evidence is available, why hasn't it been handed over to the authorities? After all, the South African government promised to get to the bottom of the matter, then later said it would not be re-opening the investigation into the plane crash. Why was this evidence not referred to the TRC, which was conducting its own investigation into the incident and eventually drew the following conclusion: 'The investigations conducted by the Commission raised a number of questions, including the possibility of a false beacon and the absence of a warning from the South African authorities. The matter requires further investigation by an appropriate structure'?

Why does Machel's trusted lieutenant, now hiding in Italy, not name the names and let justice take its course? Writing for the same publication some three weeks earlier (*Electronic Mail & Guardian* 19 June 1998), commercial pilot Robert Kirby said: 'In the Tupolev crash, the board, chaired by Judge Cecil Margo, a retired supreme court judge and a highly experienced civil aviation administrator, included Sir Edward Walter Eveleigh, former lord justice of appeal; Colonel Frank Bormann, congressional medal of honour winner, former test

Prime Minister John Vorster in the border area, South West Africa/Namibia

Prime Minister Vorster accompanies SADF officers in South West Africa

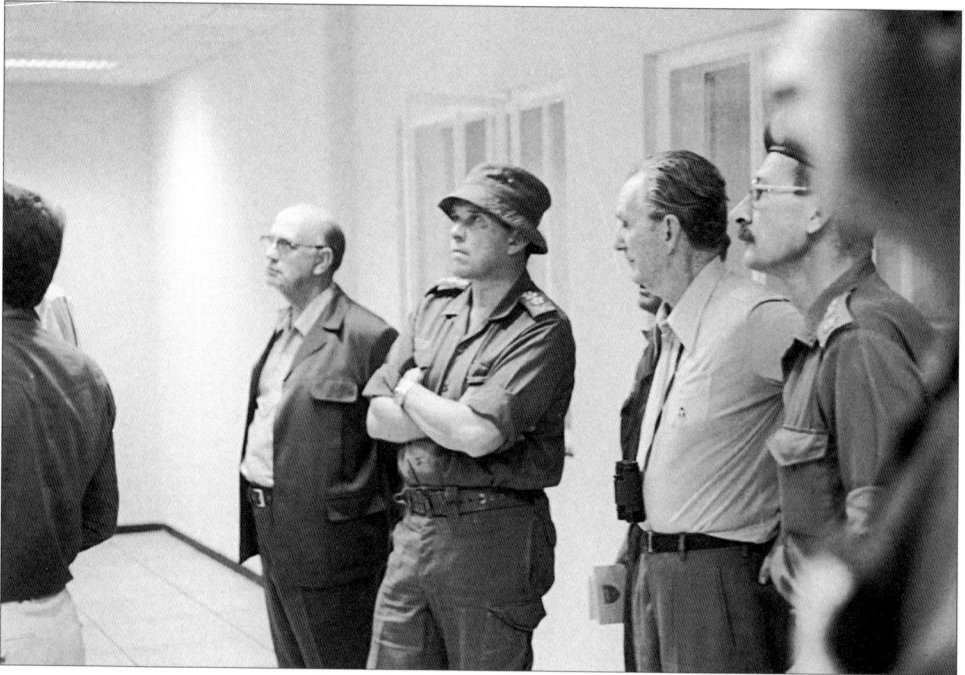
P.W. Botha and Magnus Malan at the Ruacana hydro-electric scheme, March 1978

Major General van Deventer, Magnus Malan, P.W. Botha, Jonas Savimbi, Mr J. de Wet and Minister Chris Heunis, during Operation Savannah

P.W. Botha salutes withdrawing troops after Operation Savannah

Lieutenant Generals Rogers and Viljoen and Brigadier Kat Liebenberg, 1979

Lieutenant General Hein du Toit, Chief of Staff Intelligence during Operation Savannah

P.W. Botha inspects troops in the operational area

Magnus Malan becomes the first honorary member of 31 Batallion, 1984

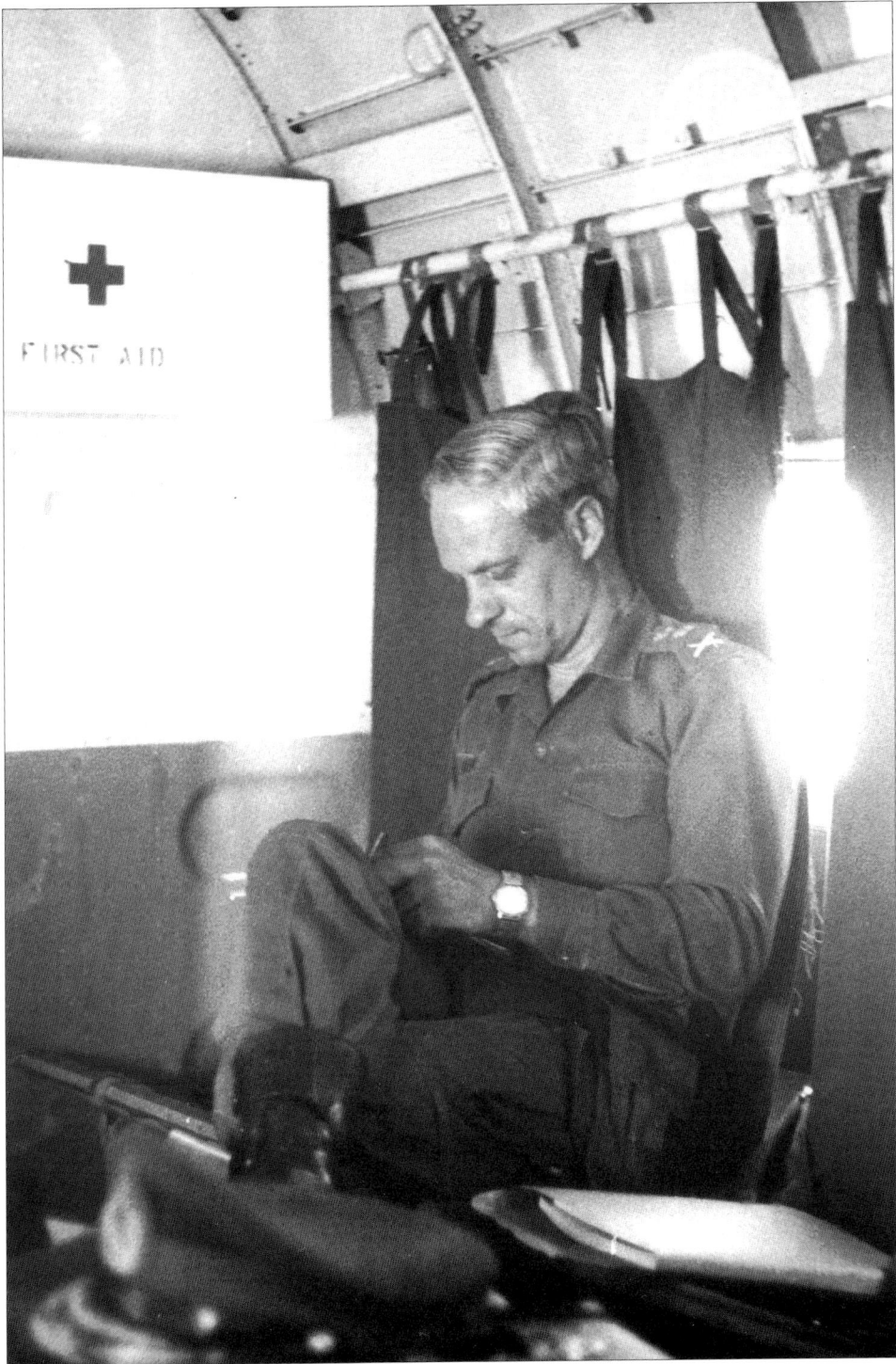

General Constand Viljoen in a Dakota DC-3 aircraft

General Constand Viljoen in a light reconnaissance spotter plane

General Viljoen keeps his hand in at the General de la Rey Firing Range, Potchefstroom

Lieutenant General J.J. Geldenhuys

Lieutenant General J.J. Geldenhuys talks to SADF officers

Lieutenant General Geldenhuys hands over command to Major General Kat Liebenberg, 1985

Chief of the Army Lieutenant General Liebenberg visits a base on South Africa's northern border in 1987

General Georg Meiring and General John M. Shalikshvili, Chairman Joint Chiefs of Staff, USA

General Georg Meiring and General Mboma, Chief of Tanzanian Armed Forces

General Georg Meiring and Field Marshal Peter Inge, Chief of Staff of British Armed Forces

Major General Pierre Steyn, author of the Steyn Report that led to the 'Night of the Generals'

General Chris Thirion

General Georg Meiring with President Nelson Mandela at Mandela's inauguration in 1994

pilot, astronaut and aeronautical engineer, and president of Eastern Airlines in the United States; Geoffrey Wilkinson, chief investigator for the accidents investigation branch of the British Ministry of Transport; J.J.S. "Jock" Germishuys, former commissioner for civil aviation of South Africa; and P. van Hoven, chairman of the Airlines Association of South Africa. A doughty collection, and Margo's own. For obvious reasons he accepted the brief only if these choices remained solely his. The board went further than required under the Chicago Convention of 1944, accommodating the other states – USSR and Mozambique – by inviting their attendance to participate in the inquiry and offering the right to representation, cross-examination and the calling of their own witnesses. (They took no advantage of this.)'

Kirby echoes the findings of the commission of enquiry: 'The Tupolev was on a flight from Zambia to Maputo. Approaching Maputo from the north-west, at 100 km out but directly on track for the Maputo airport, the Tupolev made an unexpected turn to the right – of some 37 degrees. The decision to initiate this turn was the navigator's and in reply to the captain's query about such a sudden change in course, the navigator answered: "VOR indicates that way." A rather cursory explanation but one with which the captain apparently agreed. He never again questioned the decision. The Tupolev was now flying on a new heading, towards the mountains of the escarpment.'

There was no cross-checking at all, as is required, and it appears the navigator had mistakenly locked onto the beacon at Matsapa in Swaziland – the frequencies of Maputo and Matsapa are close together: 112,7 and 112,3 respectively. From the transcripts of the cockpit voice-recorder it is clear that the crew were more concerned with finishing the flight than with following standard aviation procedures and cross-checks. The captain was busy arranging a drinks order of 'three beers and one coke' with his flight engineer. When the plane made its 37-degree turn even the most rudimentary of cross-checking would have shown that if the navigation beacon they were homing in on was in fact that of Maputo then they were some 100 km off course over the ocean.

The Tupolev was low on fuel: certainly it did not have enough to divert to Beira, so the crew had to land in Maputo whatever the case or the weather. When they saw no lights where they thought Maputo should be, they assumed power to the city had been cut. In radio communications with the control tower at Maputo the Tupolev's radio operator repeatedly asked if the runway lights were lit. He asked the air-traffic controller to check the lights. When the terrain proximity warning alarm sounded – a system that warns the crew the plane is flying dangerously close to the ground, the captain ignored it for 30 seconds until the plane crashed into the side of the mountain.

This is a transcript of conversations recorded on the cockpit voice-recorder in the last few minutes of the doomed flight. Time is UTC. For local time add two hours.

19:19:38   **Capt:** It should be lit …

19:19:40   **Capt:** There to the right lights are seen.

            Co-pilot: Runway is not lit … (?)

            Capt: Runway is not lit? … there is a problem … (?)

19:19:50   **Radio Operator:** Maputo Charlie Nine Charlie Alfa Alfa, check your runway lights.

19:19:56   **AT Controller:** Charlie Charlie Alfa Alfa roger, cleared visual approach runway zero five, join position left down wind, surface wind zero nine zero, one zero knots.

19:20:01   **Capt:** (Interjection) I can see

19:20:06   **Radio Operator:** Roger Charlie Nine Charlie Alfa Alfa, and we request to join right downwind.

19:20:13   **AT Controller:** Charlie Nine Charlie Alfa Alfa roger, right downwind is approved and report position right base for runway zero five.

19:20:18   **Capt:** What right? Wait, heading … 24.

19:20:22   **AT Controller:** Roger Charlie Alfa Alfa.

19:20:22   **Capt:** I understood nothing.

            Radio Operator: Don't you see the runway yet?

19:20:28   **Capt:** … and what runway, what are you talking about?

19:20:32   **Navigator:** We are going to do straight in approach?

19:20:35   **Capt:** We are going to do straight in approach.

19:20:38   **Radio Operator:** No, well, can you see the runway?

            Co-pilot: No, there's nothing, there's neither city nor runway.

            Radio Operator: and so he says that …

            Capt: … he says …

            Co-pilot: What does he say?

            Radio Operator: I asked him to check the runway.

            Capt: I don't understand what he's saying … ?

            Capt: Nothing can be seen, chaps …

            Co-pilot: Tell him once more to check the lights.

            Capt: So no, surely it is indeed cloudy to descend.

19:20:54 **Navigator:** Some 18–20 kilometres left.

19:20:57 **Radio Operator:** Maputo Charlie Nine Alfa Alfa, check again runway lights.

19:21:02 The terrain proximity alarm begins to sound.

19:21:05 **AT Controller:** Roger you are cleared to visual approach runway zero five, join right down wind and report position right base.

19:21:12 **Capt:** Damn it!

19:21:17 **Radio Operator:** Charlie Nine Charlie Alfa Alfa, runway lights out of service?

19:21:17 **Capt:** No, it's cloudy, cloudy, cloudy.

19:21:18 **AT Controller:** … firm, runway lights out of service?

19:21:22 **Radio Operator:** Affirmative, lights not in sight.

19:21:27 **AT Controller:** Affirmative and join right down wind runway zero five, surface wind zero nine zero, one zero knots.

Capt: (Interjection) No! Normal!

19:21:32 Alarm stops.

19:21:34 **Radio Operator:** Roger Roger.

19:21:36 **Navigator:** No, no, there's nowhere to go. No NDB [non-directional beacon], there's nothing.

Capt: Neither NDBs nor ILS [instrument landing system].

19:21:39 Impact is registered by one half second of silence.

19:24:10 **AT Controller:** Charlie Nine Charlie Alfa Alfa request your position.

The idea of a decoy beacon makes a good story but there is not one scrap of hard evidence to support such a claim. Sure, there are plenty of unnamed national servicemen, ex-Koevoet members, double-agents and people who worked at Air Force bases whom the media and the TRC say they have interviewed but as yet there is not one piece of documentary evidence. Not one person has applied for amnesty and no one actually saw the decoy beacon – which somehow had no effect on a scheduled Mozambican Airlines flight that was in the air at the same time.

If the South Africans had been able to lure Machel's plane into a mountain in South Africa it would have required a sizeable logistics exercise with troops and vehicles and much of the paraphernalia that goes with a military operation. There would have had to have been agents both in Maputo and in Manzini in Swaziland who would have had to switch the navigation beacons off at the same time. 'If the military had done this surely somebody would have seen and known about it, yet no-one has come forward,' said General Meiring.

The fact is the hard evidence shows the crew of flight Charlie Nine Alfa Alfa displayed a lack of basic airmanship and the air traffic controller at Maputo airport was incompetent. It was human error plain and simple.

7

'TOTAL ONSLAUGHT'

'We can't fight a bush war in South Africa,' Thabo Mbeki told the *New York Times* on 20 June 1980. 'Look at the map. It is all developed. There are roads, radios, and landing strips everywhere. This isn't a forest. The machine would smash us if we try to send an army from the outlying areas. Also 87% of the whites are in towns and cities. Our masses have to serve as our bush. The Black community is our bush ...' It was obvious that if the ANC were to have any hope of achieving their goals in South Africa, a change of strategy was desperately needed.

In 1978 the ANC leadership began to undertake study tours to many Third World countries. This was followed by a high-powered delegation which included Oliver Tambo, Thabo Mbeki, Chris Hani, Joe Slovo and Joe Modise to Vietnam to study that country's struggle and victory against the United States of America. In their report, presented to the ANC executive in Luanda, they outlined the key strategies of the Vietnamese struggle, pointing out the need for 'the combination of a political and military struggle, the mobilisation of the whole of the people to fight the enemy; the unity of the internal situation and international solidarity; and the party's leadership role over the armed forces.'

If P.W. Botha and his military advisors believed they'd faced a 'total onslaught' they hadn't seen anything yet! After the visit to Vietnam a new strategy was devised and presented. Officially it was termed *The Four Pillars of Revolution – a Strategy for People's War*. These four pillars were:
- the all-round activity of the underground structures of the ANC;

DAYS OF THE GENERALS

- the united mass action of the people (mass mobilisation);
- the armed offensive; and
- the international drive to isolate South Africa.

But what did it mean in practice? ANC and SACP publications spelt out the details only too clearly. *Sechaba* said: 'The role of the workers and trade unions will be to bring South Africa's economy to a halt. White anti-apartheid movements must be created to oppose compulsory military service and the war in Angola. The people's army must be strengthened so that the ANC can march in the vanguard of semi-spontaneous mass upsurges and the masses must be armed and trained as part-time guerrillas.'

Another edition of *Sechaba* stated: 'The goal of transforming the armed offensive into a people's war remains one that we must pursue with the greatest vigour. Our mass military offensive must aim to increase the number of casualties among the enemy's armed forces, to disperse and reduce these forces, make it increasingly impossible to defend themselves and undermine the material-economic base ... In other words it must become part of a policy to involve more and more armed people as organised contingents in support of our struggle and acting under our leadership.'

The *African Communist* wrote: 'By people's war we mean a war in which a liberation army becomes rooted amongst the people who progressively participate actively in the armed struggle both politically and militarily, including the possibility of engaging in partial or general insurrections. The present disparity in strength between the enemy forces and ours determines the protracted nature of the struggle ... such a struggle will lead inevitably to a revolutionary situation in which our plan must be the seizure of power through whatever ways might present themselves.'

The plan was beginning to take shape. In 1985 the ANC held a conference at Kabwe in Zambia to examine its strategy. There amongst other things it was recommended the organisation should establish cores in existing youth organisations, be in charge of the process, and educate youth, religious groups and other cultural organisations to translate their beliefs into the rejection of apartheid and to become more involved in the struggle.

One of the biggest problems the ANC faced was the fact that it had no military bases inside South Africa. To launch attacks MK cadres had to travel from surrounding countries.

In the 1960s the headquarters and training facilities of the organisation had been based in Dar es Salaam, but around 1980 these were moved to Lusaka. In 1976, after Operation Savannah and the coming to power of the MPLA, Umkhonto we Sizwe's main training facilities were moved to Angola. Between October 1976 and August 1977 Lusaka was the main operational centre, while Botswana, Lesotho and Swaziland provided the main transit routes for the infiltration of men (and women), weapons and equipment destined for South Africa. Eighty per cent of MK members arrested in South Africa between January 1977 and April 1978 infiltrated through Swaziland. After April 1978 Mozambique played a pivotal role in the ANC's armed action, although MK was prohibited from acting directly from Mozambican territory (a stipulation that was hard to enforce and monitor). By 1980 the organisation had set up regional headquarters in Botswana, Lesotho, Swaziland and Mozambique from where planning, monitoring and control of MK operations took place. The Swazi government was uncomfortable with the situation, being reluctant to provoke the wrath of its bigger and stronger neighbour, and continuously took political and security action against armed MK members.

When Zanu-PF came to power in Zimbabwe in 1980 the country's territory became accessible to both MK and the Azanian People's Liberation Army (Apla) as an assembly and transit area. Infiltrations from Zimbabwe began in 1983 and by 1985 the ANC had established two operational and two sub-headquarters. Although the Nkomati Accord of 1984 seriously dented the ANC's facilities in Mozambique, the organisation continued to operate clandestinely from the country In the last part of 1985 the area, and particularly Maputo, once again played a major role in the ANC's armed campaign. In 1988 the structure in Swaziland was disbanded and all subsequent operations for the area were controlled from Maputo.

The plans of infiltrating MK cadres were often known by South African agents and intelligence before they even set out – and they had to cross the border and make their way to the urban centres without running into the security forces. It was a hazardous occupation and many never completed their missions. It was therefore imperative for the ANC to develop, organise and train, inside the country, MK cadres whose main task would be to lead the revolution.

The new strategy foresaw MK guerrilla units operating in the rural areas of South Africa where farmers, who were seen as providing a major support base for the government, would be targeted for military-style attacks. Their workers and the rural population would be encouraged or coerced into joining the revolutionary effort. In the urban areas underground fighting units were established. Their primary tasks were sabotage and the elimination of opponents. Self-defence units

(SDUs) were established in township areas. Structures were set up to acquire, transport and supply weapons to MK cadres and ANC supporters in the townships. Specific efforts were made to spread the message of the movement; targets were identified and information gathered.

Once that was in place the second pillar of the four-part strategy – that of mass mobilisation – could be implemented. On 20 August 1983 the United Democratic Front (UDF) was established as 'a broad front of popular resistance'. It claimed affiliation with over 700 different groups and though it denied links with the ANC there are few who believed that to be the case. In 1986 the government banned the organisation but three years later the Mass Democratic Movement (MDM) was formed, which was in fact little more than the old UDF with a new name. In its submission to the TRC the SADF said of the MDM: 'The MDM saw its aim as to deepen the isolation of the regime, maximise unity against it and weaken its ability to resist the struggle for a democratic and non-racial South Africa.'

As the strategy began to take hold, the ANC created what it termed 'liberated zones' which were no-go areas for the police and other administrative functionaries. The aim was to make the country ungovernable and to establish political and paramilitary control over communities using the self-defence and combat units. This would then provide safe areas for MK from which operations could be carried out. Once an area was 'liberated', alternative structures were set up. Civic organisations mobilised the people of the area and enforced discipline using fear and intimidation to gain maximum compliance. Anyone found guilty of stepping out of line was dealt with harshly by the 'comrades'. Shoppers found buying goods from white-owned shops were forced to eat their soap powder or drink their cooking oil.

On 21 March 1985 Benjamin Kinikini and his sons had petrol-filled tyres draped around their necks and were set alight and burned to death while a Dutch television crew filmed the incident. Their crime? Kinikini was a town councillor. Anyone seen as a 'collaborator' of the South African government could expect the same fate. The 'necklace' was to be used to kill 399 people between 1984 and 1989. It was a method of execution the ANC refused to condemn and in fact encouraged. According to the SADF's submissions to the TRC, Chris Hani, MK's commander at the time, wrote in an article in *Sechaba*: 'The necklace was a weapon to remove this cancer [of collaborators] from our society … to cleanse the townships from the very disruptive and even lethal activities of the puppets and collaborators. I refuse to condemn our people when they mete out their own traditional forms of justice to those who collaborate.'

There were many other ANC statements supporting necklacing. Tim Ngubane, the ANC's representative in the USA, told a group of students at California State University on 10 October 1985: 'Collaborators and informers live in fear of petrol, either as petrol bombs being hurled at their homes and reducing them to rack and ruin, or as petrol dousing their treacherous bodies which we set alight and burn them to a charred despicable mess. We want to make the death of a collaborator so grotesque that people will never think of it.'

In addition to necklace killings a further 372 people were burnt to death between 1984 and 1989 in their homes or after petrol was poured over them and set alight. 'We convey messages and tell people what has to be done,' ANC leader Oliver Tambo told the German news magazine *Der Spiegel*. 'Our followers often decide for themselves what targets they want to attack.'

'Our people must organise themselves into groups, manufacture traditional weapons which can be used against the enemy,' Joe Modise commented in a Radio Freedom broadcast on 1 December 1985. ANC General Secretary Alfred Nzo said in a London *Sunday Times* interview on 14 September 1986: 'After arming ourselves in this manner, our people must begin to identify collaborators and enemy agents and kill them. The puppets in the tricameral Parliament and the Bantustans must be destroyed. Whatever the people decide to use to eliminate those enemy elements is their decision.' 'If they decide to use necklacing we support it.'

Comparing the ANC to other liberation movements in the region, General Viljoen said that 'Zanu and Zapu in Zimbabwe and even Swapo were much stronger from a military point of view. They had more of a military ability than MK. But eventually MK – and you can give the credit to Mbeki – went for another formula. Up until 1985 we had very little trouble with the ANC. But then they went to Vietnam and had discussions about revolutionary war. When Mbeki returned and reported to his people he said: "The SADF is far too strong. If we try to attack South Africa in the same way that Zapu and Zanu had done in Rhodesia then we will have to cross the border, the Limpopo for example, and travel hundreds of kilometres before we get to the heartland of SA." He said: "We will never succeed, they will crush us."

'On the advice of the Vietnamese they decided to make this a people's war. That's why they took the war to the townships. Instead of establishing bases in neighbouring countries and operating across the border as they'd started to do, they changed their strategy and went directly to the townships. They infiltrated the townships, revolutionised the youth and the whole situation and presented not only the Defence Force but mainly the police with a very big problem as to how to deal with it. You could not identify the terrorists – they wore no uniforms. They operated in civilian clothes and were protected by the blacks in the townships. This gave them the opportunity to create a revolutionary spirit inside South Africa. It created the impression of our not having a solution to this kind of war. How do you deal with it? At that stage we were unable, for example, to really protect the black councillors in the townships and the ANC was targeting those people for murders.

'This is how the internal thing developed,' said Viljoen. 'First on the pattern of Zanu and Zapu and then a people's war and then with a revolutionary urban situation which is a very difficult situation to deal with. [Militarily] we could have kept going against MK indefinitely provided the government was able to fund it. The problem with sustaining the military effort was not a military problem. It was financial and diplomatic.'

There can be no question that the ANC succeeded in turning up the heat and putting the South African government's feet to the fire. Between September 1984 and May 1986, 3 477 private black homes were destroyed or badly damaged, 1 220 schools were destroyed or badly damaged, education in non-white areas ground to a halt, black local authorities crumbled and 573 people were killed in black-on-black violence, including 295 who were burned to death by the necklace method.

At the same time an international campaign of unprecedented intensity was launched. Centred in the United Nations, it was driven by the ANC, the Soviet bloc and a variety of international anti-apartheid organisations. At one point no fewer than 15 United Nations committees or surrogates were solely dedicated to opposing South Africa.

'The international campaign affected every aspect of South Africa's international relations and ultimately led to the imposition of arms, oil, sport, cultural, economic and financial sanctions against South Africa,' said former State President F.W. de Klerk to the Truth and Reconciliation Commission. 'The objectives of this campaign included an unprecedented international propaganda offensive, the isolation of South Africa through the imposition of comprehensive sanctions, support for the "armed struggle" and the ultimate overthrow of the South African government. The government's response to this "total onslaught" was to develop its own "total strategy".'

'It was the international isolation of South Africa that started to count,' said General Thirion. 'It was about the economy – how much more could it spend on the war and the military budget? It was about a lot of things. It was about the total strategy. Today if people talk about the total onslaught they say: "We know that story. That was a lot of political bullshit." But the ANC and the international community decided they'd fight the South African government at every level and all over. One must not just see this in a simple military perspective. The core of the revolutionary strategy was to make South Africa ungovernable. That's where the 'total onslaught' phrase was born. The ANC said they would use every court case as a platform to make a stand. They would use the education system as a front to take on the government and [employ] civil disobedience at all levels. Let's face it, once you start going that way then the government must have the support of the majority of the people in order to survive. And let's face it, it was a white minority government. This whole concept of civil disobedience, in the trade unions, the education system, in the courts of law, is the thing that moved the government and forced F.W. de Klerk to move faster.'

Armed attacks and incidents arranged by the ANC began to increase. From October 1976 to August 1983 the organisation carried out 362 violent acts. Of these 172 were acts of sabotage directed mainly at railway property, police stations, government buildings and the electricity infrastructure. Forty-eight acts were offensive, comprising 24 attacks – mainly against police stations – and 24 contacts with the SAP. Approximately 40 MK members were killed and 155 arrested, while 11 security force members were killed and 24 wounded. Eighty-eight per cent of the attacks took place in urban areas and from 1981 onwards explosives experts noted most saboteurs used limpet mines – it appeared that conventional explosives and detonators had been discontinued. Some of the more newsworthy incidents included:

- A bomb explosion at the Carlton Centre in Johannesburg in which 17 civilians were injured (24 November 1977).
- Sabotage at Sasol 1 and Natref in Sasolburg and at Sasol 2 in Secunda (1 and 2 June 1980).
- A rocket attack on the Voortrekkerhoogte Military base in Pretoria (12 August 1981).
- Sabotage at Koeberg nuclear power station (19 August 1982).
- Car bomb at Air Force Headquarters in Church Street, Pretoria: 19 people were killed and 200 injured (20 May 1983).
- Three MK members of the Special Operations Group infiltrating from Maputo attempted to launch an attack on Sasol 2 with 122 mm rockets. All three were killed in the follow-up operation (27 November 1985).
- A civilian vehicle detonated a landmine in the Ellisras area near the Botswana border. Two civilians were killed and two were injured (4 January 1986).

- A limpet mine exploded in the Benmore shopping centre in Sandton, causing extensive damage (7 May 1986).
- A car bomb exploded in front of the Garfunkel Restaurant in Durban, killing three civilians and injuring 69 others (14 June 1986).
- A limpet mine exploded at the Wimpy Bar at the President Holiday Inn in Johannesburg, injuring 20 civilians (24 June 1986).
- An SADF vehicle detonated a landmine near Mbunzi in Mpumalanga. Six SADF members were injured (6 October 1986).
- A civilian vehicle detonated a double landmine in the Northern Transvaal near the Limpopo River. Four occupants were killed and one was injured (28 March 1987).

From 1983, with the adoption of the People's War strategy, the distinction between 'hard' and 'soft' targets began to blur – in fact the emphasis shifted to 'soft' targets. In 1983, 80 per cent of MK's armed attacks had been aimed at what were generally accepted as 'hard' targets. Three years later the figures had more than reversed and 83 per cent of the total number of incidents were directed at 'soft' targets.

Just as the ANC had to revise its strategy, so too did the SADF. 'In our internal actions we had to find an answer to curb these grotesque violations of human rights amongst the black population,' said General Dirk Marais, former Deputy Chief of the Army and the man mainly responsible for co-ordinating the SADF's submission to the Truth and Reconciliation Commission. In a document titled *The Military in a political arena: The South African Defence Force and the Truth and Reconciliation Commission*, he wrote: 'The previous government had a responsibility to protect the people – a task for which they looked to us. We realised that normal overt operations of the type that we traditionally applied would get us nowhere in the new strategic situation where the bush we had experienced on the border had now become a bush of people. New methods to obtain intelligence and conduct operations had to be researched to avoid leaving the great mass of black people to the mercy of the methods of the revolutionaries.'

Major General B. Mortimer told the TRC during the Defence Force's submission: 'The SADF was pre-eminently a peace-keeping task force, but owing to the perceived threat and the increasing instability in Southern Africa, the SADF strategy was directed at ensuring the security of the people of the RSA by taking pro-active steps.'

The SADF Strategy, a formal document drawn up in terms of the Defence Act of 1957, and various strategic guidelines from the State Security Council, said that the SADF should have the ability to exercise the following actions:

1. In the *SADF Area of Responsibility* (defined as the RSA including Prince Edward and Marion Islands, the National States, the TBVC states and adjacent maritime areas and air space):
   * conduct conventional military operations;
   * conduct counter-insurgency operations;
   * conduct intelligence;
   * conduct strategic communication operations; and
   * support the SAP in maintaining law and order.

2. In the *SADF Area of Influence* (defined as Botswana, Lesotho, Swaziland, Angola, Zambia, Zimbabwe, Mozambique, Malawi and the adjacent maritime area):
   * conduct restricted conventional operations in support of counter-insurgency operations;
   * conduct special and retaliation operations;
   * conduct full-scale conventional operations if necessary;
   * conduct intelligence; and
   * conduct strategic communication operations.

3. In the *SADF Area of Interest* (Zaire, Rwanda, Burundi, Tanzania, Gabon, Uganda, Kenya, the Comores and Mauritius and adjacent maritime area) the SADF had to be in a position to:
   * conduct intelligence;
   * exercise special and retaliatory operations;
   * exercise air and maritime reconnaissance; and
   * deploy (restricted) ground forces, and render support to friendly governments.

It was thus policy and strategy to be able to conduct cross-border and special operations and the SADF undertook a number of well-publicised raids against ANC and later PAC targets in surrounding countries. 'The security forces will hammer them wherever they find them,' Minister of Defence General Magnus Malan told Parliament on 4 February 1986. 'We will not sit here with hands folded waiting for them to cross the borders ... we shall settle the hash of those terrorists, their fellow travellers and those who help them.'

On 30 January 1981, in an operation code-named Beanbag, Special Forces commandos attacked and destroyed three houses said to be the ANC's Mozambican headquarters in Matola near Maputo. Intelligence for the operation was mainly obtained from captured ANC members and suspects. Three security force members died in the raid, and 16 South Africans were killed. These included a number of senior MK operatives and members of the elite Special Operations Group, including Motso Mokgabundi, the commander who had led the first attack on Sasol. Two MK guerrillas and one Mozambican were captured and taken back to South Africa for questioning.

According to evidence presented at the TRC hearings, the operation was planned by Section A of the Security Police, headed by Colonel (later General) Jac Buchner and Callie Steijn of Military Intelligence. 'This is how the counter-operations worked,' said General Viljoen. 'The intelligence people would get the information and someone would suggest we do this or that and it would be discussed. I remember the Matolo raid, for example, which would have to go past a Frelimo military base. I posed a question to the planning group in which I asked: "What would happen if, while our convoy was passing the base, people started chasing us? We don't want to get involved in a running battle before we even get to our destination." One security policeman asked why we didn't use horseshoe mines – the nails with four points so one always stands straight up. We quickly had them manufactured at EMLC and that's exactly how it happened. That evening [the raiding team] reported they were being followed. We told them to toss out their horseshoe mines and that stopped [their pursuers].'

At midnight on 9 December the following year, Special Forces commandos once again struck, this time in Lesotho. A number of houses and a block of flats were targeted. Forty-two people died – 30 of them South Africans and the remainder Basotho. Four SADF members were wounded. Among those killed was Zola Nqini, the ANC's chief representative in Lesotho, and Gene Gugushe, a prominent SACP activist. The planning was reportedly done by the same security force members who planned the 1981 raid on Matola.

'We used to have a policy where operational commanders would be decentralised if they were deployed next to the border. They were allowed to carry out hot-pursuit operations up to a certain distance,' said General Viljoen. 'I can't remember what exactly it was – I think 150 km. Lusaka was too deep for that – and Lusaka had very specific international and political implications. So in a case like that we would certainly use the State Security Council before a decision was made. Because of the sensitivity of these sort of operations I used to personally check the intelligence gathering and make sure we were absolutely 100 per cent correct and I also personally involved myself in the planning, the detail of the planning, so we could make 100 per cent sure the operation was carried out in an efficient and proper way.'

But things didn't always go according to plan. On 23 May 1983, in retaliation for the Church Street car bomb three days earlier, the SADF once again raided Maputo in an operation code-named *Skerwe*. The targets were a missile site, a command post, a training centre, a logistical base and logistical headquarters. According to Military Intelligence files, the raid was a disaster. None of the intended targets was hit. Instead private homes were destroyed, along with the crèche of a jam and fruit juice factory, while five Mozambican citizens and one South African refugee were killed. Although after the attack General Malan announced that six ANC bases and a missile battery had been hit, the damage report in the files concedes that target identification was erroneous and that civilians were killed and private property damaged.

In a harshly worded memo dated 14 June 1983, addressed to General Jannie Geldenhuys (then Chief of the Army), General Viljoen (then Chief of the Defence Force) described the results of the attack as 'not merely a disappointment but a shock ... our image with government and abroad has been seriously damaged. This operation is precisely what I referred to after my visits to 32 Battalion near Cuvelai [in Angola]. We accept poor results far too easily without analysing why they are poor and taking steps to remedy the situation. If we were to analyse our operational effectiveness and to make the results public we would be ashamed.'

It appears the South African government, and particularly P.W. Botha, had been extremely keen to show an angry (white) populace that it could strike back and punish the ANC for the Pretoria bomb. The government was more concerned with making a firm gesture than with acting on proper intelligence or formulating a proper plan. State Security Council minutes show that the raid was discussed at an SSC meeting on the day it took place. It was undertaken after consultations with P.W. Botha, the chairman, who explained it had not been possible to call the whole council together for consultation.

In Botswana the ANC was also attacked on 14 July 1985, resulting in 12 people being killed. Although the attack was carried out by Special Forces commandos from 5 Recce, it was a joint Security Police–SADF operation in which the police did most of the intelligence gathering. In an amnesty application, police General

Johan Coetzee said that the raid had been in response to the attack on the Cape Town home of a Deputy Minister of the House of Representatives. He also said that Foreign Minister Pik Botha had not been at the State Security Council meeting at which the raid was discussed. Coetzee had been instructed to contact Botha to tell him the raid was going to take place and to get his comments and authorisation. P.W. Botha had signed the authorisation subject to the Foreign Minister's approval, which was later given.

Once again the attack was a public relations disaster. Few, if any, of the ANC casualties appear to have been prominent military figures. In fact, among the dead were a well-known artist, a white South African draft-dodger who had just graduated from the University of Botswana with a degree in mathematics, a schoolteacher, a six-year-old child and a 71-year-old refugee. So serious was the international condemnation of the SADF raid that, according to evidence presented to the TRC, security cop super-spy Craig Williamson was tasked with planting stories in *The Citizen* and the *Sunday Times* under headlines like 'The Guns of Gaborone'. Photographs of a large selection of 'captured' weapons were published but the Commission's report says that convicted Security Police murderer Eugene de Kock revealed that some of the weapons displayed had in fact been borrowed from him by Williamson.

On 19 May 1986, in an operation code-named Leo, attacks were launched against targets in Harare, Botswana and Gaborone. The SADF said they were in retaliation for recent MK attacks on Sasol 2, but some observers believe that their real purpose was to derail the efforts of the Commonwealth Secretariat's Eminent Person's Group, which had undertaken a study mission to the area. The Zimbabwe Defence Force must have had prior warning of the SADF attack, as it took the occupants of the targeted house to a place of safety, and when the helicopter-borne South African commandos arrived the house was empty.

Though they are loath to say so publicly, counter-intelligence sources privately admit the SADF had a number of ANC moles within its ranks. 'One of my colleagues, a very senior officer in the new SANDF, tells the story of how he had the top secret plans for a South African Air Force attack against an ANC base in Angola on his desk in Maputo days before the attack was due to take place,' said Major General Bertus Steenkamp, recently retired Chief Director of Defence Intelligence in the SANDF. 'He flew to Angola to tell the ANC people there about our planned attack and everyone in the base was moved out before the SAAF bombers arrived. Once the planes had left, and they were sure it was safe, all the MK people simply returned and carried on as normal.'

General Malan confirms that security was by no means watertight. 'There was a plan to rescue some chaps held in Zimbabwe as SADF agents. The idea was to launch a rescue attempt with helicopters when the guys were taken from the prison to the court. But it was leaked,' he said, 'the Zimbabweans were waiting and the plan was abandoned.'

But just who was responsible for giving the final go-ahead for cross-border operations? The answer is not at all clear. General Malan's explanation is as follows: '[Right at the beginning] we went to Vorster's place and I asked him: "If there's a lieutenant and he crosses the border and is caught or makes a flop that causes an international crisis, whose responsibility will it be? The Cabinet's or the lieutenant's?" He said: "The Lieutenant's." I said: "Sorry, sir, but we can't do it that way." With the communications facilities we had at that stage and the unpredictability of Swapo on the other side, we could not always come through to the Cabinet to get approval. I said: "You'll have to do something about it. You'll have to decentralise responsibility."

'Eventually they gave me 200 km that, as Minister of Defence, I could operate in in Angola (without first getting further permission). I delegated authority to the Chief of the Army and the Air Force – they could operate 150 km inside, except if it was a major operation, when they had to get permission from me. I operate higher up. They needn't even know about it. Whether or not I go to the State President doesn't matter to them. I take the responsibility for it. So there we got it from Vorster. But to cover the military I wrote a document in which I took all the neighbouring countries and wrote a specific instruction for each country. This was reconsidered quarterly or every six months to see whether it remained the same.

'Angola was totally different. If it was a Special Forces operation in Angola and it was deeper than 200 km, or even if they [just] felt I should know about it, they'd come and get permission. For instance, the bridge at Quito. They never came for permission because it was part of the bigger operation. But they couldn't operate in any of the other neighbouring countries without my permission. I have an idea that I said we needed the State President's permission for the other countries. I'm not 100 per cent sure, but I think so. So what would have happened, for example, is, if Jan Geldenhuys came to me and said: "I've got a target in Lusaka," I'd say: "Fine, you can plan, carry on. I'll come back to you. I'll go and see the State President." He [the State President] had his own way of doing things. Certain operations he would have called in one or two ministers. In certain other operations he never called in anybody because of the secrecy of it. Civilians don't always understand that. So that's the way it operated. They needed permission to do it and it was given either by myself or by him depending on the situation in the country, etc.'

General Geldenhuys's explanation differs somewhat from that of Malan: 'There was a very definite categorising of responsibilities. The Chief of the Army is responsible for all landward operations. This included internal security and anti-revolutionary warfare and operations. It was immaterial if you had the participation of the Air Force or Navy or medics – the Chief of the Army was responsible. In seaward operations the Chief of the SA Navy was responsible, period – even though the Air Force may play a major role in certain maritime operations. So cross-border operations intended against MK, Apla or Plan were the Chief of the Army's responsibility and I was Chief of the Army for five years. So at a Command Council meeting the Chief of the Defence Force would be in the chair and the others would be the key members. Operations could be initiated from the top or from the bottom.

'Let's consider the following scenario, where I am Chief of the Army: one of my subordinate army commanders or a staff officer, like for example the operations or intelligence officer, could come to me and say: "This and this and this is the situation and I think we should do something about it which will entail an operation." Or I might say: "If what you say is true, shouldn't we do something about it?" I could initiate it myself or someone could put it to me. Whatever the case, at that stage I would take the responsibility. If the homework was done and we were sure of ourselves I would then ask for a meeting with the Chief of the SADF.

'At one stage an amendment of the procedure came into being. The Chief of Staff for Operations on the Chief of the Defence Force's staff is responsible for the co-ordination of all operations. As a commander I could bypass him and go straight to the Chief of the Defence Force. The latter would, however, want to know if I had discussed it with the Chief of Staff Operations because I wouldn't know about operations planned by the Navy or Air Force. As the person responsible for co-ordination he should know about my proposed operation so it didn't clash with anything else. If it was a cross-border operation the Chief of the Defence Force wouldn't give me an answer because he didn't have the authority to do so. He would then in all probability ask me to prepare a presentation for him and would probably say: "Okay, I'm going to get the political authority, I'll let you know." Or he might say: "I want you to make the presentation on my behalf to the politicians appointed to make the decision." And then you'd get the decision. For sure the bottom line is: the politicians give the ultimate go-ahead. The minimum was the Minister of Defence and the President. The exception was in the case of hot-pursuit – but that only applied to Angola.

'Make no mistake, the politicians sometimes put pressure on the military to do certain operations. For example – though I can't say which operation or what year it was – there was a spate of murders in the Transvaal. Delegations were sent to the President wanting to know what the government was doing about the situation. In at least one case I can think of we were pressurised and harsh words were spoken. The President said to us: "I've spoken to you before. Haven't you got the intelligence to do it, or are you afraid? What the hell's the matter? Why don't you do something? Do something now! I want to see results."'

So that's how the system worked … or is it? According to General Malan, the Department of Foreign Affairs didn't see it that way. 'I only discovered afterwards that Foreign Affairs said we [the military] don't have [legal] coverage in cross-border hot-pursuit operations,' Malan said. 'We said that from a legal point-of-view we did, and that internationally it would be acceptable. They disagreed. Then there was an attack at Messina on a farm. When Pik heard I was going there he asked if he could come along. We went to the farm and there was an RPG-7 [rocket launcher] which I showed to him. He stood there aiming across the border, saying: "I'm coming and we're going to fuck you up," or words to that effect. There were pictures and a report in the newspaper, which I still have – [I kept it] just to cover my back in case Foreign Affairs came out and said that's their standpoint [regarding cross-border operations] then I could say: "That's what the minister said."'

'We went to get the President's [F.W. de Klerk's] approval for a raid in Umtata once,' said General Meiring. [The raid was against a supposed PAC transit facility and took place on 17 October 1993. As a result of faulty intelligence five sleeping youths including two 12-year-old children were shot dead at the Mpendulo residence in Northcrest suburb.] 'He said he couldn't give the approval on his own but there was a Cabinet meeting coming up and he'd ask the Cabinet members to stay on a while and he'd also get the Security Council together. I had to brief them. It was me and Kat Liebenberg, who was Chief of the Defence Force at the time; I was on the verge of taking over from him. I was there as Chief of the Army. Pik was there, as was Kobie Coetsee and a number of other people [including] the Commissioner of Police and other people from the Security Council,' said Meiring. 'After I'd given them the briefing the President said: "Colleagues, you have heard. What do you say?" He went around the room getting their answers. 'Yes'...'yes'... Pik: 'yes' ... Good, we're in this thing together. General, you're excused. You heard, we've all said yes – go ahead." I stood up to leave and when I passed Pik Botha he said to me: "Fuck them up, General, fuck them up!" The next day when this thing seemed to be a bugger-up we faced a media conference at which Pik was also present. "I knew nothing about this!" he said. "Nothing! I wouldn't have allowed anything like this to happen."

'I don't like Pik Botha at all,' Meiring said. 'I think he's a political entrepreneur. Just look at him now in the ANC camp. He works for nobody other than Pik Botha.'

In its second submission to the TRC the SADF said: 'There seems to be a difference of opinion as to how specific the military authority for operations had been. A former Chief of the SADF is of the opinion that specific authority for operations had to be obtained according to prescribed procedures, while the command structure within the Special Forces believed that general approval of targets was sufficient.'

So that's the definitive answer on the question of authority for cross-border operations? Yes, definitely, maybe!

8

'DIRTY TRICKS'

In the late 1960s the SADF hierarchy realised the need to establish Special Forces that would undertake tasks ordinary soldiers could not. The SADF Joint Warfare manual describes Special Forces operations as: 'High-risk covert or clandestine operations that are conducted by specially trained and equipped troops, normally supported by elements of the Army, Air Force or Navy. Medical support is provided by the SA Medical Service. These operations are normally conducted beyond the borders of the RSA to promote national objectives, without the risk of military escalation.'

In 1971 the SADF established the present Special Forces as a cost-effective force-multiplier for use against sensitive targets and to serve as a deterrent to potential aggressors. Four reconnaissance units, popularly called Recces, were formed and were numbered 1, 2, 4 and 5. For a time there was a 3 Recce Regiment, but this name seems to have been changed to D-40 and then eventually to Civil Co-operation Bureau or CCB. Although all of the Recce regiments received training in all aspects of special forces activities, each tended to have specific areas of expertise.

- 1 Recce, based at the Bluff in Durban, specialised in airborne operations. Its members were experts in high-level parachute techniques like Halo (high altitude, low opening) and Hiho (high altitude, high opening) techniques.
- 2 Recce, based in Pretoria, was manned mostly by former Rhodesian Special Forces operatives who joined on short-term contracts after leaving Zimbabwe

when Zanu-PF became the government. As many of its members used the units merely as a means of getting into South Africa and then left to find other jobs as soon as they were able, it was eventually mothballed and considered a Citizen Force Unit.

- 4 Recce, at Saldanha on the west coast, specialised in waterborne operations. Members were often deployed by submarine and were expert divers.
- 5 Recce, stationed at Phalaborwa, drew many of its tactics and techniques from Rhodesia's Selous Scouts. Manned mainly by black members, the regiment specialised in 'pseudo-ops' where members, often dressed in the uniforms of the enemy, infiltrated local villages and guerrilla groups. Extensive use was made of turned terrorists to gather intelligence and sow confusion among the enemy. These were the real bush fighters of the SADF, men who were experts at survival and evasion techniques.

By 1986 it was clear that a covert element within Special Forces was needed, to operate under the command and umbrella of the General Officer Commanding Special Forces. The proposed unit was not planned to be an organisation separate from the SADF's institutional framework, so it can in no way be considered a 'Third Force' in the sense of being an autonomous entity – despite later claims and accusations to the contrary. It was to be an additional arrow in Special Forces' quiver. While the Recces would continue operating as they always had – mainly in cross-border operations that were acknowledged by the government – they were now to be supplemented by a secret, apparently civilian, strike force which neither the government nor the SADF would admit even existed.

A small group originally known as D-40 and later as Barnacle was organised to function as the civilian component of the Special Forces. As its activities expanded it became known as the Civil Co-operation Bureau or CCB. At the time of writing, one of the CCB's most prominent members and the former head of the SADF's chemical and biological warfare programme, Dr Wouter Basson, was being tried in the Supreme Court for a number of charges including murder, conspiracy to murder and drug-related charges. The charge sheet presented the following information:

- During 1979/1980 the unit was established under the code name Barnacle.
- Major Niel Kriel was the first commander of the unit. He was succeeded by Commandant Charl Naudé.
- The unit was stationed on a smallholding in the Broederstroom area. Its members, black and white, were mostly soldiers from the former Rhodesia.

- The cover name of the unit was NKTF Properties, which was later changed to President Security Consultants.
- In an SADF document the goals and functions of the unit are described as follows:
  - Goal: To conduct special operations of an extremely sensitive nature.
  - Functions:
    1. Eliminations.
    2. Ambushes against people of strategic importance.
    3. The carrying out of other super-sensitive operations as instructed.
    4. The gathering of combat intelligence with regard to above-mentioned operations.
    5. The gathering of intelligence as required in instances where other sources cannot be used for such.
    6. The carrying out of certain special security tasks for Special Forces, e.g., the monitoring of sources/agents and the carrying out of security penetration tests (*sekerheidsteekproewe*) as instructed …
       - The elimination of members of the unit who posed a risk by revealing the actions of the Special Forces and so ensuring the actions of the unit were kept secret.
       - The administering of substances, primarily toxic or narcotic in nature, played an important role in the elimination of the above-mentioned members.

Further on, when referring to the objectives of the CCB, the state's charge sheet reads as follows: 'To cause maximum disruption to the enemies of South Africa. Maximum disruption included the use of swear words, the breaking of a window or other intimidation, to the killing of people considered enemies of the state. The people and institutions regarded as enemies of the state were inter alia:
- the African National Congress, its members, collaborators, supporters and sympathisers;
- the South African Communist Party;
- the United Democratic Front;
- the South African Council of Churches and associated organisations;
- Swapo members, supporters, collaborators and sympathisers;
- own forces that threatened or suggested that they would reveal the activities of the Special Forces, and
- other organisations/persons that criticised the government of the day.'

It should be noted that these were claims made by the prosecution and at the time of writing had not been proven – in fact some had been dropped.

According to SADF documents, 'The CCB was a covert military front organisation, managed by a managing director under supervision of a senior officer of Special Forces. Its functions were infiltration, penetration and disruption of the enemy.' The CCB was organised into 10 regions, seven of them operational regions. Each region was responsible for collecting its own intelligence – including Region 6, which collected military intelligence internally. The idea was to create a global network of 'underground' companies that would consist of both legitimate businesses and front companies that would be used for gathering operational intelligence. Each enterprise was to be headed by a businessman who was well established and entrenched in his community but who was also a skilled covert intelligence operative. According to Christoffel Nel, who was the CCB's head of intelligence, the CCB was a long-term plan that would require at least 10 years to reach fruition. It would take a long time for a career soldier to transform himself into a career businessman.

In his submission to the TRC, General Malan said: 'The CCB organisation as a component of Special Forces was approved in principle by me. However, F.W. de Klerk, in his book *The Last Great Trek – A New Beginning*, said that Malan had told him he did not know of the existence of the organisation. But Malan seems to have known about it. 'Special Forces was an integral and supportive part of the South African Defence Force,' he said. 'The role envisaged for the CCB was the infiltration and penetration of the enemy. The CCB was approved as an organisation consisting of ten divisions, or, as expressed in military jargon, regions. Eight of these divisions or regions were intended to refer to geographical areas. The area of one of these regions, Region 6, referred to the Republic of South Africa. The fact that Region Six was activated, came to my knowledge for the first time in November 1989.

'The CCB provided the South African Defence Force with good covert capabilities. During my term of office as Head of the South African Defence Force and as Minister of Defence, instructions to members of the South African Defence Force were clear: destroy the terrorists, their bases and their capabilities. This was also government policy.'

The name Civil Co-operation Bureau was arbitrarily chosen because the inner circle of Special Forces commanders didn't want to speak about covert operations while seated around a conference table. Colonel Johan 'Joe' Verster was appointed managing director. To create an adequate cover framework, all members of the

CCB were required to resign from the SADF but were then secretly rehired with full pension and medical benefits. By 1988 the organisation was fully functional and although originally intended to operate externally it also had an internal component, Region 6. Members were recruited from the Special Forces, the SADF, the South African Medical Services and the Police as well as outsiders, most of whom had no idea they were involved in a covert military front operation. In fact, outside a small 'inner core', many of the other security force members in the CCB were kept in the dark. Everything was on a need-to-know basis. 'Covert operations were not even referred to by code names amongst colleagues, for those who knew would not tell and those who did not know were not supposed to ask,' the SADF said in its submission to the TRC.

The CCB's primary task was to cause 'maximum disruption to the enemy'. According to a CCB planning document, this disruption had five dimensions: death, infiltration, bribery, compromise or blackmail – not necessarily in that order.

In an amnesty application General A.J.M. 'Joop' Joubert, who was the General Officer Commanding (GOC) Special Forces from 1985 to 1989, said: 'In the mid- to late eighties, one of the major goals of national security policy and strategy was to bring the revolutionary organisation and mobilisation of the liberation movements, particularly the ANC, to a halt … by this time it was also clear that the ANC was not going to be stopped by normal conventional methods and that revolutionary methods would have to be used.

'As the institution for external operations, Special Forces would also have to intensify its external operations … since the necessity for unconventional war and revolutionary action was already clear, it was also clear that clandestine and covert operations would have to take place internally, for which Special Forces members would have to be used. It was more or less then that the name CCB was adopted as a replacement for D-40 or Barnacle. The revolutionary and covert nature of the plan, amongst other things, involved:

a. that ANC leaders and people who substantially contributed to the struggle would be eliminated;
b. that ANC facilities and support services would be destroyed;
c. that activists, sympathisers, fighters and people who supported them would also be eliminated.'

Operations carried out by the CCB included campaigns to destroy enemy infrastructure through sabotage attacks, as well as the collection of intelligence for specific operational purposes. In Maseru the CCB set up a communications company run by black operatives that sold and installed communications equipment like telephones, faxes and telexes. One of its clients was an office used by the ANC, which meant all communications to and from the office were monitored by the CCB. The information gathered was used against the ANC, particularly in the Western Cape. Many of the plans and devices made would not have been out of place in a James Bond movie. Explosive devices and special weapons were made at the Electronic Magnetic Logistical Component, EMLC, a Special Forces technological resource facility in Pretoria.

Employees at EMLC were all highly qualified specialists, back-room boys who really knew their stuff. One was a former Rhodesian – identified only as Mr Q when he gave evidence in the Wouter Basson trial – who joined EMLC at the beginning of the 1980s. I met Mr Q at a restaurant in a northern Johannesburg suburb, and was struck by the deceptively benevolent air of the man everyone said was an explosives and 'dirty tricks' genius, a real-life Q. In Rhodesia Mr Q worked for the Selous Scouts building specialised weapons and explosive devices, then he was approached by the South Africans. 'I was just told there would be a job for me down here if I decided to come down,' he said. 'It didn't look like there were any good prospects there. Certainly not military-wise. [Name known but removed] told me that. He wanted me to do the same sort of stuff down here that I was doing up there. He was leaving by the time I got here because [General] Fritz Loods [the GOC Special Forces at the time] insisted on EMLC moving to the Kop to the facility that had been made for them. [Name known but removed] said no way was he ever going to share premises with Spec Forces because it would blow the cover of EMLC totally.

'Sybie van der Spuy was the boss at the time. He was a commandant. Kat Liebenberg was the head of Special Forces. He was a general. There was an empty room and they said: "Make a list of the stuff you want: the sky's the limit. It'll be your own workshop, you're in here by yourself with a key-code on the door which you don't need to give to anyone except your immediate boss," and that was it. I made a list and the stuff arrived like magic,' Q said. 'One of the first things they said they wanted me to do was to build a timing device. They had a variety of electronic timers but the operators were always nervous about electronics because the wires break and the batteries go flat and it becomes an unknown quantity. You always have this sneaking suspicion that when you connect the two wires you're going to be the first one to know about it – in a big way! So they preferred mechanical things. The operators like to know: when you push this pin it gets armed and then they've got 15 seconds buggering-off time or whatever. So the first thing they asked me to do was think about a mechanical timer. I stopped at a hardware shop on the way home that night and bought an Aussie mechanical timer for a garden tap. I took it to work the next day, modified it and said to them: "Here, here's your mechanical timer,"' said Q. 'In 90 per cent of the timers they wanted a delay from zero up to an hour. Sure, there's a use for longer timers as well, but most are shorter. For instance you would screw something into a grenade and leave it under a table in the target area and walk out or something like that. An hour is more than enough to get well away from there!

'Then they wanted me to look at letter bomb mechanisms. They'd had some drastic failures with their current model and weren't happy to use it again. They asked me to look at the possibility of making something that would be more reliable and foolproof. So the electronic guys were tasked with coming up with something and so was I. In the end they went for my version. It used a small 2 mm blank pin-fire cartridge to fire an S-4 detonator which had been specially flattened to no more than 3 mm thick so it would fit in an envelope. That in turn initiated the sheet of plastic [explosive] in the envelope. It was very nice. It had good safety devices and you could arm it after it had been totally sealed and addressed and everything else. When you removed the paperwork from inside the envelope that would initiate the explosion.'

The letters – and Christmas cards, in the case of one particular batch – were deadly. 'An ounce of PE [plastic explosive] on someone's body would be enough to kill him,' said Mr Q. 'This would probably blow both his arms off. They were definitely used. As I understand it they were posted in Lesotho and received in Zambia. I believe they were deployed quite successfully. I would make the devices and they would be handed over to the Special Forces guys. They were instructed on how to pack them but in some cases they were packed by EMLC staff because the average operator is very well aware that this is an extremely sensitive, potentially dangerous device – so they didn't like fiddling with it them-selves. No one's better than the designer to do it, because you know exactly what's potting. I don't know how the targets were selected or who gave the approval. The request would just come from the Special Forces liaison officer, Colonel Hekkies van Heerden. They may also have gone to the police or National Intelligence, but that's something I wouldn't know. We're talking about the early to mid-1980s – '83, '85, around there.

'I was also used for other things – funny weapons that were untraceable ballistically. The electronics people were also busy with things like that, but everything operated on a need-to-know basis so it wasn't as if we swapped ideas over tea. [There were also] non-standard military tactics – car bombs, etc. I was involved in car bombs. One was sent to Maputo. It was a big balls-up because it wasn't packed right; in fact it blew half the PE out of the car onto the pavement without even detonating it. There was a lot of shit about that. Also Botswana. ANC people were targeted and they were quite successful.

'Before I got there they'd tried all sorts of methods of attaching the device to the car. They had two-part epoxies, etc. but they weren't real successful. Some of the epoxies generated a lot of heat and it meant the operator had a good chance of getting quite badly burnt on his hands while he was mixing it and attaching the bomb under the car. Magnets weren't very successful because of all the anti-rust coatings applied to cars. In the end I'd be supplied with a car that was the same as the target vehicle and it would be custom-made to suit that car. It would be, for example, a custom-made sheet-metal box made up to fit under the car – but to fit perfectly, with a quick on–off catch so the operator had to spend the minimum amount of time lying under the vehicle to fix it on. The clamps were designed to be clamped onto the various pipes and structures under the car. That was the purpose of their supplying me with one that was identical. We normally initiated [the explosion] through one of the universal joints on the prop-shaft. We dropped a lead through there and the detonator would be in a can that could swivel to take whatever angle was required from that lead to the prop-shaft. As soon as the prop-shaft moved half a turn that was it. It was instantaneous!

'Initially I did the research and development at EMLC but after a while it got to the stage that when people saw me driving around in a car that was not my own they knew some bugger was going to have a *moer* of an accident. It got a bit embarrassing so sometimes I'd have to do the work at home. I'd at least take the operator there so I could demonstrate and train him there with no onlookers. I also used to prepare a lot of vehicles for transporting all sorts of illegal contraband, whether it was cameras or hand grenades or weapons or radios or explosives.

'Then there were the requests concerning poisons. I was asked if I could open various sealed cans of beer or cooldrink so they could inject whatever into it. The beer was a non-starter because it's got too much effervescence. As soon you make a hole in the can it blows foam all over the place. So eventually we used cans of Game cold-drink. I used to drill a tiny hole through on the solder joint of the can and then a guy would inject into it and I'd solder it up again. I don't know how or where they were used. It was done very clandestinely. Sybie van der Spuy didn't even know it was happening. It was just something that the doctors wanted done and they wanted to do it with the least amount of people knowing about it. It's quite possible they didn't get approval from higher up. It's also possible the reason was if Sybie knew about anything he would want to take over and run the show. Even if he didn't have the expertise he'd still want to be there, dictating how things should be done.

'A whole lot later,' Q said, 'I made up a poisoned walking stick and a poisoned umbrella. That came from Doc Basson's side of operations. It was a walking stick that fired a little polyester ball filled with poison. I think the poison was called Renkin. There was also an umbrella I made with five needles. As far as I know it was used against an ANC guy, but that was just the talk – I couldn't say with any certainty. It was a walking stick that was hollowed out to take a small-bore barrel and fired with a finger release under the hook of the walking stick. It propelled a small polyethylene ball and was pretty quiet. The ball was maybe 3 or 4 mm in diameter. As far as I know it was never used.'

During the trial of Wouter Basson a number of screwdrivers specially modified by Mr Q to deliver a lethal payload of poison were displayed. 'I made quite a few of those. A screwdriver is like a traditional African weapon, so I guess whoever was investigating in the cases of deaths would be quite used to seeing wounds caused by screwdrivers: it's just that with an extra dose of *muti* going in he has a whole lot less chance of survival. I also doctored a lot of grenades. I don't know what happened with them. I just did the zero timer on them and then they were taken away.' As it turns out, the grenades were put back into discovered ANC arms caches. In the mid-1980s a number of ANC cadres died when they pulled the pins on grenades and had them blow up in their faces.

According to Q, General Kat Liebenberg, Officer Commanding Special Forces, knew exactly what he (Q) was up to in his workshop at Speskop. 'Doc Basson had obviously spoken to him and told him he needed me to do some work for him but that he didn't want me to do it at EMLC. Maybe it was because various people would stick their noses in and want to know what was going on. He wanted me to do it at home. I do not know if Kat knew what the job was going to be but he just organised that I got the leave to go and do the job. In fact the people at EMLC were quite pissed off because I was doing things directed by Kat and they couldn't argue against him, but they obviously felt they were being cut out of the line of command.'

Did Q think Basson would have had the authority to do anything he liked, or did he think there was a command structure? His answer: 'As far as I'm concerned it stopped at Basson. But whether or not he was dictated to by some-one else – I believe he was P.W.'s personal physician, so there must have been lots of talk at night between those two – but I don't know.' And remorse or regret for making the things he did? 'Look, it was a job,' Q said. 'I got told what to do. Because I knew so much about those things I wouldn't have done myself any good if I refused or started querying the end use. But again, at that time everyone was told they were fighting communism and [the targets] were enemies of the state and people who were placing bombs and going around blowing up civvies here in South Africa. So if that's the way we had to fight them that's what we did. At that stage I had intimate details of lots of ops and who said to do this and who did what; and people did used to come short in mysterious circumstances. I didn't really see it would do my health much good if I started raising objections along those lines.'

Who knew about the existence of the CCB? Not many people, it would appear. Whether P.W. Botha knew about it or not, no one seems to be saying. General Malan says he did not. F.W. de Klerk claims he did not when he became President. In his book *The Last Trek – a New Beginning* De Klerk writes: 'At the beginning of 1990, after I became President, I learned that in the mid eighties an elaborate front organisation, the Civil Co-operation Bureau, was established outside the normal framework of the SADF which was given responsibility and the means for the prosecution of a secret war against the ANC and its allies. ... Allegations were also made about bizarre and horrifying chemical and biological warfare activities and experiments carried out by the SADF.

'I do not know the full truth about all these charges, or who within the security forces authorised these gross violations of human rights. Certainly they were never discussed at any meeting of any body that I ever attended ... After the existence of the Civil Co-operation Bureau had been exposed by the media at the end of 1989, General Malan assured me that even he had no prior knowledge of its existence.'

Later on, De Klerk writes: 'My concern over third-force allegations deepened during the summer holidays early in January 1990 while I was vacationing at Botha House, a presidential residence on the south coast of Natal. I realised there was a serious problem when General Magnus Malan, the Minister of Defence, informed me that he wanted to fly down to Durban to discuss a very serious matter with me. After he arrived at Botha House, Malan told me he had just discovered the nature of the operations of a secret SADF front organisation, called the Civil Co-operation Bureau (CCB). He said that he had learned that the CCB, which had been established within the framework of the underground structures of the South African Defence Force in the mid-eighties, had been using totally unacceptable methods and strategies against the ANC and other revolutionary organisations. General Malan appeared to be as shocked as I was and assured me that he had taken immediate steps to investigate and disband the organisation. Although I had been given a supposedly full briefing on the activities of the SADF soon after I had become president, I had not been informed of the existence of the CCB.'

At an interview at his Waterkloof home, I asked General Malan to comment on Mr Q's statements. I asked him if he would have known about the car bombs, letter bombs and poison umbrellas. 'No,' he said. 'But it depends on a lot of things. Special Ops had, to a certain extent, freedom of movement outside the country but not inside the country. The surprise they caught me with was the CCB. They caught me when they said the internal section was activated. I'm coming back to the police responsibilities and the Defence Force and there they overstepped the line.

'I called in … I can't remember who: I think it might have been Chief of Intelligence and they explained to me – can you recall that incident where a woman and her whole section of ANC were caught down in the Eastern Cape – they [the Intelligence people] used that as an example. They tracked them from the other side [of the border] and they said that if they then had to hand them over to the police when they arrived in South Africa they could easily get lost again because they were the chaps intimately involved. They most probably had someone inside tracking them down to Cape Town where they were arrested.

'So I said okay. This [incident] happened ages after the CCB was approved,' said Malan. 'Now if they'd killed those people I would have said: "You can't just kill people without getting approval from the top echelon. If you are doing things that are against the law you require permission to do so. I wouldn't even take it on myself to give you approval." I would then have gone to the State President and said: "We've got a request, this is the situation, you've got to decide." That's where the buck stops.

'Now, regarding the CCB, which was basically there to get intelligence and basically worked in Africa: they overstepped. They went into Europe. I don't know how. It might have been a misunderstanding or it might have been the same type of situation where they said: "If I want the intelligence here I've got to go and pick it up in Europe and follow it through to the place where it is my responsibility." And they had to disrupt the ANC. They could have interpreted "disrupt" as killing the people or as putting sugar in their vehicles' petrol tanks. They had to decide what they could do and what they couldn't do. Nobody ever came and asked me whether they could assassinate anyone. You can argue again, that if it was Oliver Tambo, for example, and he was sitting in Algiers, you haven't got time to ask the chaps in Pretoria. It's a once-off opportunity. Then you take the responsibility on your own.

'It's very difficult to define where the responsibility lies,' Malan explained. 'Let's talk about the chaps who are sitting in jail in Harare. They blew their own cover and they were caught, but when they became agents of CSI [Chief of Staff Intelligence], or whoever it might have been, I wasn't notified that we had agents there. That's part of the system. I don't expect to be. But then your coverage must be of such a nature and your responsibility and your risk (as well) that you understand: "If I'm caught I might be killed – it's my responsibility." I gave instructions that no Zimbabwean could be employed in security or sensitive operations because they always seemed to be getting drunk and talking.'

And the bombing of the ANC offices in London? 'I wouldn't know. I doubt whether we were involved,' Malan said. 'If we were, I never knew about it. This is a good example of the problem of what were the responsibilities of NI [National Intelligence], the police and the military. I think it was the police who did it, but they could just have easily said it was the military – or NI, who had the responsibility for overseas. You see, there are certain other things that develop if you're in an operational situation like that. I've got a soft heart for the military because their way of thinking was: don't get the minister or the politicians involved, because if we do it's a hell of a risk politically in this country. The government could fall. So let's take the responsibility on ourselves. That's what I think one or two chaps did. But there's another type of attitude that develops. For instance, [there was] a brigadier who was kicked out of the force because he decided he'd steal cars here, take them through Botswana to Zimbabwe to go and blow up facilities there. He never had permission. We caught him and he was kicked out of the Defence Force.

'It was the prerogative of the State President to decide whether something like [the bombing of ANC offices] could be done or not,' said Malan. 'If he didn't tell me, how could I know about it? Take the ANC bomb. There was probably a rumour spread that there was a bomb inside [the offices] and that was what blew it up. That satisfied any minister. I can't really recall it because it wasn't my responsibility.'

What about letter bombs being sent? If Kat Liebenberg knew about it, would he have been the guy who made the decision, or would the buck have stopped with Malan? 'First of all, I can't say Kat did it – sending letter bombs, that is,' said Malan, 'because that's something that Kat would have to answer, which is obviously impossible. Even though there may be affidavits, if you don't have a cross-examination you can't know for sure. But for argument's sake, let's say he did it: I never knew about it. But that's not my problem. My problem was something much greater than that – who decides on whom to eliminate. I think that's the prerogative of the politicians. If it was a question of military people – well, then, I have to change my story a little bit. I'll tell you why I'm saying this. I don't know if you saw that article about a chap who's taking the ANC to court for a landmine they exploded that killed a lot of people. I think his name is Van Eck. I went to the scene ... on 15 December 1986. At that stage, I picked it up, I think it was from the Commissioner of Police, [that] it was eight chaps [who planted the landmines]: they gave me the names. I gave the telex back to the police, but I said to myself, shouldn't we target those eight? I couldn't care less where [they hid] – I would make the decision. I would most probably go to P.W. It depends.'

'Politically it's very difficult for a security man to decide who is a political man to target,' Malan explained. 'I'll give you a classic example. Sam Nujoma was flying into Windhoek in 1967. I was OC [SWA] Command. The Police Commissioner there was a chap called Theo Krauss. The Hereros were having a march as a show of force. Their information was that Nujoma was flying in at 15h00 in the afternoon. The chap who flew him in was called Nash. He came over the radio and said: "My pax [passenger] is ..." and he spelled it out. Nujoma didn't pick it up. The chap who was in the control tower was called De Villiers: he phoned through to Krauss and said, "Nujoma's coming in, he's landing at 11h00." The two of us went there and arrested Sam Nujoma and took him to jail; the Hereros arrived there late in the afternoon, Sam Nujoma never turned up. We kept him in jail for about seven days. The military made an analysis and said: "Please send him back: he has fantastic lieutenants, whilst he's useless." The police agreed. We sent him back. So it depends upon the individual. We consulted with the Prime Minister and he said: "Send him back."

'At that stage it would have been up to the Prime Minster to say: "Eliminate him" or not – although I wouldn't have advised him to do so. Apart from the military situation this is the type of risk that shouldn't be taken by the head of a state, because if you crack that then you crack the country,' said Malan. 'That's why in my testimony in front of the Truth Commission I requested that they should give the 37 ANC members amnesty without a hearing, because the President [Mandela] was involved. It's my President. It's my country. We can never allow the international community to see what he's done!'

'Letter bombs were not the Defence Force's way,' said General Viljoen. 'I was operationally involved until 1985 and our Special Forces operations were mainly confined to attacks in military-style cross-border operations. It's not impossible this could have happened, but I can't think of any specific operation. No car bomb attack ever took place under my authority. You're creating the impression that only the military used poison and bombs. Have you been briefed on the Matola raid, in the Lebombo mountains [Operation Skerwe], and we went on the tar road to Maputo where we attacked three houses which we blew up? Those are the kind of operations that we did – or the attacks on the houses in Lesotho and Gaborone. But I can't recall one single incident where I authorised letter bombs. Just bear in mind that the fact those things existed does not mean they were applied. Remember that there were people such as EMLC and even Wouter Basson. Their scientific knowledge was available not only to the Defence Force but also to other security agencies, for example Boss. In the world of spying the use of this kind of thing is perfectly possible. Those were not instruments used in the Defence Force. Not until 1985. Maybe the CCB.'

When asked about Mr Q's poisoned umbrella, Viljoen said: 'Then it must have been an intelligence operation. Because there is no way the military by itself would have enough intelligence-gathering [capability] abroad and that would certainly have been together with Boss and with the Security Police. [I presume] they would gather the information and eventually make a joint plan, and maybe it was executed by some or other chap, but it was certainly not approved by me. If you take a man such as Eugene de Kock and what has come out there I don't think this ever went as far as P.W. Not even as far as the State Security Council. I would say if we authorised a raid on Gaborone and these people [the Special Forces, security police, CCB] have these special weapons available without our knowledge, it's not impossible they could have taken them with. Remember the story about the human bush. I often said that the dirty methods applied by the security forces were actually an effort to solve the problems caused by the idea of using the blacks as the human bush.'

When asked about his knowledge of letter and car bombs, General Jannie Geldenhuys said: 'There were many operations of which I knew the detail for the simple reason I had to be briefed on what the plans were and how they were going to be executed. One doesn't automatically have to go to the minister or the

Chief of the SADF. You could shoot it down at your level. But you couldn't do that unless you'd heard all the details. I saw many presentations. I can't recall any in which letter bombs or poisoning were involved, but yes, I can remember explosive devices. I think that was in Mozambique. Kat Liebenberg has an advantage over me in that he was the General Officer Commanding Special Forces – I wasn't. I would definitely not know the details he knew. I think you could ask any Chief of any Defence Force anywhere in the world and you'd get pretty much the same response.'

But what about the politicians: would they have known about the clandestine and covert operations – for example, the Wouter Basson story? 'There is no way I could have known about it without my minister knowing about it,' said Geldenhuys, 'because I can't authorise it. If I know about it I must either disapprove or take it up to him. I would say no, Special Forces couldn't send a letter bomb on their own. No, they can't. But I can foresee that such things might have happened, especially with operations involving the police. I testified in court that internally there was a very specific policy decision and statement that for all internal operations the SAP was responsible. From the time I joined the Army, the system – which was copied from the Brits – was that the military was available to the police at their request.

'If we wanted to initiate an internal operation,' said Geldenhuys, 'we'd have to go to the police and ask them to do it. I don't think it ever happened, but it's possible, I suppose. The police, if they wanted to do an internal operation and needed military assistance, could ask for it and it could be given to them. But then the police would be responsible for getting approval for the operation. If we wanted, for example, to do an operation in Mozambique and we wanted police assistance, we had to ask for it. But then we had to get the approval for that. Operations you have talked about could have happened in that context with the police. I called in General "Joop" Joubert (GOC Special Forces at the time) and told him: "Even if the police have obtained approval for an operation, I still want to know about it." This illustrates how it worked in practice.'

General Meiring said: 'I worked with the police since 1966 and I never liked working with them because they are inherent liars, they never give you all the facts, they never trusted you and they always have another agenda. When I heard about the workings of the CCB and I learnt the police were involved, I immediately said: "That was where you went wrong. You should never have hired the Ferdie Barnards and those people." In the process of firing – the "Night of the Generals" [discussed later] – I said to General Liebenberg: "If [De Klerk] is so upset with us and he wants us to fire people, fire the CCB people who we said we're going to fire, and who are still in service; fire them, they have an axe hanging over their heads, so continue with that and get rid of this cancer that is within us." But it wasn't the entire CCB. It was one cell of the CCB. The CCB, per se, did a very good job. It was only the one cell – Cell 6 – made up of mostly riff-raff policeman who then got together and did things far beyond what they were entitled to. That left a sour taste in my mouth more than anything else.'

On 29 March 1988 Dulcie September, chief representative of the ANC in France and Switzerland, was shot five times in the face with a silenced .22 calibre firearm while unlocking the ANC offices in London. She died instantly. A South African, most probably CCB, hit-team was blamed, and this is the explanation generally accepted. The TRC sent an investigation team to France, where they examined the files of the investigating Judge, Ms Claudine Forkel. In her findings Forkel said she was unable to identify the assassins but that it was clear in her view that September was killed in the context of a plan by the South African State to eliminate senior ANC figures in Europe. French names connected to the Comores Presidential Guard, an outfit claimed to be financed by South African intelligence, were also mentioned by Forkel.

In 1998 security cop killer Eugene de Kock was interviewed by the TRC and said the September assassination was a CCB operation co-ordinated by Commandant Dawid Fourie. He said the two who pulled the trigger were members of the Comorien Presidential Guard. Also testifying before the Commission, Christoffel Nel, the CCB's head of intelligence, described the murder of Dulcie September as one of the CCB's 'successes'. The TRC report states: 'Pressed on this, he [Nel] stated that "… from the general atmosphere at the CCB head office whenever reference was made to Dulcie September's death, I had never any doubt in my mind that it was a CCB operation."' Based on that corroborating evidence, the commission made the following finding: 'While it is not able to make a definitive finding on the assassination of Ms Dulcie September, the commission believes, on the basis of the evidence available to it, that she was a victim of a CCB operation involving the contracting of a private intelligence organisation which in turn contracted out the killing.'

'Those [kinds of operations] may well have been operations that took place without approval,' said General Geldenhuys. 'You need to remember how some of these things work from the lowest to the highest. If the thing is presented to the lowest commander, it's in great detail. Then as it goes a level higher it's in less detail. By the time you get to the top it's a much abbreviated briefing compared to that which was first presented at the lower level. If P.W. Botha claimed he didn't know certain details I would believe him. He would in all probability not deny knowledge of an operation but if he denied the detail I could understand that perfectly – and even if he can't remember certain operations. He would probably say he agrees many such operations took place but don't ask me do I remember this one in Botswana, or that one in Lusaka, etc. I'm absolutely sure he speaks the truth when he says that.'

But even among the generals there seems to be some confusion about to whom the CCB was ultimately answerable. The impression in military and government circles is that they operated on their own and that nobody seemed to know for sure where the chain of command started and ended. 'I think that's true, said General Thirion. 'For me it was a sad day when General ['Joop'] Joubert said he discussed the murder of the Ribeiro couple. I'm not 100 per cent sure whether he referred specifically to that operation, but definitely [to] the idea of the military becoming involved in eliminating enemies of the state inside the country in unconventional ways – that he [certainly] discussed with General Geldenhuys at an Armscor party. That was a sad day for me, that things like that should be discussed at a place like that. Joubert testified that he then gave a broad layout of his plans, how it should be done, to Geldenhuys and Geldenhuys said to him: "It's a good plan." He took those words from Geldenhuys as, "Yes, go ahead." And then, with the involvement at certain levels of police and military, some actions took place of which we didn't know at the time. One heard about them at the Truth Commission.'

While the TRC investigating team flew all the way to Paris to investigate the Dulcie September assassination, it failed to read or mention an article that appeared in the South African *Mail & Guardian* of 12 January 1998, or to interview the author or any of the people mentioned in it. Journalist Evelyn Groenink, in 1990, uncovered a large body of evidence that indicated the ANC representative may in fact have been killed by elements within the French Secret Service and that it may have been done with some French government knowledge. According to Groenink's article, 'the idea that Pretoria or Paris, or both, could have felt threatened by the political activities of the ANC office in Paris seems far-fetched ... She made speeches in community centres and sold badges and stickers. Her political influence was non-existent. September, in other words, would not have been killed in a professional, risky and costly operation just because she happened to say anti-apartheid things to a few hundred people in a small town or city hall every once in a while. Pretoria was in the late eighties desperately looking for a thaw in its foreign relations. Especially with the West: they wouldn't risk all that just to kill Dulcie.'

Even ANC colleagues interviewed by Groenink are convinced there must have been a reason that the French government or secret service saw as sufficient to allow the killing to take place. It appears from Groenink's article that September stumbled across information about French arms deals with South Africa that were taking place despite the UN arms embargo. Groenink wrote: '"In the autumn of 1987, some French diplomats and secret service and military people were here, ostensibly to negotiate a prisoner swap between Angola and South Africa. But in the meantime they were dealing arms all around," former apartheid spy Craig Williamson told me. "And if September stood in the way of that, she would surely have been killed."'

Groenink's article does not establish who killed Dulcie September. It does, however, present convincing evidence that the French Secret Service and possibly even elements of the French government were deeply involved. Perhaps the TRC investigators should take a look at it.

From the mid-1980s the ANC made increasing claims that there was some sort of 'third force' at work in South Africa. As time went by these allegations became louder and increased in intensity. The truth – according to the generals and minutes of the State Security Council marked top secret – is that there never was a third force in the accepted sense of a paramilitary force that operated outside the military and police. 'Despite the persistent propaganda to the contrary, no "third force" ever existed,' General Malan told the TRC.

In 1985 the State Security Council examined the possibility of establishing a third force, separate from the police or SADF, to deal with the unrest situation. It was felt that such a force, which would be legally constituted and openly established, would be in the interest of the SAP and the SADF with regard to their image and primary functions. On 4 December 1985 it gave instructions for a feasibility study to be done. Military attachés at South African embassies in countries where third forces were in existence were instructed to research their structure, role and jurisdiction. At the same time, instructions were issued to a working committee of the SSC, in conjunction with the security forces, to investigate the possible establishment of a third force that would operate parallel to the SAP and the SADF.

'I was the unofficial military attaché in Germany, stationed in Bonn,' said General Bertus Steenkamp, recently retired Chief Director of Defence Intelligence of the new SANDF. Then he was a Lieutenant Colonel. 'My rank was First Secretary. The reason for that was that my predecessor was there for several years and the Germans were not prepared to take in a new attaché but were prepared to receive an unofficial one. I was military attaché, but in an unofficial capacity. At the end of 1985 I was instructed to research the situation in Germany where three separate forces existed, that is, the *Bundeswehr* (the Defence Force), *Kriminalpolizei* (the police) and *Bundesgrezschutz* (BGS, the border police).'

In Steenkamp's report, dated 7 January 1986, to the Chief of Staff Intelligence he explained the different functions of each German force: 'The task of the defence force and the police is broadly the same as in South Africa – in other words, the defence force is primarily responsible for dealing with an external threat and the police for internal problems. The BGS, in contrast, is primarily responsible for border control but has both internal and external operational forces. The elite anti-terrorist unit, GSG9, is part of the BGS.'

Two comprehensive reports were produced by the State Security Council and the South African Police. The second was written by a Lieutenant Colonel Gijsbers. The police document examined the existing capabilities of the SAP, pointing out that the force already had some R86 million worth of counter-insurgency equipment as well as all the relevant accommodation, etc. The recommendation was as follows:

1. In the light of the above, the formation of a so-called 'third force' is not recommended.
2. As an alternative it is suggested that the Counter-Insurgency Unrest component of the Force be expanded and become a separate branch of the SA Police on the same level as the Uniform, Detective, Security and Criminal branches is organised.

The Working Group of the State Security Council under the chairmanship of the Deputy Minister of Defence and Law and Order, Adriaan Vlok, examined all the pros and cons. In the end the recommendation in their report dated 13 March 1986 read: 'The Working Group recommends that the existing capabilities of the SA Police be restructured. It must be a specialised ability that possesses police skill and techniques but that can also carry out paramilitary functions and that is equipped and trained to prevent and control internal terror, unrest, riots and public violence.'

The SSC's top-secret minutes of the meeting read as follows: 'It was decided ... that a "Third Force" would not be established but that the existing capabilities of the SA Police will be restructured and increased. Other recommendations in this regard will be presented which will include structured, integrated security force procedures and actions.'

But what of the evidence found by, among others, Judge Richard Goldstone? What about the reported train violence, hit squads, weapons deliveries to political opponents of the ANC? The simple answer is: I don't know for sure. After going through thousands of documents and interviewing dozens of people, I can only say what I believe to be the truth, based on my personal perceptions, my experience in and with the SADF and a healthy dose of educated supposition. What I do know is: intelligence operatives lie. That is the nature of the beast and their job. The better liars they are, they better they are at their jobs. They are taught to lie with the straightest of faces and will lie to save their skins or advance their cause. They love to create an aura of mystery and invincibility about them and will happily take credit for operations they may not have done but which make them look better in the eyes of their peers or superiors.

What I believe is that some operatives lied to a gullible TRC – which in many cases appeared to have decided on its findings before any evidence was even heard. They told the TRC what they believed it wanted to hear. I believe there was no 'third force' but that CCB operatives, Unit C-10, the SAP equivalent based at Vlakplaas and members of the National Intelligence Service took the broadest possible latitude they could from the instruction 'disrupt the enemy'.

I think the generals probably knew of the existence of the CCB, but only in its 'purest' form. Apart from the General Officer Commanding Special Forces, I do not think they knew the specific details or even the existence of all operations. 'The idea of the CCB was really good,' said a former member, 'but when they started hiring all those shit-bag ex-cops the whole thing fell apart. [A number of policemen linked with criminal activities were employed, including Ferdi Barnard, a former low-ranking policeman, now serving a long-term jail sentence for murder and other criminal activities. Some of the ex-policemen owned and ran a brothel – 'because,' they claimed, 'it would be a good way of gathering intelligence'.] What did they expect, putting criminals and scum in charge of life and death matters and giving them access to huge sums of money?'

'As a professional soldier,' General Malan told the TRC, 'I issued orders, and later as Minister of Defence I issued orders which led to the death of innocent civilians in cross-fire. I sincerely regret the civilian casualties, but unfortunately this is part of the ugly reality of war. However, I never issued an order or authorised an order for the assassination of anybody, nor was I approached for such authorisation by any member of the South African Defence Force. The killing of political opponents of the government, such as Dr Webster, never formed part of the brief of the South African Defence Force.'

9

ARMAMENTS AND ARSENALS

In 1977 the United Nations slapped an arms embargo on South Africa in the mistaken belief that it would bring the Pretoria government to its knees. What it in fact did was to make South Africa one of the world's largest producers of armaments, and led to the development of some of the world's finest weapons and military equipment – the G-5 and G-6 155 mm field guns are examples. The international action saw the establishment of Armscor and a wave of sanctions-busting activities.

The schemes the government employed were sometimes comical and sometimes daring. High on its shopping list in the mid-1980s were submarines needed to replace the ageing fleet of four French Daphne-class vessels, which had already undergone extensive refurbishing. Submarines were seen as being a major deterrent by a government that was increasingly concerned about Soviet and Eastern bloc shipping around the South African coastline. But submarines were also used extensively to infiltrate Special Force teams for operations in African countries. The following exploit caused a furore.

'Before I left here for my posting in Germany as military attaché [1984–87] I was asked to go to Armscor for a briefing,' said General Bertus Steenkamp. 'They told me there were two projects running. One was an armoured car and the other a submarine. They told me I must just support them where necessary. My main job was to represent the Defence Force. I also had to do overt collection of information of a military nature to tell the people in South Africa what was going on and how the situation in South Africa was perceived in Europe. What I also did was present several lectures to try to explain what was going on here,' said Steenkamp. 'I was under command of the military in South Africa but under functional control of the Ambassador. I operated under the rules spelled out by the Ambassador and the Department of Foreign Affairs but reported directly back to the Chief of Staff Intelligence. First it was Pieter van der Westhuizen and then Admiral Putter. It was an intelligence function. The intelligence was on a strategic rather than operational or tactical level.

'The German government were very adamant they opposed the South African government's policies. They also made it quite clear that they disagreed with the policy of that time. But from person to person it boiled down to personalities. If you had the personality that allowed you to go around and talk to people it was easier. The Germans were very open to me personally. At the end of my time we had a function which more than 300 people attended and the Chief of the *Bundesgrezchutz* flew in with a helicopter and supplied the guard of honour to say goodbye to us. I was briefed by Armscor as to what projects we were involved in with the Germans at the time. We were categorically told that we were not in any way allowed to spy and were not allowed to become involved in covert work, but we did give the necessary support to Armscor members who were in the country. It was part of the function of the military attaché to do that. As far as I'm aware Armscor had an office in the embassy in Paris from which people came to see us from time to time. They didn't necessarily brief us on what they were doing.'

The support Steenkamp gave to Armscor put him into the spotlight and had the German opposition and media baying for his blood. 'At one point the Armscor representative was delayed and wasn't going to arrive on time to collect certain items,' said Steenkamp. 'So I was phoned and asked to go to Lübeck to collect some stuff for them which they would later collect from me. This is how my signature came to be on the receipt for the [submarine] blueprints. It was a collection of circumstances. I went there and signed for them. My involvement increased because I took over some of the liaison for them. Regularly I and my assistant, Dries van Heerden, went to see the people to get certain documents, etc.

'I'm not sure if the Germans knew about us getting the submarine plans,' Steenkamp goes on. 'I was told that there was a contract, but when the whole thing became known we couldn't make the contract public knowledge because it would have caused a political storm in Germany. If that's true or not I don't know. I never saw the contract myself. The idea was for us to build [the submarine] in

South Africa. I think Armscor had already got quite far with construction facilities in Durban. The blueprints were on microfiche. These were handed over to Armscor. I don't want to give the details of how this was done but they were handed over to Armscor.'

On one occasion when Steenkamp went to make a payment to his German contacts things almost went horribly wrong. 'I went to Munich by train,' he said. 'I had my briefcase with me and on the train I sat writing a report. Then I took a taxi from the station. When I got out of the taxi I realised I had everything with me except my briefcase, which contained all my documents. When I looked up I saw the taxi had stopped at the robot and I managed to run after it and stop it by hammering on its roof. It was a very close shave. In my briefcase was a receipt for money I'd paid to the firm involved in the submarine project. There were signatures and names and details stating exactly what the payment was for. If this had become public it could have caused an international incident. I would certainly have been thrown out of the country and the fall-out for the German government would have been huge,' he said.

As it was, the German–South African submarine deal was blown after a dispute between two employees at the company that supplied the plans. 'I was told that two staff members at the company became involved in a conflict and one said: "If you don't stop, I'll go to the press." The other said: "I don't believe you. If you do so your neck will also be on the line." The first guy called his bluff and went to the press. It was in-fighting. It was in no way caused by mistakes on our side,' Steenkamp said.

'When the thing blew Dries van Heerden and I were with one of the contacts who was supposed to give us certain documentation. He said: "Have you heard on the radio what's going on?" We immediately got into the car and drove back to the embassy. The initial press reports said both the embassy and I were involved. It was a huge shock to me because my involvement was relative. I was a go-between, that's all. I didn't have the full details. When I got back to the embassy I asked to see the Ambassador but he wasn't available. I was worried because the Ambassador hadn't been completely informed about what was going on. [He] was not happy. The big problem for Foreign Affairs and the question asked by the German opposition was – did I use the diplomatic bag to send the documents to SA? The Germans said it was in contravention of the arms embargo: in other words I may not do it. My argument is it was documentation. It contained no dangerous substances. Once or twice I sent a few bits of the documentation in the dip bag. But the majority was not sent in the dip bag, it was handed over to a representative of Armscor, not always in Germany. I didn't get any trouble from the military in Pretoria. I was told to maintain a low profile. I was never rapped over the knuckles.

'At Armscor I know I was recommended for a prize (I didn't get it). There were a number of nominations for the Chairman's Prize. I believe I came second. But I was officially thanked by them for the work I'd done. The whole story broke in the first quarter of 1987. There was a lot of noise made in the press and German Parliament but I experienced no ill-effects regarding my contacts with people in Germany. I still believe it was a great pity this thing came to naught because at that stage I believe we'd progressed quite a long way and it would have meant a lot to South Africa.'

In March 1993 President F.W. de Klerk announced that South Africa had secretly developed a small nuclear arsenal containing six nuclear devices. 'I revealed for the first time what the international community had long suspected,' he wrote in his book *The Last Trek – a New Beginning*, namely, 'that South Africa had, at one stage, developed a limited nuclear deterrent capability. The decision to do so was taken in 1974, against the background of the Soviet expansionist threat in southern Africa, the deployment of Cuban forces in Angola from 1975 onwards and the knowledge that because of our international isolation, we would not be able to rely on outside assistance in the event of an attack. The programmes included the construction of seven fairly simple nuclear fission devices (in the end only six were completed) similar to the bombs that destroyed Hiroshima. The weapons were considered the minimum for testing purposes and for the maintenance of a credible deterrent capability.'

Full preparations had been made to deliver the bombs – either by aircraft or by missile: a successful missile test was apparently carried out. 'We could have delivered them by missiles,' said General Malan. 'But there were a lot of other means we could have used. We could have delivered them by aircraft. But the main thing is if you could deliver it by missile you could do a lot of things. We made all the preparations, everything at Overberg, on the other side of Bredasdorp. Arniston. There was a hell of a fight about Arniston. People criticised us for claiming the area there for military purposes.

'The instruments and facilities were all in place. It wasn't like the American ICBM [inter-continental ballistic missile] system. You could fire it from a mobile vehicle (an enormous vehicle – the size of the wheels was about two metres high). It was a very successfully kept secret. It was very difficult explaining to the people down there why we needed the land. The Green Party was against it, the local farmers and fishermen were against it, the holidaymakers and Nature Conservation were against it because it was right in the centre of a conservation area. Everybody was against us. We had to explain without telling them what it was. They said: "To hell with this man. Why do you want this area? Why can't you take the desert area around Klawer?"'

Why did South Africa build nuclear arms? Most observers believe they would never have used them, as to do so would have been tantamount to committing national suicide. According to David Albright, writing in *The Bulletin of the Atomic Scientists* July/August 1994 edition, the weapons came out of the technological 'can-do' mentality that coincided with the country's increasing international isolation in the 1970s and 1980s. It was much more of a political strategy based on forcing Western governments to come to South Africa's aid in the event of an overwhelming attack by Soviet-sponsored military forces in the region. Albright wrote: 'An official who described this "strategy of uncertainty" said the government would have revealed its nuclear arsenal only if "the country found itself with its back to the wall".

'South Africa's strategy of nuclear deterrence had three phases,' Albright claimed. 'The first phase was uncertainty, in which the county's nuclear status was neither acknowledged nor denied. If the country was threatened militarily, it would enter phase two. The government would covertly acknowledge the existence of its nuclear weapons to leading Western governments, particularly the United States. If phase two failed to persuade the international community to provide assistance against military attack, the government would publicly acknowledge its nuclear capability or demonstrate it with an underground test.' In essence it was a very expensive political bluff aimed at blackmailing the United States and the Western powers into coming to South Africa's defence if the pawpaw really hit the fan.

General Malan sees the situation slightly differently. He agrees there was very little chance of South Africa ever using a nuclear device, but says the reason for developing the bombs was somewhat different. 'If your enemy is sitting with a nuclear bomb and you don't take any precautions about it there's something wrong,' he said. 'The Russians had one and we had the Russians in Angola. There was nothing preventing their using it, other than the international community. But you couldn't say for sure they wouldn't use it. And if they used it ... what then? We would have been sacrificing all South Africans if we had no means of countering. We had to do it. Apart from that, we were forced. We couldn't get any uranium for our power station at Melkbaai, so we had to enrich uranium here. So why not continue with it and see whether we couldn't develop a nuclear [armaments] capability?

'We were forced in that direction, so we did it,' Malan said. 'The gravest mistake we ever made was not using that ability as leverage in our negotiations with the international community. Some of my colleagues were prepared just to give it away. Why not ask for something? For instance ask for a nuclear-free southern Africa. Get the other countries involved. Put responsibility on them, because tomorrow there might be a new India or similar country in Africa with nuclear power. Where are we then? We haven't got the formula, we haven't got the technicians, we've got bugger-all. We're playing second league again.'

Until De Klerk's announcement, South Africa never publicly admitted it had any nuclear weapons, but Malan claims the international community knew. 'They knew about it,' he said. 'Can you recall the Upington hole with all the satellites watching it? Hell, the Americans were mad. And we had a leak. So they knew about it but we never got anything out of it.'

In 1977 the Vastrap testing facility in the Kalahari Desert north of Upington was completed. Two test shafts were completed – one 385 metres in length and the other 216 metres. Atomic Energy Corporation officials say a 'cold test' (a test without Uranium 235) was planned for August 1977. It was to have been a fully instrumented underground test with a dummy core, its major purpose being to test the logistical plans for an actual detonation. But the test was cancelled after Soviet Intelligence detected the preparations and alerted the United States. US Intelligence quickly confirmed the existence of the test site and the story was leaked to the world's media. The ensuing publicity and the pressure exerted on South Africa by the West caused the cancellation of the test, and according to Atomic Energy Corporation officials the holes in the Kalahari were sealed.

In the late 1970s a gun-type device was tested at Pelindaba near Pretoria in a building called Building 5000. 'When the Manhattan Project scientists conducted this dangerous experiment, they called it "tickling the dragon's tail",' wrote David Albright. 'For a brief moment the Highly Enriched Uranium went critical, causing nuclear fissioning and providing confidence that the device would have worked as predicted by theoretical calculations.' It was the only test ever carried out.

According to a retired senior military counter-intelligence officer who was intimately involved with the nuclear weapons programme, Armscor took over the nuclear weapons programme in the late 1970s. Facilities were set up at Kentron, south-east of Pretoria. (The site was later called Advena.) In 1980 work on a new building called The Circle was started. Underground storage facilities were built under the Gerotek vehicle testing facility. 'That test site provided a very convenient cover,' he said. The Circle, completed in 1981, consisted of two floors with the second, lower floor dedicated to making nuclear devices. 'The top floor looked like any other office block with reception areas and conference rooms and that sort of thing,' said the officer. 'There were no antennae or anything else around that could give any external clues. Nuclear waste was taken away for reprocessing at night in disguised vehicles. As you can well understand, everything was incredibly hush-hush and security was extremely tight. Our job (counter-intelligence) was to scrutinise everyone, from the highest to the lowest, and that we did – very vigorously!' Only South African nationals who held no other passport were considered for employment. By the time the programme was shut down in 1989, around 300 people were employed, 100 of whom actually built the devices.

The device built at Pelindaba was transferred to The Circle and placed in a special vault. It had been temporarily stored in an abandoned coalmine at Witbank, a former military ammunition depot.

In April 1982, Armscor manufactured its first device – a 'pre-qualification' model – which, according to an Armscor official, could be kicked out of the back of a plane. Safety precautions and measures to prevent accidental firings or detonations enjoyed the highest of all priorities. A high-security vault was built at The Circle with a number of smaller vaults inside it. Each device was divided into two halves, kept apart in separate vaults. The enriched uranium was divided between the two halves to minimise the possibility and effects of an accidental detonation. It was forbidden to work on both halves at the same time. In fact, both halves could only be removed from their respective vaults at the same time after three top ministers and the head of government inserted their separate sections of the code into the vault. No single person had the complete code. There were also a multitude of other safety devices.

So what did South Africa's bombs look like? According to David Albright, 'the total mass of a completed device was about one metric ton. It had a diameter of nearly 65 centimeters and was about 1.8 meters long. Each device contained an estimated 55 kilograms of HEU (Highly Enriched Uranium). The cores of the second through seventh contained weapon-grade uranium. The reflector was made of tungsten. The calculated yield of each device was about 10–18 kilotons when the core had weapon-grade uranium. Using 80 percent enriched material halved the expected yield.'

In the mid-1980s, as Cuban force levels rose sharply in Angola, and South African military involvement escalated in that country and in Namibia, the highest of government and military circles decided that the strategy of political pressure and blackmail of the West should be driven home once again. The government wanted to know how long it would take before an underground test could take place.

Armscor began with the preparations. The sealed shafts at Vastrap were reopened. A large shed was built over the openings to prevent their being seen by the prying eyes of foreign intelligence agencies. At the same time the SADF conducted shooting exercises on the site. Water pumped from the shafts was not simply pumped onto the dry desert sands where it would provoke suspicion, but carted away in tankers and discharged off-site. 'Of course we knew the satellites would see the whole thing,' said the retired counter-intelligence officer. 'While we went out of our way to cover our tracks, that was part of the plan. I cannot say for sure, but I heard from impeccable foreign intelligence sources that the reopening of the Vastrap facility gave the West and the Soviets a hell of a fright. They believed we were getting ready to first-test a nuclear device (which we would have been forced to do if they'd called our bluff), then deploy it. Soviet and Western intelligence were suddenly convinced we were serious about nuclear weapons and the West began to put pressure on the Soviets to get the Cubans to withdraw from Angola.'

The nuclear weapons programme caused wide differences in South Africa. Even among the SADF's senior generals there were wildly divergent views. 'I'm on record at the TRC where I said I was never in favour of the whole idea of nuclear capability,' insists General Viljoen. 'Remember I was a student of revolutionary war: I knew you don't win a revolutionary war with a nuclear bomb.

'I think the whole idea of nuclear potential was very closely involved with P.W. Botha and also the politicians of the National Party, because it would be of great advantage that SA was known as a country with a nuclear capacity. It doesn't matter that we denied it. The intelligence people knew it. I have no reason to believe that we ever carried out a test. I know that we prepared in the Kalahari to do an underground test. That we did and we were part of the planning for it. But it never took place. My resistance to the nuclear programme was not against the idea that South Africa would have a nuclear potential. I think that did have some advantage, but at that stage I felt the threat was from a revolutionary war. It was not one in which nuclear capabilities would have counted. I often said: "Let's rather buy tanks or guns."

'I was not in favour of the programme. I was often offended by the great amounts of money we spent on the developments, but it was a matter of political pride for the government,' said Viljoen. 'But however much I was against the programme, it did have a certain deterrent value. The way in which we agreed to dismantle them was admitting we were wrong. I think it was bloody foolish. I was told De Klerk briefed Mandela completely about the nuclear capabilities. Eventually the ANC got the credit for the whole operation. From our shame of dismantling the millions and millions of rands spent on this, they got the propaganda value.'

General Meiring felt differently. 'I attended a meeting where we were told we were going to fold up our atomic programme,' he said. 'I knew about this [the programme] because I was in logistics and was in on part of the knowledge. We had to assist in the dismantling of these things, which I thought was bloody stupid. I said so, and Geldenhuys who was Chief of the Defence Force nearly bit my head off. I still think it was stupid,' he said.

'The nuclear programme started in 1975 or before,' said General Geldenhuys. 'I was too low down to know what the position was. I had virtually zero knowledge until the day I became Chief of the SADF. In that first week people came to me and said: "We need to brief you about this." From what I've heard it was the stereotype nuclear strategy followed by most countries apart from the superpowers. It was a deterrent and it gave that country status and some clout around the negotiation table and put you in a position where you were seen as someone to be reckoned with.

'Of course we could never have used them. But you have to think about the human psychology behind this. People would say: "South Africa would never use them, but on the other hand you never know." That's why you don't acknowledge that you have them, neither do you deny it. Keep them guessing and on their toes. It creates the idea: you've got to be careful. You can't just bump them and if you really got them in a corner you don't know what they'd do,' explained Geldenhuys. 'If the "new South Africa" had come in 1985 or 1986 instead of when it did, we would have had big problems because then the revolutionary forces and their backers, the Soviet Union, the Cubans and the East Germans, were all on a high. Their demands would have been those of the revolutionaries of the time. We would have had a totalitarian state such as they created in Angola, Mozambique and so on. On the other hand if [the government] had let it go on a few years it might have been a better South Africa. I don't think they allowed us enough time to capitalise on what we'd achieved. The negotiations were very much in line with the model for a takeover rather than a politically agreed settlement. The same applies to the bomb. We would never have used it. But that was never the aim.

'If you have the money, and I think it was done on a shoe-string … it might have served some purpose to have maintained the status quo for a few more years,' said Geldenhuys. 'How have we benefited since banning the bomb? There was always criticism that the military and national service was killing the economy of the country. Why couldn't we use all the money spent on defence to make more ploughshares? Do you see any trace of more ploughshares and tractors and less joblessness [now]? What's happened to that money? It almost seems as if that money saved on the defence budget has vanished into thin air.'

After Operation Savannah, as Cuban troop levels increased in Angola, the SADF began to worry about the increasing possibility of its soldiers being subjected to attacks with chemical and biological weapons. In 1981 General Malan gave approval for the establishment of a programme in which the Defence Force was to develop a chemical and biological warfare capability. The idea, according to Malan, was to develop defensive capabilities to be able to counter biological and chemical attacks against the SADF. Code-named Project Coast, it has since evoked heated discussion and condemnation in the media and forms a major component of a criminal case against its former head, Dr Wouter Basson. At the time of writing, the accusations against Basson were still being considered by the court, so detailed examination will have to wait until the judicial process has run its course.

'At no stage did I authorise the use of any chemical or biological capability developed by Project Coast,' Malan told the TRC. 'This project never had any sinister connotation. I have been informed that the members responsible for this project briefed President Mandela fully on the existence, scope and ambit of Project Coast and that he thereafter granted his approval for its continuation.'

On 16 March 1990, General Jannie Geldenhuys, as Chief of the SADF, signed a letter marked 'top secret' addressed to the Minister of Defence, General Magnus Malan, requesting authorisation for funds to be allocated to Project Coast from the Defence Special Account. The letter was apparently written by Project Coast leader Dr Wouter Basson, and his contact details were listed in the event that the minister wished to make further enquiries. In his motivation he wrote: 'The purpose of Project Coast is, in a clandestine and covert manner, to do research and development and to establish a production technology in the sensitive and critical arena of chemical and biological warfare [and] to give the security forces a chemical and biological warfare capability in line with the CBW philosophy and strategy.' The following were listed as the goals of Project Coast:

- the establishment of facilities required to run basic CBW research;
- the establishment of the necessary security measures required for the CBW research facilities;
- the establishment of the necessary safety measures required for CBW research;
- the operation and management of basic CBW research;
- the establishment (in terms of the guidelines of HS Ops/Hs Plan and in co-operation with Armscor) of an industrial capability for CBW;
- the operation of a CBW technical intelligence system;
- the carrying out of CBW operations;
- the supply of operational and technical equipment and support to the SADF with regard to CBW operations and related actions; and
- the effective financial and administrative management of the project.

Attached to the letter of motivation was a schedule listing the money spent on Project Coast from April 1985 to March 1990. It reads as follows (the amounts are in millions of rands):

85/86	86/87	87/88	88/89	89/90
28,79	27,34	32,9	45,46	31,7

Geldenhuys/Basson's request was approved by Malan and the then Minister of Finance, Barend du Plessis, although Du Plessis added a handwritten note that reads as follows: 'In the light of the fact that I have been given the assurance that the activities being carried out under the code name, Project Coast, will be acceptable to the international community should they become known, I hereby give approval for the expenditure of the above funds from the Defence Special Account.'

There can however be little doubt that Project Coast was on numerous occasions used for more sinister purposes. There have been a number of amnesty applications from former Vlakplaas and CCB members for crimes in which poisons were used, while Mr Q made a variety of instruments intended to dispense poison and stated that it was put into cans of cold-drink. There has also been a large body of similar evidence presented at the trial of Dr Basson – none of which, it must be pointed out, has been proved at the time of writing. However, the state believes it has a strong case and the charge sheet is like something that might have been read out at the trial of a Nazi concentration camp commandant. Included in the over 60 charges originally brought by the prosecution (some have since been dropped) are:

- In a wooded area in the Duku Duku area of KwaZulu-Natal five unknown black men were tied to trees and smeared with a jelly-like substance in an experiment to see if the substance was lethal or not. The ointment did not have the necessary effect, so the captives were injected with Tuberine and Scoline, which killed them. Their bodies were then loaded into an aircraft which flew out to sea and dumped them in the ocean.
- A Special Forces member, Lance Corporal Victor M. de Fonseca, developed brain cancer and, in hospital, began to talk about clandestine operations the Special Forces had carried out. It was decided he had become a security risk and must be eliminated. Poison given to him in the hospital did not kill him, however, so a week later, after his release, he was given poisoned orange juice. After another week he became ill and died in 1 Military Hospital on 10 April 1986.
- In August 1986 orders were given for a member of 5 Reconnaissance regiment to be eliminated. CCB members went to Phalaborwa, where an unidentified black man held in custody was handed over. The CCB members made the man do a series of exercises then gave him a cold drink containing a sleeping drug. Thereafter a CCB operative took the man to the airfield at Barberton, where he was injected with a chemical substance. His body was loaded into a Cessna Caravan aircraft and dumped in the sea off Mtubatuba.
- The state also claims that a project code-named Baxil came into being in 1992, in which the drug Ecstasy was manufactured in large quantities and a facility to manufacture Mandrax tablets was set up at Special Forces Headquarters which manufactured some 100 000 tablets. These were allegedly to be sold on the streets of South Africa.

Basson was arrested in a police trap on 29 January 1997 in a parking lot at Magnolia Dal in Pretoria, allegedly delivering Ecstasy tablets to a dealer. When arrested he apparently had 1 040 Ecstasy tablets in his possession. 'With the Wouter Basson trial,' said General Meiring, 'if I listen to the people as reported in the media, and I listen to Wouter's legal people, they laugh all the way because they say there's no substance to a lot of what these people are saying – because in the cross-examination phase it comes out that this or that bloke is talking shit, he's got no real hard evidence – but those things are not reported in the media. There might be things that are true that Wouter did, but a lot of things are not true. A lot of things are quoted out of context.'

Did South Africa ever use chemical weapons on the battlefield? There is no evidence to support such a claim. However, there have been accusations that South Africa tested a biological weapon on Frelimo soldiers on one occasion: this is reported by Klaas de Jonge, who was sponsored by the Dutch government to research alleged atrocities by the SADF. His report was presented to the TRC. 'The claimed incident took place on 16 January 1992 when Mozambican government forces consisting of three commando companies and one company of provincial troops, totalling approximately 300 to 400 soldiers were attacking one of the largest Renamo strongholds in southern Mozambique (Ngungwe), very close to the South African border,' De Jonge reported. 'As they approached the camp on foot, in box formation, one company forming each side of the box, a white jeep-type vehicle was seen in the vicinity of the camp. At about this time, also an unidentified light aircraft was seen flying above the area. The troops passed into the recently deserted Renamo base. They left the base again and a few kilometres away they came under limited small arms fire, not more than 15 shots. They took cover and then an explosion occurred overhead within the outline of the box between 150 and 250 feet above their heads, releasing a dense cloud of black smoke which then dissipated. The wind was blowing towards the rear of the formation.

'After 15 minutes the first complaints occurred: "It became very hot. Some of us were going crazy," told Second Lieutenant Joaquim Jonassa. He said they felt severe chest pains, were tired and thirsty, and when they drank water the next morning some of them vomited. Others said they had difficulty seeing (*The Guardian*, 28 January 1992). As a consequence a considerable disorganisation of the troops occurred.

'The UN Report on this incident concluded:
- that the effect (of the reported attack) on the troops was consistent with the use of a chemical warfare agent and also with severe heat stress;
- that in the absence of analytical data, they could not conclude that a chemical warfare agent was used in the attack;
- that because a considerable delay occurred between the attack (16 January 1992) and the investigation (23–27 March 1992) it might not be possible to detect traces of the agent if a chemical warfare agent has been used in the attack. The offsite laboratory analysis of samples taken indeed did not show traces of chemical weapons.'

Despite the fact that investigation teams from five countries could find no evidence of a chemical or biological attack, De Jonge reported: 'We think that there remains a fair possibility that the above incident was, however, an example of the testing of chemical weapons in a combat situation against foreign soldiers as part of South Africa's chemical and biological weapons programme ... Until now there is not real hard evidence that nerve gas, BZ or other chemical agents were used by the South African forces during the wars in Southern Africa. In the case of the Mozambique incident we are missing reliable physical tests of the victims and of the site. In the majority of cases of alleged use of chemical weapons one does not have conclusive proof. But based on more knowledge about the South African Chemical and Biological programme than was available in 1992, we think that there exists enough circumstantial evidence to state, that the 1992 Mozambique incident was probably an example of the testing of chemical weapons on foreign soldiers.' A case of condemning a man as a being rapist simply because he has the equipment ... or in this case perhaps doesn't have the equipment?

'Everything that we did in the biological and chemical warfare programme is documented and was handed to Mandela the day he took over,' said General Meiring. 'We were cross-examined by the British and American experts about this matter – and our own people – and we told them everything.'

Did the higher echelons of the SADF and government know and approve of the alleged atrocities committed in the chemical and biological warfare programme? I seriously doubt it – and not one single source has said otherwise. They say it was once again a case of 'power corrupts and absolute power corrupts absolutely.' It was a small group of men with low moral values. Perhaps they had genuinely bought into the 'total onslaught, total response' philosophy or, in the case of some of the former Rhodesians, were angry at having lost their country. When given the keys to the pharmacy, together with an open, signed cheque book and a secretive type of 'work' that made them accountable to no one, they simply ended up out of control.

'I was on the biological and chemical warfare committee when I was Chief of the Army, so before the time I was Chief of the SADF I knew what was supposedly going on,' said General Meiring. 'I can't tell you what Wouter did from day to day; I can't tell you whether he was working clandestinely with Neethling [the police's head of forensics] or the police or Magnus Malan, or things that are still being said today. What I know is he did nothing wrong in terms of the programme. The programme we had going was concerned with two major things. One aspect was to enable us to find the correct protective clothing for the troops.

That was why we had to be able to manufacture the [chemical and biological] agents, even the newest ones.

'The other aspect we were looking at was to find agents that enabled us to control a mob. A mob is a very difficult thing to control. It's got a mind of its own and if it gets out of hand there's only one way to control it and that is to shoot them. If we could find something that would negate bloodshed, then we would be in the pound seats,' Meiring explained. 'What we tried to do was to get an agent that caused disruption, and we were working on a number of them. One way was to make them feel so good they'd sit around and laugh. The other was to make them feel so bad they would want to go home immediately. One was easier to do: it was made from the ingredients found in Ecstasy. We stopped it because we lacked enough of the ingredients to enable us to deliver it effectively. The other was a more active teargas that we could use with a water cannon. You could also put dye in it. There's nothing you can do to get it away from you. It's like teargas, only 20 times worse, it sticks into you, you feel as if you are going to die – it's a terrible feeling. What we weren't able to complete was putting it in a foam barrier that people couldn't cross. We weren't able to get enough foaming agent to make the foam stable for long enough.

'We had these things and we made them so that if things got out of hand during the negotiations we could stop a mob without major bloodletting. That was the reason we did this,' Meiring said. 'Before it became illegal, as a result of the new [international] protocols, we worked on non-lethal gases. We tried to put them into [artillery] shells. With biological warfare one of the aims is to delay people. They can't go further, that is the main object of biological warfare: it's not so much to kill people but to stop an advance because the troops don't want to go into an area. It's like a minefield, only much worse, and only a limited number of people can go through because only a limited number of people have protective gear. They must first clean the area and only then can the others go through. If you fire this sort of gas or agent in a battle you can stop the enemy immediately. We wanted to use it to assist Unita if they were threatened by a major advance against Jamba.'

But the weapons were never used. Before they could be finally developed or deployed, new international protocols concerning the use of chemical and biological weapons were introduced outlawing the use of non-lethal gases in military applications. South Africa signed the protocol, and the stocks of chemicals were loaded into the back of a C-130 transport plane and dumped into the sea some 200 miles off the coast.

However, not all covert Military Intelligence operations aimed at 'disrupting the enemy' involved violence or bloodshed. 'In the mid-1980s there was a rash of "free Nelson Mandela" and anti-apartheid concerts in various parts of the world,' said a senior Military Intelligence officer who served in London and Europe. 'We got to know of a concert that was to take place in Hyde Park in London and our agents managed to get copies of the official printed programme a few days before the concert was due to take place. We then printed our own programmes, retaining the outside cover, but inside we had pictures of necklace and ANC bomb victims and information about the terrorist activities of the ANC. These programmes were then sold to concert-goers in their thousands. We also had balloons with anti-sanctions slogans printed on top of them. These were handed out to concert patrons who, because they were filled with helium, could not see the top of the balloon. They were tied to trees, put on rooftops, etc, because we knew that when the news and television stations zoomed in for aerial shots of the crowd, millions of viewers would see the slogans. At the same time agents poured quick-setting cement into the public toilets.'

10

THE NIGHT OF THE GENERALS

In many ways, the power and influence of the securocrats began to wane on 26 February 1986, though no one would have known it at the time. It was the day that President P.W. Botha first suggested that the positions of leader of the National Party and State President be separated.

Historically the leader of the majority party – the Nationalists, from 1948 – was also the leader of the government, first as Prime Minister and then from 1984 as State President. Botha believed that, as State President, but not leader of the majority party, he would somehow be above politics and more acceptable to the people. History was to prove he grossly misread the situation. Over the years – and particularly from the time he created the position of State President – Botha had adopted a style that was more like that of an emperor than an elected head of state. He tolerated no questioning of his authority or decisions and increasingly became the stern, finger-wagging figure that newspaper cartoonists portrayed him as. His inner circle of advisors closed ranks about him, carefully screening his visitors and in many ways providing him with the news and intelligence they wanted him to hear.

Botha seemed to be more and more out of touch with the real situation in South Africa, and his Cabinet ministers appeared more concerned with retaining their positions by not antagonising him than with good governance. Decisions began to be made based on how the government wanted things to be, rather than how they really were. 'You will come across people who will say "We lacked intelligence",' protests General Chris Thirion, former Deputy Chief of Staff Intelligence. 'I say bullshit. I'm not saying that tactically we were always on the ball. But what was our job? Strategic intelligence! No one in the [previous] government can turn around and say they were ill-informed. If they were, it's because they either didn't listen or they didn't have time for intelligence.

'To give you an example, I was flown from Windhoek to Cape Town with the instructions to give a briefing on the situation in SWA and Angola. I was told it was a half-hour briefing so I prepared myself for that. It was a briefing for the State Security Council. When I landed in Cape Town I was told to urgently make contact with the Chief of National Intelligence, Dr Niel Barnard. I went to Parliament to his office. He said to me: "I notice they said you've got half an hour, but can you do it in 15 minutes?" I said "If that's what I have, I'll cut down on the detail." That night I sat in the hotel and changed the briefing, maintaining the mainstream of the intelligence that we believed should be said. When I arrived in Parliament, where the State Security Council was gathered, I was called in by Kat Liebenberg and asked if I could do the briefing in five minutes. I said to him: "General, do you really want to have this briefing?" "Yes," he said, "after all, we've flown you all the way from Windhoek to Cape Town. We want the briefing, but you've got five minutes."

'If you were to compare them with [well-known businessman] Anton Rupert and his guys, Anton Rupert would spend four hours listening to the intelligence and then take 10 minutes to make the right decisions. Government leaders of the day didn't have time for intelligence. So for them five minutes was fine – but then they'd spend four hours making the wrong decision. I can tell you they made the wrong decision, because after I went there, and Pik Botha was present at that meeting, he set up someone with a hell of a budget to support Kalangula in Ovamboland. Kalangula was the leader of the Christian National Democratic Party in Ovamboland. He was a clergyman turned politician who opposed Swapo.

'A guy in Military Intelligence who was an SSO, a hell of a good intelligence officer, gave a briefing to South African military attachés who were back in the country for a short conference,' said Thirion. 'He briefed them on what was going to be the outcome of elections in Namibia and the route Namibia was going to go. We [Military Intelligence] cleared the briefing around an intelligence conference table and it reflected our evaluation. His words were exactly what we wrote in that briefing. The words were: "There is nothing SA can do to avoid Swapo winning the elections in Namibia." Only a fool at the time could differ from that. Yet I was called in as Chief Director Military Intelligence, by General Witkop Badenhorst, shat upon and told to transfer that guy out of the head-quarters because "he is not a good influence on his subordinates."'

General Bertus Steenkamp, recently retired Chief Director of Defence Intelligence of the SANDF, confirms Thirion's story: 'During the election process in Namibia we presented a picture that the DTA [Democratic Turnhalle Alliance] was not going to win or do very well. They would not believe us,' he said. 'The person concerned, who gave the briefing, Colonel Roelf Kotzenberg, resigned and is now out of the system.'

Increasingly Botha began to feel his leadership was under threat, and Cabinet sources tell of a number of clashes within the inner sanctum of power. In his book, former president F.W. de Klerk tells of Botha's aggressive and bullying tactics. He writes: 'I was one of those who was becoming seriously concerned about President Botha's increasing aggressiveness. I watched with alarm how he frittered away opportunities to promote better relations with the leaders of our various population groups and international visitors who came to see him.'

Botha clashed violently with the Revd Allan Hendrickse, leader of the Labour Party and Chairman of the coloured Minister's Council in the tricameral Parliament. De Klerk recalls: 'The next clash between the two leaders came on 19 August 1987 in the coloured chamber of Parliament. After President Botha had listened to a number of quite aggressive and strongly critical speeches from mem-bers of the Labour Party, he lost his temper. He launched a personal and humiliating attack on the Revd Hendrickse and another member, Mr Chris April. He furiously shouted: "I don't allow myself to be pushed around. I have never allowed myself to be pushed around – not by the House of Assembly (the white chamber of Parliament), not by this House or the House of Delegates (the Indian chamber of Parliament). My colleagues know me." He also said: "I am heartily sick and tired of being pushed around by threats and destructive criticism. The honourable members have tangled with the wrong person." A few days later the Revd Hendrickse hit back at a public meeting with a sharp attack on the presi-dent. P.W. Botha reacted by informing Hendrickse in a letter that his continued membership of the Cabinet had become unacceptable. Hendrickse resigned from the Cabinet. This was the end of voluntary co-operation in a multi-party Cabinet that many of us felt had held so much promise.'

Botha also began to alienate many leading figures in the National Party, many of whom had been his ardent supporters. The once unified party was starting to split from the inside, and the cracks were widening faster than they could be papered over. On Wednesday 18 January 1989, P.W. Botha suffered a stroke and was taken to hospital critically ill, although government spin doctors tried to make it look otherwise. Other than acting State President Chris Heunis and Dr Willie van Niekerk, Minister of Health and a medical doctor, Cabinet ministers were kept away from him. In the party and the Cabinet, meetings took place in which it was decided to try to persuade Botha to bow out gracefully and retire – his poor health presented a face-saving window of opportunity. 'That was our first course of action,' said a Cabinet source, 'but we knew he probably wouldn't, so we decided if he wouldn't jump we'd have to push him.'

When P.W. was released from hospital he made it clear that he intended it to be business as usual once he returned from a period of recovery. He also indicated in a letter to the National Party caucus that he believed it was now a matter of urgency to separate the office of the State President and that of the leader of the party. He wanted the caucus to elect a new party leader and intended to remain on as State President. For the party it was an impossible situation: party policy and direction could effectively be vetoed by the President. 'P.W. had to leave, whether we liked it or not, or whether we liked him or not,' said General Malan. 'That was immaterial and I agreed with that. He had to leave but he wasn't prepared to take advice. There were people like his own padre who convinced him to leave and then an hour or two later he'd phone back and say: "Sorry, I'm not leaving," because there were people behind him trying to keep him in his position – his wife and his children, people like that. He was incompetent. He couldn't run it.

'He had certain disadvantages after he had the stroke. His left side – when you get older you'll see it – there are certain things you lose. Your balance isn't as good and certain other faculties slow down. For example, it's easier to bump your face. Earlier on it wouldn't have happened. In P.W.'s case he couldn't control his left side – control in the sense that he wouldn't notice the first two ministers seated on his left side. Even if they started talking or protesting or making suggestions. He didn't try not to notice them – he couldn't because of the stroke. I sat next to F.W. (de Klerk) who tried his best to say to his colleagues: "Gentlemen, if we have problems let's try to first solve them and bring the solutions to Cabinet. Let's not bring the problems here and discuss them here because we can see the situation." There I take my hat off to F.W.'

In a closely fought leadership battle F.W. de Klerk was elected the new leader of the National Party, who had all pretty much agreed it was time to put P.W. out to pasture, although his advisers told him he still enjoyed the support of most of the caucus. It was easier said than done. Despite voicing fierce opposition to the date, Botha called a general election for 6 September 1989 – he wanted it to take place early the next year after a new constituency delimitation had taken place. In the meantime, Pik Botha arranged trips to and meetings with foreign heads of state for De Klerk. 'The success of my foreign visits received wide and favourable publicity – something that apparently irritated President Botha,' De Klerk wrote. A meeting was arranged for De Klerk and Pik Botha to brief Zambian President Kenneth Kaunda – it was to be the straw that broke P.W.'s back.

'Then this thing happened about F.W. and Pik going to Zambia,' said General Malan. 'In actual fact P.W. forced it, because he phoned me that night and wanted to know: "Do you know about them leaving and going to Zambia?" I said I'd heard about it but I didn't know anything first-hand. P.W. said: "You'll read about it in the newspapers!" I replied: "No, no, sir!" This was 12 o'clock at night and I made some notes. I said: "Give me some time, sir, I'll phone F.W. and Pik and see whether we can't solve the problem."

'I phoned Pik and said: "Boy, you've got some problems coming. You'd better do something about it." He said he'd phone F.W. – and I phoned F.W. afterwards just to be quite sure that Pik had phoned him. (He had.) F.W. asked me what he should do. I said: "Just leave it. I'll go back to P.W. tomorrow morning and tell him you'll contact him tomorrow morning: if you contact P.W. now you're looking for trouble,"' Malan said.

'I think they were going to see Kaunda, because at that stage it was already clear F.W. was going to be the future president. Pik has that craze to take the president to whichever country he can and I think at that stage he was polishing his marble. So I phoned P.W. and he said: "You'll still read it in the newspapers." I asked him please not to do it. The following morning I got a message to meet F.W. at his office and when I got there, there were a couple of chaps sitting there. Then he and Pik took over and P.W. refused to see them. I was also involved; they nominated me to go and see if I could pacify him, but he wasn't prepared to see anyone. So on the Saturday a meeting was held and it was decided we'd have to go and see him and have a meeting with him. On the Sunday evening they sent a group of people down to his office to see him. I was with the others sitting and waiting for the results. They came back and said: "We're in for a stormy session tomorrow, but it seems we'll have to do something. We'll have to accept our responsibilities and tell him he can't continue."

'We did it at the meeting. He was furious but he resigned then and left. I think that was right. It was the right decision, although it could have happened a month or two earlier. There were people advising him who were giving him false infor-mation, saying that every politician or at least 90 per cent were behind him. That wasn't true. I spoke to people in the caucus meeting and saw that everybody was against him – they wanted him out, rightly or wrongly,' said Malan. It was 14 August 1989: P.W. Botha resigned, F.W. de Klerk was sworn in as acting State President the next day and the hammer was poised to drive the first nail into the coffin of the military.

'In 1990, just before I became Chief of the Army, there were a number of things that worried me a lot,' General Meiring remembers. 'De Klerk had just taken over from P.W. During that period leading up to De Klerk's speech in 1990 things started to happen. I attended a meeting where we were told we were going to fold up our atomic programme. And, on the first occasion where I met De Klerk and his wife she said to me: "General, don't you think we should do away with national service?" I said: "No, Madam, I don't think so. I think it is a good thing." She said: "*Ag, die arme ou kindertjies* [those poor little children]." I said to my wife when we drove home that night: "Watch, this woman is going to make us lose national service." And it was so,' said Meiring.

'The next thing was the speech where he unbanned the ANC which made life terrible for us. We knew what was going on, we had good intelligence, but we could do nothing about it. We didn't know about De Klerk's plans to unban the ANC. It was a complete surprise. Nobody knew about it, but when it happened we had a major problem on our hands. We still had the increasing internal unrest to handle, but we had nothing – no more laws – to do it with because these people were now unbanned and we couldn't take any preventative measures.

'After that we had to do things in a com-ops [Communications Operation] way,' Meiring said. 'There are two incidents I can remember specifically. At one stage of the game, we knew, we had very good intelligence, that [the ANC] were planning to kill Oupa Gqozo [the leader of the "independent" Ciskei homeland]. He was outside our jurisdiction because he was in an independent country. We couldn't do anything to prevent it, so I went public saying we had intelligence that the ANC intended murdering Gqozo that weekend. They made a terrible mistake by denying it, which made Oupa Gqozo the safest man in the country that week. On Monday the ANC said: "See, Meiring is a liar!" I didn't care what they called me. All I cared about was we'd achieved our aim and they weren't able to carry out their action,' said Meiring. 'On another occasion there was going to be an IFP march in Durban and we knew there were going to be seven or eight ANC cronies amongst them who planned to start firing indiscriminately to cause a riot. I also went public with that and it resulted in their having to sit in the Elangeni Hotel the whole day drinking whisky because they could do nothing. We had to resort to those sort of things,' he said.

After his inauguration as State President in 1989, De Klerk began to consolidate his power base, and one of his first actions was to begin dismantling the structures the securocrats had established under P.W. Botha. On 28 November 1989 he announced the disbanding of the National Security Management System and ordered an investigation into all secret projects. Inconceivable as it may seem, most of the generals, with the possible exception of Constand Viljoen, were firmly behind De Klerk.

'F.W. wanted to gain control over the security forces,' said General Thirion. 'I could see the writing on the wall, but I believed in what De Klerk was doing and where he was going. I was one of the people who said we don't have much of an option. I had no problem with the direction he was going. But playing his trump cards – which, amongst others, were the security forces – so quickly, I thought was a strategic mistake. I listened to De Klerk and I know that the intelligence community at one stage sat down formally – in something like a work group (NI, the police and the military were all present), and the question was: "Must Mandela be released or not? If the answer is 'yes', then when and how?"

'Out of that whole exercise, which was a big exercise with a lot of senior people involved, the answer was: "No – it's going to cause havoc inside the country." I know it was a silly answer, because on the other hand he was an ill man and could not be allowed to die in jail. I think it could be understood that the intelligence community said: "Yes, at some or other time he must be released,"' said Thirion.

'The meetings took place at Intelligence Headquarters and NI conference rooms. A document was produced. Then one day De Klerk addressed a group of generals. He said he was advised not to unban the ANC and not to release Mandela, but had decided to do so against this advice. As a simple answer, he said: "I'm going to release Mandela because in jail nobody can make mistakes." I thought – that's very clever: De Klerk is continuing on the road that was started by Vorster and P.W. Botha. He's moving forward faster, but maybe he knows exactly how it should be done. I also believed that the alternative was a civil war.' Later, De Klerk, in what appeared to be a gesture of appeasement to the ANC, fired Thirion.

General Malan fully agrees with what De Klerk did, but denies him some of the credit: 'Remember he was elected in September 1989, when – and this is the critical factor everybody forgets – the Berlin Wall came down, and when that happened that was the trigger that we could recognise the ANC ... that we could at least begin to advance. There was no Act that had to be changed. All discrimination, everything had been removed prior to that by P.W., not by F.W. F.W. was not the reformist, it was P.W. All that F.W. did was unban the ANC and release Mandela, but nothing else. Everything else was already done when he took over.'

De Klerk was slowly but surely starting to squeeze out the military. When still-imprisoned ANC leader Nelson Mandela was smuggled into Tuynhuys, De Klerk's official residence, on the night of 13 December 1989 for his first meeting with the leader of the National Party, Malan was conspicuous by his absence. Present at that occasion were Ministers Gerrit Viljoen and Kobie Coetsee, General Willemse, Commissioner of Prisons, Dr Niel Barnard, head of the National Intelligence Service and his deputy, Mike Louw.

After the release of Mandela and the return of key ANC and PAC exiles, negotiations between the government and the liberation movements began in earnest. A key strategy of the ANC was first to discredit the security forces and then to negotiate itself into a position where it exercised a large measure of control over them. Mandela made use of every opportunity to accuse the security forces of being involved in violence and committing atrocities – which had a measure of irony to it, considering that at the time of the claim the ANC's Operation Vula came to light. In terms of the plot the ANC infiltrated operatives, including Mac Maharaj, Siphiwe Nyanda and Ronnie Kasrils, into the country to set up an underground structure whose aim was to organise and prepare for revolution. Maharaj and eight others were caught and charged with attempting to overthrow the government by force. Operation Vula was authorised by ANC leader Oliver Tambo in the mid-1980s and kept in place as an 'insurance policy' to be activated if the ANC was not able to achieve what it wanted at the negotiation table.

On 5 April 1991 the ANC wrote the government an open letter in which, amongst other things, it demanded the firing of Magnus Malan and Adriaan Vlok (Minister of Law and Order), the dismantling of counter-insurgency units, and the appointment of an independent judicial commission of inquiry to investigate the security forces. That same year De Klerk appointed a commission of inquiry into the Prevention of Public Violence and Intimidation under the chairmanship of Judge Richard Goldstone, who has since become a prominent international jurist.

As the negotiations moved along, despite members of the previous government's claims to the contrary, the ANC outmanoeuvred and outnegotiated the Nats. De Klerk's government appeared so keen to break ties with the military that there were times they simply disregarded intelligence because they didn't like it. 'By definition, intelligence is the truth, timely, well told,' said General Thirion, who was soon to become one of the victims of a De Klerk purge. 'Although you do evaluation and interpretation you are supposed to deal with the truth all the time, whether it's bad news or good news. I experienced some cases where the intelligence picture of the day wasn't as positive as some of the top command structure would have liked it to be, then they would go for a second opinion from within the com-ops arena.

'I once gave a briefing to the Command Council. At that time Roelf Meyer was Minister of Defence and he was present. It wasn't a very positive picture. It was about the ANC and their strategy and what they would like to achieve at the negotiations and how they intended to keep the back door open to be able to continue with the armed struggle if the negotiations failed – how they would keep the back door open and use it as a trump card, not committing themselves to stop all violence or the armed struggle – something they never did formally,' said Thirion. 'They went right through the negotiation process and they got away with it. We told [the Command Council] that was going to be the case. Under no circumstances would [the ANC] refrain from keeping the guys outside, they'd keep on training and move equipment.

'At the time we got information, which turned out to be hard intelligence: how they were formally helped by the Zimbabwean forces to move equipment towards the South African border. That was the situation. At that stage Roelf Meyer was already very involved in the sort of prelude towards final serious negotiations. He differed from me completely, to the extent that he said· "Military Intelligence, and specifically General Thirion, must make sure they don't spread ANC propaganda."

'The ANC said after the first round of negotiations they wanted to have a say in finance, in all the media, specifically the SABC, and they wanted a say in all security matters, also in terms of promotions – and they got it. They got what they wanted. Plus they never agreed to refrain from the armed struggle. Before the start of the negotiations I told Roelf Meyer those were their aims and never has he come back to me and said: "You were right,"' Thirion said. 'Our intelligence indicated the ANC believed if they could achieve those things in the first round of negotiations they would then be sure they would win the political war.'

Why did the government's negotiators cave in so easily? Thirion has some firm opinions: 'I would say first and foremost the unity within the top structure of the National Party and the Broederbond at the time was falling apart,' he said.

'You had more than one idea. The leadership wasn't what it was like under P.W. Botha – I'm not saying he was a messiah – but De Klerk took the reins over and he went his way ... I was present at a very serious meeting attended by General Malan, Pik Botha, Barend du Plessis and Kobie Coetsee when the then Deputy Chief of Staff Military Intelligence, Admiral Du Plessis, said: "The options are the following" – this was long before the negotiations started – "destroy the ANC or talk to them." He said he did not believe the National Party and/or the government had the will or the means to destroy the ANC, therefore the only option was to negotiate. I'm now talking about 1988–90.

'At the end of that year Du Plessis retired. He had to. They said to him he was going to go nowhere and they were appointing guys over him from outside who couldn't spell "intelligence". He never said negotiate at all costs. The input was – negotiate from a strong position, and he told them they were in a strong position then,' Thirion said. 'When it came to the negotiations [the government] was outmanoeuvred. The ANC definitely had outside support in terms of international lawyers. But that wasn't the crux of the matter. They were very skilful at negotiating. Ramaphosa came from a long school of negotiations. You must remember, Ramaphosa, then, as Chairman of Cosatu, was constantly involved in the inner ring of negotiations with the mining houses – and who did the negotiating for the Mining Houses? – top strategists, top guys. And he was on the other side of the table. He came through a schooling of negotiations where you have to go back to the people you represent with results. If you go through the history of negotiations between the mining houses and Cosatu, which was basically the schooling process of Ramaphosa, then you can see exactly from what angle he came and how skilful he was.

'Then there was also outside support and strategy planning. The National Party was outmanoeuvred in the sense they thought: hell, we're talking to nice guys, and how unfortunate we've gone through this war. Look how nice these guys are. All the time we've been mislead by the military, by the securocrats, who told us these guys are a bunch of communists. They were simply outplayed. It wasn't a matter of rolling over, they were outmanoeuvred. At the time Pik Botha was flying all over the world with De Klerk introducing him to international forums and saying: "This is the messiah, this is the man who is going to save South Africa."

'It's true that a small inner core of the National Party knew what was going on with the negotiations; the others got feedback monthly or fortnightly. What they got back was the feedback that the negotiators themselves were giving them and not what the overall intelligence picture was. What happened in actual fact was, to speak in military terms, the com-ops guys were also giving the ops picture.'

On 16 November 1992 the Goldstone Commission raided the headquarters of Military Intelligence's Directorate of Covert Collections. It seized files showing that members of the disbanded CCB were employed by Military Intelligence. Goldstone alerted the press with 'startling revelations'. It did not make F.W. de Klerk happy. 'I was, nevertheless, shocked and dismayed by Goldstone's statement in November 1992,' he wrote in his book. 'It indicated that elements of the South African Defence Force might be contravening the direct undertaking I had given after the Inkathagate imbroglio that the security forces would no longer involve themselves in actions in favour of, or against, political parties. I also did not like the sensational manner in which Goldstone had publicised preliminary and untested findings.'

'There's no simple answer to the whole thing,' said General Thirion. 'I think there was a long process stretching over a couple of years. The basic background is there was a feeling that the military, being the main force of the securocrats and the State Security Council, was like an inner circle and the guys [who were part of it] were trusted and knew what was going on and what the strategy was. Within certain political and government structures there were, so to speak, the insiders and the outsiders. There were people who felt they were left outside – and in some cases that was true, because not everyone was trusted. The insiders were, among others, General Malan, at times Gerrit Viljoen, at times Barend du Plessis (because I saw him at the Security Council meetings), Kobie Coetsee featured at a time, Pik Botha was around because he was the spokesman for Foreign Affairs stuff. But a man like F.W. de Klerk, I never saw him as a real insider, because you never saw him around much,' Thirion said, 'but then of course he followed P.W. Botha, and I think he had a strong feeling that what he saw as the power of the securocrats had to be broken down.

'I think De Klerk functioned to a large extent on advice from National Intelligence – Niel Barnard. And I think he thought it wise to play the three organisations, the military, National Intelligence and the police, off against one another and so get himself into a strong position with regard to how he was going to dismantle this Securocrat image of the government. The government must be seen to govern. The other thing is he also, to a large extent, came up with the idea that the various government departments should refrain from becoming involved in the political mainstream. They were part and parcel of the administration, and he said that where they were involved in activities outside of their line function, that had to stop. He tried to define the different roles of, for example, the military, the police and National Intelligence. In an insurgency war situation, that process is not easy. I think it was a problem to him and he felt he had to sort this out, to get government departments to concentrate on their line functions and not become involved in anything outside of that, least of all become involved in local politics.

'With De Klerk came a change of climate,' said Thirion. 'He referred to that in his book when he said that in the beginning dealing with the security forces reminded him of a man who got two Rottweilers from his predecessor. With the previous boss the dogs had had the freedom to hunt cats and kill and do what-ever they liked and in so doing they even got the best food from the boss-man. These were the dogs he inherited – the security forces. This is indicative of what he experienced. So there was definitely a change of climate taking place. At the same time, he became subjected to very, very strong ANC propaganda about the role of the military – but more specifically about the role of Military Intelligence. The ANC went all out to discredit MI and portray it as being like a rogue elephant.

'De Klerk's wife once told me how Mandela, just before the elections, would at every meeting he had with De Klerk, present accusations about MI's involve-ment in a third force, about third force activities inside the country and that the brains of the third force were inside MI. This was all part and parcel of the build-up to what made De Klerk act in the way he did. His wife – after their divorce, she came to *Die Werf* [the restaurant Thirion now owns and runs] – explained to me how he was hammered by Mandela. De Klerk himself didn't trust the security forces all-out. So in a sense he started believing Mandela. Mandela wasn't producing any details that could be investigated, but De Klerk came to the point where he decided it was no use us investigating these allegations because we were masters at wiping out and leaving no tracks. He said so in the newspapers,' explains the former Deputy Chief of Staff Intelligence.

'The allegations were about our having a third force and in so doing killing people. Also of having been involved in military coups in the former national states and in supporting dissident groups fighting against neighbouring govern-ments – specifically the Unita and Renamo types of operations and what went on in Lesotho.'

Was there any truth to those allegations? 'Yes. I would say in a sense yes. But one must see it in perspective,' Thirion explains. 'I was never involved in third force activities inside the country. I always warned against the Defence Force's involvement inside the country. I said this in the presence of Generals Malan and

Geldenhuys. I maintained that in fighting the so-called revolutionary onslaught, the Defence Force's enemy was MK. We had to spend our budget, energy and time fighting MK. But then there was the argument that such clear lines couldn't be drawn. There was a strong school of thought in the military that the military should become involved in the psychological battle – the psychological battle against the revolution, the ANC and the PAC, and that the military's activities should go far beyond simply fighting the psychological war. That was one terrain where the military went beyond its defined borders. The involvement in what people like to call third force activities wasn't a very open thing among generals. I got hints here and there. We saw [in the media] that Ferdi Barnard said he killed Webster, and it was from within the framework of the military where he served at the time. Not in uniform, not in the capacity of a soldier. So yes, I think here and there are indications that the military did get involved in this kind of operation, should one choose to define it as a third force operation.'

But whatever De Klerk said about being displeased with Goldstone's revelations to the press, it did not stop him from setting off a chain of events for which the old SADF generals and much of the SADF have never forgiven him. On 18 November 1992 he launched a further investigation into the SADF. He appointed Air Force general Pierre Steyn to carry out the investigation – or so he says.

General Meiring does not see it that way. 'Liebenberg was away, or somewhere, and Steyn, a Chief of Staff at Defence Headquarters, was sitting in for him at a meeting – I assume it was a Security Council Meeting or something like that. It was just after the Goldstone raid on an intelligence-gathering organisation of Military Intelligence where they raided a house. Because they [Goldstone] didn't know the whole story they immediately attached certain wrongdoings to this. Steyn didn't know his arse from his elbow – he was confronted with this thing at a Security Council meeting, he wasn't briefed, nobody knew about this. Liebenberg would have said: "Give us time to study the details and allegations," but Steyn just sat there and accepted everything. De Klerk said: "You people must eradicate this thing. You must ensure this does not happen again. You must investigate all the wrongdoings in the SADF." Steyn then went back to Liebenberg and said: "I've been appointed to investigate this thing." But on a council like that, if they say "you" it doesn't mean Georg Meiring or Pierre Steyn – it means you, the military, must do it.

'His job should have been to go to General Liebenberg and say to him: "We've got the job to do this," and Liebenberg would have appointed somebody to do it. It might even have been him [Steyn], but that would have been the right way to do it. But Pierre Steyn took the authority of the President; he went to see General Liebenberg when he came back and said he, Steyn, had to investigate the ungodly things happening in Military Intelligence. So Liebenberg called me (I was Chief of the Army) and Joffel van der Westhuizen, who was Chief of Staff Intelligence, and said: "You must give full support to this bloke,"' said Meiring.

'Joffel had, as you always do in counter-intelligence, lots of rumours about people – every one of which has to be investigated, because you can't afford not to do so. So there were a lot of files of uncorroborated information or rumours about people and he showed these to Pierre Steyn because he'd been instructed to give him everything he had. What Steyn then did was construct a table listing the names of the people and the possible things they were involved in. He took that to the President and said: "I only have this and it's unsubstantiated." De Klerk said: "Have you been to National Intelligence yet?" Steyn said: "No." De Klerk said: "Go and speak to Dr Scholtz." Scholtz was one of the senior officials at NI.

'Scholtz showed Steyn a lot of files which he wouldn't allow him to take with him – he had to make notes there,' said Meiring. 'He also read him a lot of stuff. Steyn took this information, gave it to his Staff Officer and said: "Make me the same sort of table as this" (showing him the table he'd made from Van der Westhuizen's files). He took the new table to the President, for whom it was manna from heaven – he saw the same things he already had because Scholtz had given him some stuff already, only now it had been substantiated from another source. De Klerk said: "Aha, now we've got them." But Steyn's stuff was the same hearsay evidence that Scholtz had.'

Even Steyn admitted that the evidence was shaky. 'General Steyn told us he believed all this to be true, even though his information was generally based on unconfirmed reports which would not stand up in a court of law,' De Klerk admitted in his book. 'In the briefing General Steyn stressed the point that the greatest part of the information that was presented to us was based on untested allegations which would have to be confirmed or refuted by further intelligence and investigation before a proper evaluation would be possible.' Yet despite that, De Klerk was determined to make a grand gesture to, as he put it, 'puncture the steel-belted culture of the SADF'.

'When this Steyn stuff went to De Klerk he called Liebenberg, Van der Westhuizen and me and said he wanted to see us,' said General Meiring. 'We went down to Cape Town. We sat outside his office. Liebenberg and Minister Eugene Louw, who was then the Minister of Defence, went in to see him. [Malan had been moved to the Department of Water and Forestry by then.] When they came out Liebenberg said: "He wants to see you. Come and see me in my office when you're finished."

'We went in and sat down. The President was there, [Pik] Botha was there, and one or two others. [De Klerk] said to us: "Chaps, things are not going well in the Defence Force. There are people meddling in things and they must be rooted out. If there are people working against the State they must be rooted out. Go to General Liebenberg, he'll tell you more. Thank you." Then we left and went to see Liebenberg. He said: "Here's the list, I want these people gone." I looked at the list and the names on it and thought – you're mad, man! I said: "No ways! Not in a month of Sundays!" I said to Liebenberg: "Go back to the President!" which he did. In the meantime we sat and waited. When he and Louw came back he said, "He said if you don't fire them, I will. I can."

'So I said to the general, "Are these the people he wants to fire by name, or does he want to fire as many as possible?"' said Meiring. '"What does he really want?" He said: "Both. These names he wants, but he also wants to show he's eradicating this." I said: "Okay, some of these people listed here have asked for early retirement. Let us put them on early retirement and give them all the benefits they can get. But let's go back to him and ask him to give us two weeks to come up with a plan so we can talk to these people, tell them about it, tell them what's going on – that this bloke has made up his mind, that there is wrong information about them but if it suits them they can go on early retirement." Liebenberg went back to De Klerk, who said yes, he'd give us two weeks. But when we landed in Pretoria he'd already announced the names. They'd already been leaked to the media,' said Meiring.

In what has become known as the 'Night of the Generals', 23 senior SADF officers were fired by De Klerk. This number included two generals and four brigadiers. Later many sued the government and won. In one case, De Klerk was forced to write a document admitting he was wrong. 'I was at the stage where I'd said to myself: "Okay, now you can leave [government],"' said General Malan. 'I was Minister of Forestry and Water. F.W. called me. He said I had to come and see him at Tuynhuys. I flew to Cape Town where I saw him. He gave me a document to read which I scanned through then said: "I'm not sure what this is, can you please enlighten me?" He said: "I'm sacking 23 officers and you have the opportunity to leave as well if you like. You have three choices: you can resign now – I'll be announcing this on Saturday (this was around about Wednesday or Thursday, I'm not sure), or you can resign with them or you can ride out the storm." I looked at him and said: "I think you're doing the wrong thing because

I can assure you there are certain members you've mentioned here that are better Nationalists than you or I. I don't know what you're doing but I know each and every person on the list. I have full confidence in them; they served during my period. But why did you bring me in?" He replied: "Because it happened during your period." I said: "Oh? So I'm taking the blame?" He said: "Well ... yes." I looked at him and said: "I tell you what, you announce it, I'll phone you and tell you what I think of it."

'The announcement was made on the Saturday (I think it was the 20th of December). I phoned him on the Sunday after I'd read the newspapers and seen the television broadcasts, and said: "Mr President, I'm leaving, but I'll decide when I'll leave. You made the wrong decision, but I'll be leaving." In mid-January I went to him and told him I'd be leaving on 28 February. I acted until 28 February with all the loyalty I could. I never went to the public. I read a lot of things after-wards. I read the Steyn so-called report. I saw there was no report and a lot of decisions had been made without the evidence required. I still have the minutes of a meeting that the Attorney-General of the Witwatersrand, some police officers, Steyn and someone else had. It was around 4 January 1993. The Attorney-General turned around and said: "This is not evidence. We can never prosecute them on these things. There is no evidence." It was apparently about discussions that took place between one or two chaps during coffee breaks, and they called that evidence. They used that and Steyn had a look at that and said: "We've got them, here's something,"' said Malan.

In old SADF circles it is generally accepted that De Klerk was pressurised by the Americans to make a gesture to the ANC that showed he was serious about the negotiations, which were in danger of breaking down. By sacking the 23 officers he could kill a number of birds with one stone: he could emasculate the conservatives in the SADF, send a message to the other security forces, show the ANC he was serious about the negotiations and get rid of Magnus Malan, whom he reportedly disliked intensely.

'I think [his motivation] was in connection with America,' agrees General Malan. 'This is hearsay, but at that stage Roelf Meyer was in America. Apparently [Meyer] phoned and said there was a lot of pressure on him from the Americans that he should act. These guys were then thrown to the wolves.'

'The Americans were putting pressure on De Klerk to make a gesture,' General Meiring confirms. 'At that time Roelf Meyer was in America. He was phoning De Klerk every half an hour or so. I think he leaked the names from America. I never had confirmation, but that's what I think.'

'At that stage I was a member of the Broederbond and I resigned as a result,' said General Viljoen. 'I said, if these are the kind of people involved then I don't want to be part of it. The Broederbond's changed its name now. It's called the Afrikaner Bond. De Klerk was a member. I'm not sure if he still is. This all happened after my time, so I'm not sure, but I got the impression it was pressure from the international world and I think through the useless person of Pik Botha. He is the most objectionable sort of person.'

11

A GENERAL FIGHTS BACK

General Chris Thirion was one of the casualties of De Klerk's purge, but he refused to go gently into the night. Thirion was determined to clear his name and refused to let De Klerk off the hook. His story presents a fascinating look behind the closed doors of the senior echelons of Military Intelligence.

Thirion grew up in what was then South West Africa, where his father was a farmer. After school he completed a degree in economics and geography. After completing an Honours degree at Stellenbosch University he joined the SADF, where he spent a year at 1 Parachute Battalion before being moved to the Military Academy, where he became a lecturer in Military Geography. 'Military Geography is Applied Geography,' he said. 'We normally say strategy has two main dimensions – time and space. That space is geography. By definition, war is, above all else, a geographic phenomenon. It's bound to the surface of the earth, moves purposefully over the surface of the earth and applies all sorts of resources. That's what war is about, and in the end that's what military strategy is all about. It's exactly what the Germans called geo-politics before and during the Second World War. I did a Master's degree and then started to work on a doctorate based on air reconnaissance using remote sensing for terrain evaluation for military purposes as opposed to agricultural or developmental purposes. I never finished that. I did 90 per cent of it but because of that was seconded to HQ in Pretoria.'

After a stint in Angola he was transferred to the Directorate of Military

Intelligence, where he spent the rest of his career, eventually rising to the rank of major general. 'I was appointed Deputy Chief of Staff Intelligence under Joffel van der Westhuizen. And at the time there was a cold wind blowing in the direction of MI in the sense that there was a feeling in the top structure of the Defence Force that MI was a bit negative. The picture we supplied was negative. It was a case of killing the messenger,' said Thirion. 'For a long time I was Chief Director of Military Intelligence and in so doing I was the guy responsible for the intelligence picture put on the table. I had one approach: I said: "Listen, this is it, this is how we see it. This is the information and this is how we interpret it." At times it was too negative for certain people. I'm talking about the Chief of the Defence Force. I went through Geldenhuys and then Kat Liebenberg and then Meiring. I even had differences with General Meiring. At the time, we made an appreciation for briefings Meiring was giving overseas or to international top banking or military visitors. They had this thing of saying: "The ANC is a bunch of communists and just a communist organisation." I stepped in and said: "That can't be said. If you as Chief of the SADF slip up on this thing, the Germans won't believe us, the Israelis won't believe us. They won't believe that the ANC is simply a communist organisation. It's also a nationalist organisation, albeit black.

'"No," [Meiring] said, "they're communist." We had a long argument about it. He said: "Let me prove it to you," and went through the list of names. He said: "This guy here, this is his position in the ANC, this is his position in the SACP." I said: "It's just a marriage of convenience." This was also the case with Geldenhuys. I believe I was looked at as somebody who did not necessarily hunt with the pack simply to be part of it. I would do my job first. I was aware of the fact that I wasn't unconditionally part of the real military inner circle. I realised that I wasn't going to make it to the top, and it was confirmed to me. The top would have been Chief of Staff Intelligence. [Then] certain things happened. When the command structure sat down with General Liebenberg to discuss promotions to the top structure, of course my name was in the hat to become Chief of Staff Intelligence. I was told by a guy who was present at the meeting that Kat Liebenberg said: "Next name is Chris Thirion – what's his political orientation?" Some of the senior generals said: "He's a right-winger. He's National Party but he's in the right wing of the party." Some other person – and I know who said what, this was told to me by a lieutenant general who was in the meeting – somebody else said he thought I was a Democratic Party supporter. Then General Liebenberg responded, with the generals sitting there not knowing where I stood politically, and said: "Do you guys realise we're talking about a senior general and we don't know where he stands politically? We don't know much about this guy." Then Liebenberg said: "I'll tell you where he stands – he's a fucking maverick." It was then I got the message: as far as he was concerned I was a fucking maverick. I lived with that. As an intelligence operator I believed that by definition intelligence is the truth presented timeously and well-told. I said that's what it's going to be. In a sense, yes, they did try to freeze me out,' said Thirion. 'They couldn't do it all the time. It was not that easy because of the position I held.

'It's important to understand the background and climate that led up to De Klerk making the decision to get rid of us. When the CCB was disbanded it was De Klerk's instructions that they should be out. That was final and none of those guys [he ordered] would ever be employed in the Defence Force in any way. For reasons unknown to me – but I can guess about them – some of the CCB guys were kept on the Defence payroll. The safe way in which it could be done was by doing it with secret funds. There were secret funds that could be spent in such a way that these guys, about seven of them, could be paid. They were kept on ice and they got paid but didn't do a day's work for the Defence Force,' said Thirion. 'To be able to keep them going with secret funds, the way to do it was to slot them in under "covert collections".

'Covert operations and covert collections. Tolletjie Botha was in charge of that but he was simply told that these guys now resided under him. He was a brigadier and Director of Covert Collections. Then something else happened. Because of budgetary constraints we were given instructions for the Defence Force to cut back on the budget x percentage. So everyone was instructed to come up with methods of how they could implement the cut-backs and what risks were involved in doing so. We had to go through that exercise as well, and being Deputy Chief of Staff Intelligence I was in a sense the operational head of intelligence, so Tolletjie Botha was under my command. He said to me: "We can easily cut back on the budget without any risk being involved." Then it came out that he had, hidden under the table, these ex-CCB guys and they were being paid from his budget but were not operationally responsible to him in any way whatsoever. He said: "What we are paying them is more or less the amount we have to cut back," and suggested we get rid of these guys. I asked him how the hell they ended up there. "They shouldn't be there!" He said, yes, he knew, but he was simply told by "Joop" Joubert, who was told by Witkop Badenhorst, that he's got these guys,' Thirion said.

Why did Badenhorst want them kept on, when F.W. had given specific instructions to the contrary? 'I think Badenhorst was instructed to do so by Kat

Liebenberg,' said Thirion. 'Botha said: "What they get paid in a year is the amount we have to cut back, and in addition we're not making use of their services.' So I said: "That's fine. Let's get some legal advice. It's now September, we can give them x months' notice and we can give them the extra three months to the end of the financial year.' Everybody said: "Okay, this is legal, it's fine, there will be no legal implications whatsoever. So we sat down and drafted the documents terminating their services. Then Tolletjie Botha called them in and said: "This is it. This is your copy – can you sign our copy so we can keep it on file?" One of the guys chucked it back across the table to Botha and said: "I'm not signing this, and you'll hear from me again." Botha reported back to me and not long after that I was called in by General Liebenberg, who was very negative about our actions. He really wiped the floor with me. He said: "We'll have a meeting, the Chief of Staff Finance will be present," and Tolletjie Botha and myself and one or two other guys.

'We had that meeting and he again said to me – he phrased the words in such a way that he effectively said: "Who the fuck do you think you are that you can fire people without first talking to me?" I explained to him what my position was, what Tolletjie's position was, the budget, and that this was our best solution. It was totally unacceptable to him. He said: "In the future, first talk to me when you have these sort of decisions to make." Then he gave instructions to the Chief of Staff Finance to make sure the money would be available to continue with that situation and that the guys could continue to get paid from a B-12 account. And that was it,' said Thirion.

'The next thing that happened to trigger a lot of things was Goldstone's raid on the Covert Collection Headquarters. Judge Goldstone laid his hands on files from which he gathered that people like Ferdi [Barnard] and Staal Burger and those guys were still on the payroll of Covert Collection Operations. He blew the whistle on that to F.W. de Klerk, who one could understand went crazy and wanted to know who was responsible for this. In terms of the command structure it ended up that I was responsible for that. Kat Liebenberg didn't step forward and accept responsibility. My back was exposed. On the "Night of the Generals" my back wasn't covered. De Klerk said: "I don't want to fire captains or majors. Who's in the line of command? Who's responsible?" That was me. At one stage during that night, I was told, he said to Kat Liebenberg: "You don't seem to know what's going on in the Defence Force."

'We got kicked out on the 18th or 19th of December 1992, and that was the night before,' said Thirion. 'But another thing happened, completely unrelated, but these things all came together. Going back some months before this, there was this thing about a guy called [Leon] Flores. He and a lady officer [Pamela du Randt] in plain clothes went to London. It was more of a com-ops operation, a propaganda operation, than anything else. They went to London, based on information that some guys in the UK, the Ulster Constabulary Group, a right-wing group, had sound information on MK–IRA co-operation. Everybody's response was that this was true international terrorism – co-operation, exchanging expertise, etc. The decision was made – without my knowledge – for two people to go to the UK, get this information and then leak it to the press in England. Once it appeared in the papers there, it would blow over to South Africa and would be a hell of an embarrassment to the ANC. So it was a com-ops operation, nothing else.

'Flores was under Tolletjie Botha's command. Tolletjie believed this was an Army operation rather than a Chief of the Defence Force operation, so he seconded Flores to the Army, which sent these two people over. They got arrested in England and it was a hell of a thing,' said Thirion. 'The British were tipped off. It appears National Intelligence tipped them off. I was told by the British and the CIA that they were tipped off by National Intelligence. There was a leak in our organisation.

'At the time Roelf Meyer was Minister of Defence. I was called in over the Easter weekend and told it was a Military Intelligence operation. They wanted to know how we could do a thing like this. It was a diplomatic blunder and we were instructed to do everything possible to keep it out of the press. When I was called to Roelf Meyer's house that was the first time I knew anything about the operation. What turned out to be the truth in the end was that Flores did a "false-flag" operation, in the sense that certain local policemen gave him money to take along to pay to the Ulster Constabulary Group to do surveillance on Dirk Coetzee. [Coetzee was a former Vlakplaas police commander who fled to England and 'spilled the beans' to the ANC. At the time he was staying in the UK.] That was the concern of the British. They got arrested, they were interrogated and so on. I was told this by Roelf Meyer in his house with two senior members of National Intelligence present. I said: "I'm afraid I know nothing about it, but I'll see what I can find out."

'I kicked off by contacting two people. One was Tolletjie Botha, who confirmed to me that Flores was there but that it was an Army operation; and I contacted another guy when I realised it was actually a psychological warfare operation, a com-ops operation. I also contacted [Brigadier] Ferdie van Wyk. They gave me sworn written affidavits as to what the situation was. As far as we, the military, were concerned, it had nothing to do with Dirk Coetzee. Dirk Coetzee was no threat to us in any way. But Flores was an ex-Vlakplaas operator who was involved with covert operations and covert collections.

'I had to move fast,' said Thirion. 'I was told by Roelf Meyer that all the conversations about the surveillance on Dirk Coetzee – they went so far as to say this was to do with killing Dirk Coetzee – were all on tape. He said we [the military] have had it – it's on tape. At the time we were not allowed to speak to the British, the declared officer of MI-5 or MI-6 and we had no contact because it was forbidden. The only people who had the right to talk to them were National Intelligence. I said to myself: now I've got these written statements by two brigadiers, I went back to Roelf Meyer's house, I showed them to him. I showed him the document where Georg Meiring authorised the trip of these two people and the purpose of the trip. Dirk Coetzee was not mentioned at all.

'The two guys from National Intelligence, specifically one, a Dr Scholtz, looked at them and said: "This is nonsense, it's lies." I said: "These are the written statements of two senior Defence Force officers and unless I'm proved wrong this is what I am able to put on the table. I also take strong exception to those statements." I also said: "The truth can only be established if we have access to the tapes." Roelf Meyer turned and said to the National Intelligence people: "Can we have access to the tapes? Can we have access to our people arrested in London?" I said I would like [personally] to have access to the tapes and access to our people. Meyer then gave instructions for us to go to London and that I should be part of that team.

'As I walked out of his house I realised I was at the short end of the stick,' said Thirion. 'I didn't like the way I was spoken to by the NI guy, Scholtz, so I broke certain rules. I went to a representative of the CIA. When I got to his house I told him I had a problem, people have been arrested in London. He said: "Yes, I know, these are their names and these are their operational names. They flew on such and such a flight, etc." He also mentioned the Coetzee thing. I asked him how he knew. He said: "I was told by [SA] National Intelligence." He asked what he could do for me.

'I asked him to find out if the local representative of MI-5 would be willing to meet me and he arranged a meeting. I discussed the whole thing with the British guy. I identified myself. I told him the people arrested were indeed our people. I identified Flores and the woman with him. I told him, as far as we were concerned, what the aim of the visit was. I told him we wanted our people returned unharmed immediately and in exchange for that – I put that on the table: it was the Easter weekend, there was nobody else available, Kat Liebenberg was hunt-ing, Joffel van der Westhuizen was hunting, even Georg Meiring was out hunting – I said in exchange we would co-operate with him unconditionally about the matter. "You can send people to SA to interrogate Flores and the woman," I said.

'The MI-5 bloke said: "This afternoon I will be talking to London, must I tell them this?" I said yes. I also asked him if we could have access to the tapes. He looked at me blankly and asked: "What tapes are you talking about?" I said: "The tape-recordings made in the hotel room." He said: "No ways. That's nonsense. There are no tapes – but I'll get confirmation from my headquarters before tonight and I'll tell you exactly what the situation is." We agreed not to play games with one another. Later he confirmed to me that there were no tapes whatsoever.

'By that time the thing had been discussed with F.W., Kobie Coetsee, Pik Botha and everyone else. They were all shitting their pants. This was a diplomatic disaster on our hands,' said Thirion. 'I told them: "There are no tapes. There is no proof the operation had anything to do with Dirk Coetzee." That turned out to be the situation, but everyone in the government, including F.W., was told about these non-existent tapes and they were the things that meant there was no way out. It was Scholtz saying this. I proved it to be a lot of bullshit. Then I was warned by senior insiders from NI that they'd have my head on a block. They cre-ated the story that I had an unhealthy relationship with the CIA, with the German BND and with the British, which was utter nonsense. They were putting this story out to De Klerk. I was told – but never confronted – that this was also one of the things that led up to the whole picture,' said Thirion.

Then came the 'Night of the Generals': 'Goldstone raided the premises at a different time and we knew there was a lot of shit coming our way,' said Thirion. 'But Goldstone also went haywire with a lot of accusations that were not true – but nobody was allowed to respond to those accusations. Then at a certain stage I was told because I'd been there a long time, and because I was aware of all the operations I was the person who would have to see the whole Goldstone thing through to its conclusion – whatever that proved to be. It was said by Joffel van der Westhuizen and Kat Liebenberg. He actually said: "We are relying on you to see this thing through."'

A scapegoat? A set-up? 'What else?' asks Thirion. 'What I don't understand up until this day is why I was refused a court martial. I never got an answer from the State President's office – and I addressed my letter to him personally, asking him to subject the whole thing to a legal process. I asked to be court martialled, know-ing that De Klerk is not a military man. I also suggested to him that if it's not a court martial then any other formal legal process, be it civilian or otherwise. I never got an answer. They acknowledged receipt of my letter but I never got an answer. This is something that still eludes me.

'That night [the 'Night of the Generals'] they were down in the Cape. De Klerk was on holiday in Hermanus or somewhere. He was briefed by Pierre Steyn and also got information from Goldstone and when he had the whole picture in front of him he was convinced it was serious and said: "We must act immediately." He met with Pierre Steyn, with Scholtz of NI and maybe also other NI people. He instructed that Kat Liebenberg, Georg Meiring and Joffel van der Westhuizen fly down to Cape Town for a meeting. They had that meeting that day, running through the afternoon, evening and into the night. At about 2 o'clock in the morning it was decided those particular 23 guys had to be out,' said Thirion.

And pressure from the Americans? 'Oh yes. I put this picture together for myself, because there are loose ends here and there. During that night there were phone calls to and from the United States where Roelf Meyer was. He was in contact with the United Nations and the Security Council. F.W. told him the whole story over the phone and the CIA picked it up. And then, according to Meiring, it was agreed that F.W. would allow the lapse of a fortnight or so for [Kat Liebenberg, Meiring and Joffel van der Westhuizen] to get us together and brief us. They had a plan. But the calls during the night were all picked up by the CIA who leaked it to the local press and the next morning when Meiring and the other guys landed in Pretoria it was on the front pages. And there was no turning back.

'I was phoned by Joffel van der Westhuizen that Saturday morning round about 4:30 in the morning and told me to report to Defence HQ as soon as possible. He said it was decided, I had to go,' said Thirion. 'I wanted to know: on what grounds? Van der Westhuizen said there was going to be an overall, broad statement issued about the planning of military coups, the planning of a miltary coup against the present process of negotiations. Also about having been involved in military coups in neighbouring states, arms trafficking over borders, Third Force activities, involvement in right-wing politics and misleading the political leadership and the auditor general. That was the list of things. When I asked him what it was all about he said he couldn't tell me. But I was out.

'I said: "Okay, I can do nothing about it. The State President as Supreme Commander of the Defence Force can decide – but I think I have the right to know." [Van der Westhuizen] said Liebenberg asked him to ask me to do one thing, and that was not to take any action. He said they would take care of me. I replied I didn't want anyone to take care of me but that I thought I should know why I was being fired. He said he couldn't tell me and should he tell me and should I say this to anyone else he would say it was a blatant lie. He said then that the State President was going to issue a press statement which was made at 1 o'clock that Saturday in which all of the accusations were made,' said Thirion.

'I wanted to have a word with Kat Liebenberg. I realised my back wasn't covered, I had no top cover. I realised I was by myself. I wanted to clear up certain things with him, so I asked Van der Westhuizen to ask Liebenberg whether I could see him. I said specifically: "I know he's a busy man, but I only need two minutes." Why I only needed two minutes was because I wanted to say to him: "I wasn't involved, not in my personal capacity nor in any group capacity, in any activities or action that could put the security of the State, or the government, the Defence Force, or Military Intelligence in any sense at risk." That's all I wanted to do. To tell them that. So they didn't have to run around trying to find explanations or wonder what went wrong. That was my reaction. I said to [Van der Westhuizen]: "Apart from General Liebenberg, I want to see the Defence Force Command Council eyeball to eyeball. When they have their next meeting can I have two minutes to say to them: "As my former colleagues and comrades-in-arms, listen guys, no matter what you hear, no matter what you read, here I stand, I can say before God that I wasn't involved in any of these activities."

'I never got an answer,' said Thirion. 'I got tremendous support [from my friends and colleagues]. They said: "We don't believe this nonsense. We've known you long enough." Relatively senior guys in Military Intelligence came to my office. They were all crying, there were tears running freely, and senior guys said to me: "Just tell us to down tools and we will not continue with any work in this headquarters." I said to them: "Listen, there are things larger and more important than we are. What I want from you is to carry on with your work; even better than in the past, do it as professionally as is humanly possible. Walk tall and know that I have never let you down." I said the same to them as I said to Joffel van der Westhuizen that morning: "I want you to tell General Liebenberg and the Minister of Defence that there's no way I'm just going to be fired. I want to be court martialled. I have 30 years of service. I don't want to be protected by anybody and I don't want hand-outs from anybody, but I'm going to carefully check what my rightful pension should be and I want every cent of my gratuity. If I don't get it I'll take the State President to court. I want you to tell them this. I also want you to tell them I'm not just going to disappear, I'm going to walk out of the front door!" I had to go back to the office and clear it out on the Monday – I had to leave straight away. I left on the Wednesday – I told my driver to take my car and to park it in the street outside the front of the Military Intelligence building in Vermeulen Street. I told him to park it right in front of the main entrance. It was around about 1 or 2 o'clock in the daytime. I worked on the 14th floor and I walked down all the floors and walked out of the front door. I told them I would walk out of the front door and not disappear through the back door,' said Thirion.

The effects of his firing and the accusations being bandied about were devastating for Thirion. 'It was severe. It was horrible, just terrible,' he said. 'My son Nico came and stood in front of me and said: "Dad, are you clean?" He was in Standard nine at the time. All I could say was: "It depends what you mean by clean." I didn't know what was coming. What was clean and what was dirty? In December I started drafting a letter to F.W. de Klerk, but I took my time with it. I asked him to initiate a court martial – you can't arrange your own court martial. I said to him I didn't know on what information he'd acted, I didn't know what information he had and that did not really matter to me. What mattered was that I was not being given the chance of having it put to trial. He never acknowledged. So then I went through other channels and I once saw De Klerk in his office at my request. By that time he was Deputy President. We went over the whole thing and I said to him that according to the law I could no longer be court martialled but I could still go through a formal trial. He said he wouldn't do that and wouldn't allow it.

'[De Klerk] said to me that that very week Mandela had signed the law implementing the Truth Commission and that was my solution. He said he would raise the matter with the TRC so it could be investigated. What I didn't know then – because I wasn't aware of their existence – was there were documents drawn up as a follow-up to investigations by the police, by the office of the Attorney-General and the military, and all of these investigations led to one conclusion that was documented: there were no grounds for any action against me. De Klerk had seen those documents, but he never said anything to me, nor did he ever apologise. I got to know about them through the Truth Commission. I did not apply for amnesty. I had no reason whatsoever to do so and no charges have ever been brought against me,' said Thirion. 'Roelf Meyer once saw me and said what happened was an injustice. He said it to me personally but not publicly. He said it very quietly but he also said: "If you want me to testify, I'm available." But that was after he'd had his political fall-out with De Klerk.'

Thirion refused to let the matter die. He instituted legal action against De Klerk. 'I made it clear to his advocates I wasn't suing him for money,' he said. 'I just wanted my name cleared. They came with an offer that he was prepared to make a statement in writing and in public. They made suggestions as to what the statement would look like and said I could have the final say in the statement. The suggestions were all about what a nice guy I was, how good a soldier I was, how loyal I was. I said: "That's not what I want and I don't want an excuse from him. What I want is for him to say that he acted on unconfirmed information, that I asked him to be court martialled and that was not done and that he never gave me an answer." I also wanted him to state that there were investigations by the Attorney-General's office, the police and the Defence Force and that it was reported back to him that there were no grounds for action against me. That was it. I wanted that written and signed by him and signed by his advocates and that I got. I have a copy of which I photocopied and gave to my children. I also sent it with a letter to the Defence Force saying I wanted it placed on my file in the archives,' said Thirion.

De Klerk's statement, drafted by his advocates but signed by him, reads as follows: 'The former State President, Mr F.W. de Klerk, hereby gives notice that he had great understanding of the stress General Thirion and his family must have undergone and for his desire to be absolved of any blame with respect to malpractices and unacceptable behaviour. In support he would like the following attachments to be placed on record:

1. I was at no stage of the opinion that Genl Thirion was personally involved in any serious malpractices or crimes. No direct allegations or information indicating such was ever presented to me. Consequently in all pronouncements I made with regard to the Steyn report, whether orally or in writing, I never had the intention of accusing Genl Thirion of being personally involved in any malpractices. In the event of readers, despite the care I took in formulating my book, drawing such a conclusion that would be incorrect.

2. At all times I regarded Genl Thirion as an honest man and believe his retirement was part of the drastic re-organisation of the Defence Force's intelligence activities which in my opinion was necessary as a result of information uncovered by the Goldstone Commission and the subsequent investigations of Genl Pierre Steyn. The list of names was compiled at my instruction but without my participation. I was under the impression that Genl Thirion was included because the post he held was part of the command structure that was affected by the intervention that I ordered.

3. I am not aware of any evidence in subsequent investigations by government institutions, commissions or anything else that in any way implicates Genl

Thirion in unacceptable actions. I am aware that Genl Thirion attempted to subject himself to a military judicial process. Despite the fact that I was not directly involved with this, I am of the opinion that the circumstances would be inappropriate because as to the best of my knowledge no evidence of any sort whatsoever was produced that would justify such a legal process.

4. In as much as an erroneous impression may have been created that Genl Thirion was guilty of any malpractice or crime as a result of those occurrences and what was written and said, that would be incorrect and unfair to him.'

'De Klerk never came back and said he was wrong,' said General Meiring. 'Never. No charge was ever brought against a single individual, because it was a lot of shit. For that I'll never forgive him. I felt fucking terrible having to tell these people this. They were my friends but they heard this not from me. For example, Ferdie van Wyk heard about it while travelling through the Karoo on his motorcycle. He phoned me from Cradock or somewhere. I said: "Ferdie, come home, I'll tell you about it." It was terrible. It was the worst experience of my career. I went around the country saving De Klerk's bacon because the blokes were up in arms. I went to every Command and specifically explained what happened. I told them how Steyn got this thing wrong, how it was all wrong information; how the politicians had already made up their minds and how it was better for us to get these people out and to give them all the benefits possible because he would discharge them anyway and then they'd end up getting nothing. I wrote letters to all of them telling them there was nothing against them.'

There is no doubt the 'Night of the Generals' caused extreme bitterness in the SADF and between many of the senior officers themselves. 'Steyn did this because he wanted to become Chief of the Defence Force,' said Meiring. 'He wanted to get Liebenberg and myself out of the way and figured he'd be in like Flint. (Steyn later took up the new post of Secretary of Defence under the ANC. At the time of writing he worked for the SA Mint.)

'I have very good relations with General Meiring,' said Thirion. 'I still wanted to sort things out with General Liebenberg, but he passed away. When I saw General Liebenberg afterwards, in a completely different situation – I was quoted in the press on the integration of the SADF and MK, and he said he needed to see me. That was six months after I'd left. I went to see him at the Military Intelligence College. I had an idea it was about the newspaper article, so I took out the clipping and highlighted what I'd said. When I got there he asked how I was. I said to him: "General, it's strange how now, six months later, you ask how

I am. I am not well. I am healthy but I am not well." I didn't ask him how he was. Then he said to me: "I see you've spoken to the press." I said: "Yes, not by my initiative: they asked me questions and I gave them my opinion. I told them about the lies and the fact the generals and the politicians did not speak with the same voice. Don't tell the troops on the parade-ground there is not going to be an integration process and then on Monday they read about meetings between generals and senior MK leaders," I said. He said it was very unfortunate that was my viewpoint and that the whole Defence Force had the greatest respect for me but that I should be very careful I didn't lose that respect. I replied: "That's what I said, and I stand by it. I have nothing else to say."

'In the beginning I asked him if he minded me putting our conversation on tape. He asked if it was really necessary, and I said: "Not from my point of view – I can just as well leave it, but I know you will have it taped anyway." I wanted him to know I knew the room was bugged. Then he said: "Hell, you've changed. You're strange [now]." He vaguely tried to tell me there was nothing he could do down in the Cape. I said: "I think the opportunity to tell me that was six months ago. When I asked to see you for only two minutes you never answered me. Now you come and ask me how I am." I stood up and said: "General, I wish you luck with your work. You have a difficult task ahead. May God bless you." Then I saluted him and he started crying. I then left.

'One day he came to *Die Werf* to have a meal here. The people in the front said to me: "Do you know who's coming to have a meal here? How must we handle it?" I said: "As professionally and friendly as possible." I was working in the kitchen that day, so I could only go out to his table much later – they were having desserts – to say hello to him and to ask if everything was okay. But it was strictly on a professional basis and his tears once again started and I just left.

'It was a sad part of my life,' said Thirion. 'As far as I'm concerned I was a good soldier. I was well respected by my subordinates. I tried to treat them as well as possible. General Geldenhuys always told us "look down" – take care of the people under you. That I tried to do to the best of my ability. I served the government of the day and I served the country unconditionally and I was respected internationally.'

12

THE MILITARY ON TRIAL

There were more names listed in the Steyn report than just those of the officers fired by De Klerk. 'Only later, when I was Chief of the SADF and got to see aspects of the Steyn report, did I see that Kat Liebenberg and I were also named,' said General Meiring. 'Supposedly as Chief of the Army I was planning a coup to overthrow the government. The reason they said this was because at the time we were studying and planning for different scenarios [in the run-up to the election]. We believed the worst case scenario for the stability of the country was if the whole process was derailed, and that could happen from two sides, the left or the right. We knew we had to make sure we got information so we could substantiate or get early warning that something was going to happen – and if it happened we had to have a plan about what we'd do. We'd take control of the main centres. Say, for example, if the right wing attempted a coup, we needed to know exactly where the town hall is, where the telephone exchange is, where the water supply is, etc., so we could guard that and prevent them from taking it over.

'We needed to know where all the key points were,' Meiring explained. 'We made contingency plans in the event of something like that happening, contingency plans to act against the right or the left. Steyn and NI said we were planning a coup. Of course that's a similar type of plan. If we wanted to do it we could have done it, but it's the old story – once you've caught the bus what do you do with it? It wouldn't have been difficult to carry out a coup. We could have done it in a morning. Because of the decentralisation of the SADF you could be in command before anyone knew what was going on. But the main thing was it never even entered our minds. In fact, since the previous year, in the process of time we had a lot of footwork going on where we tried to have discussions with the other political role players, who were also quasi-military role players, or thought themselves to be – the General Viljoens of this world, the Ferdi Hartzenbergs, the Buthelezis. Everyone had an axe to grind and was a major player in this thing and from time to time threatened to pull out and go to war. The Zulus were trying to arm themselves, the far right were trying to arm themselves, and I had to talk to a lot of them. From the PAC right through to the CP at the time. I never spoke to Eugene Terre'Blanche, because he was a non-entity. But we were really very seriously trying to let the people see the wisdom of working together and not pulling out of this whole thing. We had these contingency plans at the time and I told many of them: "If you are really going to do what you say you are going to do, we'll have to stop you." I even had to say that to Constand Viljoen. He said he understood and for a long time we discussed it. We never antagonised one another, but we were very clear in understanding what we actually meant. When he phoned me one time and said he was going to go along with the elections I was really glad. I said it seems praying really helps.'

Would Meiring really have been prepared to tackle Viljoen head-on if Viljoen had decided to take up arms at the time? 'Yes, sure, because there was no wisdom in doing it,' Meiring said. As it turned out, Viljoen and some of his followers did commit a few sporadic acts of sabotage. 'I applied for amnesty for my role in the Afrikaner Volksfront which was a reactionary movement in the 1993/94 situation,' said Viljoen. 'I had to. Unless I applied for amnesty my people lower down in the organisation would not be able to. One of the conditions of amnesty was that the actions had to be part of a bigger political plan, and in my case it was. We did blow up certain pylons and ANC offices and all that. That was a contravention of the law. We have not been granted amnesty yet. As a matter of fact I doubt that they will. They will come with the argument that I cannot apply for a general amnesty – I'm too generalised in my application because I could not furnish the names. I would send out an order saying: "I want electric pylons to be blown up." Who blew them I don't know. I never knew who the people were. That would be foolish. The purpose of those operations was to apply pressure on the De Klerk–ANC government in order to get them to make concessions regarding Afrikaner self-determination, and I think some good came of it, because eventually in the negotiations for the new constitution in 1996 we succeeded in getting some concessions from the ANC and I'm sure the whole negotiation process would not have been as well carried out in 1993/1994 had it not been for the military potential that we had.'

But according to Viljoen, his organisation never considered a full-blown coup. 'My opinion was that a coup would not have been successful because of the division of people within the country,' he said. 'Especially because some people frantically believed in De Klerk's and Mandela's attitudes – and because of the personality of Mandela. People would say this was the last hope of finding a peaceful resolution for South Africa. So a very large portion of the Defence Force would not have accepted a coup. I think the general spirit of expectation in the country was against the concept of a coup. For a coup you need some sort of great dissatisfaction. You have to have some support. That was part of my problem in 1994. I really did have a very lightly armed but a very big organisation ready and I could have stirred up things in 1994 – but for what purpose? I don't think any action from my side would have resulted in a major part of the Defence Force siding with me. That would have led to a "brother against brother" war within the Defence Force. And because of my loyalty towards the Defence Force I said I cannot do this. I have no regrets that I didn't go for the war, because my arguments were very good and I studied this thing very carefully. Up until today history has proved my approach was the right one. What I am very sorry about, is the fact I have lost my "pistol".

'In 1994 when I decided not to wage war a very large portion of my forces disintegrated, and that was not part of our agreement. We used to plan for what we called a "thick arrow" (meaning one big operation), or a "thin arrow" (meaning the kind of IRA situation that we could easily develop in South Africa). When the thick arrow collapsed and I said it was senseless to wage war at that stage, then the potential collapsed and with that also the thin arrow. The thin arrow was the potential that I regarded at that stage as most applicable. I don't regret the decision, but maybe I should say give me another five years then I'll tell you whether I regret it or not, because the situation in politics doesn't change that quickly and whether I made the right or wrong decision may only come out in another five or 10 years. Things in South Africa might take a turn like that in Zimbabwe: then I would certainly regret it.'

Deciding to get involved in the process and work within the system has left Viljoen with some wounds. There are people who see him as a traitor to the Afrikaner cause. 'Remember, when I got involved in politics in 1993 I was asked to give strategic guidance to the Afrikaner people,' he said. 'At that stage all the political parties were regarded by the Afrikaner people as being sterile. I then worked on a strategy – political, military, economic and propaganda. For nine months we worked flat out on this, also preparing the military strategy itself. During the planning, however, I always said: "I may be preparing for a military option but I will decide whether and if the time is right to launch an offensive." I always said I was prepared to wage a war and was prepared to sacrifice lives if I regarded that as the only and last possibility.

'And then in 1994 when eventually I decided the time was not ripe for a war politically I was ostracised by, among others, Ferdi Hartzenberg and the Conservative Party. Some of them called me a traitor because they somehow thought I was in a position to keep the old South Africa going. That was never my intention. It would have been foolish for me to try to keep the old South Africa standing,' Viljoen explained. 'I would say I lost about half of my support. But what I lost on the one side I gained on the other. This is how politics works. The point is, I lost my pistol, and had the military potential of Viljoen not disintegrated, I would have achieved much more politically than that which I have achieved up until now. It's true that people like Ferdi Hartzenberg have largely disappeared, but it's also true that we [the Freedom Front, the party that Viljoen led] can't say we've done extremely well. But it's like participating in boxing. You've got to get into the ring or you're not in the fight. By staying outside you're a coward.'

Malan, too, had approaches to help organise a coup. 'A lot of people say to me: "You had a lot of power." But that's not the way you approach it. You're there as part of a team, you're serving the leader – and now they expect you to get rid of the leader and get rid of the team and take over. My whole way of thinking is that you serve the government of the day and that this is a democratic country,' Malan explains. 'If you want to change it you use the ballot box. You don't change it through military might. I had a lot of approaches from South Africans living in South Africa, saying: "We'll supply the money, you do the coup." My reply was always: "Are you trying to escape from the present situation by arranging a coup and are you then sure you'll accept the new situation or are you just trying to find an escape route? Forget it. Do it through the ballot box."'

The approaches, according to Malan, were usually South African business people. Some were well known, but none, he stressed, came from the ranks of the really influential or top business people. 'The first approach was almost always jokingly,' said Malan. 'They did it light-heartedly to test the water – once you've tested the water you can get serious. So they always tested the water first. I still maintain the military I belonged to would accept my way of thinking and would never be part of a coup. You might find the odd person talking about it but in his heart of hearts wouldn't say: "Let's do it."'

That may have been so, but why did the lower-ranking members of the SADF not try to organise something? After all, they would have felt threatened and wouldn't have had access to the new politicians or the overall picture. Malan is very clear on that, although his views on the ability of the former SADF to organise a coup d'état differ radically from those expressed by General Meiring. 'The prospect of losing their jobs was at that stage just theory,' he said. 'When you actually lose your job, that's the time you know it's real and has happened. However, I also think, generally speaking, South Africans are not inclined to do something like that. It's not our nature. We're too open. But with the way the Defence Force was organised it was not something that could have been easily done ... with a Citizen Force and a Commando system that had a completely different way of thinking to that of the Permanent Force ... the Permanent Force would be loyal to the system, but a Commando Force, because it is decentralised, doesn't have a unified type of thinking. So how would you start it? It would have been difficult to do it. If a coup was planned in the Permanent Force it would have been easily or at least more readily organised, but forget about it in the Citizen Force or Commando Force. Of course, the system of decentralisation also worked against the possibility of a coup. We could have brought in Citizen or Commando Force units from other areas to put down a coup,' said Malan.

But in the end, the simple fact is that South Africa was able to negotiate a settlement and have a democratic election because the SADF was there. It was they who kept the lid on everyone, left or right, who wanted to derail the process. Before the election Meiring made sure everyone knew they were playing with fire. 'I warned everyone before the election: *"As julle 'n ding gaan doen gaan ons julle opvok: julle moet pasop!"* [If you're going to do something, we'll fuck you up: watch out!] he said. 'So everybody knew the success and stability was as a result of this.' The fact he was on the receiving end of accusations about plotting a coup still rankles. 'I mean, I saved the bloody country – I didn't "coup" it! Then they come and say I was going to instigate a coup! My fuck, man!'

In 1995 General Magnus Malan and 19 other security force members, including General Jannie Geldenhuys and General Kat Liebenberg, were arrested and charged with a variety of offences, including murder. The case revolved around an operation code-named Marion. News reports claim that the name was a shortened version of the word 'marionette', a word reported to have been repeatedly used in secret State Security Council documents at the time when referring to the government's relationship with Zulu leader, Mangosuthu Buthelezi.

Operation Marion revolved around the training of 200 Inkatha supporters at a base in the Caprivi in South West Africa in 1985. These men, according to Malan, were trained as a protection unit for Chief Buthelezi, who had broken alliance with the ANC and become embroiled in increasing violence in the province. The men were given military training and then returned to KwaZulu-Natal where it appears some became involved in attacks against civilians who either were or were believed to be ANC supporters.

On 19 December 1985, a former Military Intelligence operator, Captain J.P. Opperman, led a group of 10 of the trainees in a murderous attack in a village in KwaMakutha. Thirteen women and children were slaughtered. He claimed the attack was part of the aims and objectives of Operation Marion and alleged Malan had knowledge of the planning of the attack. In return for his testimony he was given immunity and put on the witness protection programme. Malan was arrested and charged with murder. 'They phoned me and said that Georg Meiring wanted to see me and could I come to his office,' said Malan. 'Somebody said: "You're going to be arrested," to which I replied: "Forget about it!" There were about 10 or 12 people there and I knew almost everybody. Georg said: "You'll be arrested on Wednesday" – this was on the Friday. He said: "We've got to play it down, keep quiet about it. It'll appear in the newspapers when you are arrested and there'll be an announcement."

'It was quite a shock and I said: "I'm sorry, but this is going to be in the Sunday newspapers. I warn you now I'm going to break the news." I went to *Rapport* and told them I was going to be arrested. On the day concerned I reported to the authorities so I could be arrested. They tried to keep it quiet so we were taken to the Police College (rather than a charge office) where our fingerprints were taken and then they took us to Durban where we appeared in the local magistrate's court before it was referred to the Supreme Court,' said Malan. 'It wasn't so much a traumatic experience for me as it was for my family. They didn't know what was going on. When we saw the so-called evidence, we knew what was going on. They were working on perceptions. They had the perception of certain words. They saw "offensive" as meaning "kill" or "attack". In my definition "offensive" is something totally different. "Offensive" means keeping the initiative. There are a lot of things you have to do to keep the initiative. You can defend, you can attack … but they saw it as killing. When they saw the word "offensive" they said it meant killing certain people. They believed those who testified against us, the state witnesses,' said Malan. 'But strangely they never questioned me before I was arrested.

'It was a political thing,' Malan explains. 'The ANC had a fantastic strategy. This was the first step. They had the minutes of the State Security Council where the Defence Force was instructed to train people as a kind of security guard for Buthelezi. They read into that something more – a hit team – and connected all the people there. There were a lot of heads of department there. This was an opening to eliminate any of the previous government before the election. Secondly, they had a strategy – and I thought it was marvellous – they said to themselves (and they have a tremendous support base, from the militant left even to a kind of rightish approach), if we can keep this support base together until the 1999 elections then we will have succeeded in passing all the Acts through Parliament that will create an ANC culture in South Africa. Then if there was a break-up within the ANC, which could happen, they would have established themselves and could continue governing the country or people with the same type of ideas. There could be a sort of regrouping of political parties, but the ANC would then be here for ever and ever,' said Malan.

'The case against us was the first step to nullify the previous government. The other step took place simultaneously. You can see now the cracks that are appearing from grassroots up to a higher level, left to right. It won't happen immediately. It'll happen in a couple of years. But that's their strategy, and they've done it. They believed to such an extent in their political strategy that McNally, the Attorney-General of Natal, didn't want to prosecute but was called in because there was an assistant prosecutor there – I've forgotten his name now – who went to the politicians and said: "We can catch them now." They wanted to know from McNally why he wasn't prosecuting us. He said: "I haven't got a case against them." They told him: "You will prosecute and you will take this assistant prosecutor back." So he was forced, he had to prosecute.

'The head of the Scorpions is a chap called Dutton, he was the police [investigating] officer. You should go and read what the Judge said to Dutton, because he tried to frame us. He tried to frame us on the Iscor situation – that's apparently where we'd taken the rifles and melted them. He said he'd been there and there's no security – because we said if we had done it [taken the rifles to Iscor] we'd have had to pass through security and they'd have records of us having done so. But he said he was there, and there was no security. He was testifying about the present situation. We were talking about 10 years ago. He did it purposely. The Judge was very annoyed. My question is: how can that man become the head of such a sensitive department?' said Malan. In fact, Judge Jan Hugo in his judgment said that former Military Intelligence operative Captain J.P. Opperman's evidence was often contradictory, improbable or absurd. He criticised the State's other key witness, André Cloete, describing him as 'nondescript … shabbily dressed … and weak'. Judge Hugo also described the main investigator in the trial, Colonel Frank Dutton, as a 'self-satisfied witness' who gave irrelevant testimony.

'All of the politicians, with the exception of Vlok and P.W., ran for cover,' said Malan. 'F.W. and I have never been house friends. I haven't seen him since. I don't know what his attitude is towards me. There was support prior to the trial. They came here and said: "Good luck to you." But after the evidence [started to come out] they ran – and remember this was a political set-up – there were elections [coming up]: our arrest was announced at the beginning of November, the [municipal] elections were in December, but KZN elections were postponed until March and our court case started in February. I made a statement to this effect in the newspapers. Mandela replied and said it was unfortunate I drew that conclusion but that wasn't the [government's] intention.'

Though Malan refuses to comment on this, people close to him say he went to see Mandela and had dinner with him. Mandela was apparently under pressure to grant Malan amnesty – something the former Defence Minister did not want. 'He told the President his conscience was clear and that the perpetrators of the violence in KwaZulu had to be brought to book. He was confident to face the courts,' said the close colleague. The story appears to be borne out by former State President F.W. de Klerk, who wrote: 'I had to be careful to avoid the perception that I wished to interfere with the normal process of the law. I nevertheless felt obliged to come to the defence of General Malan and the senior officers of the old SADF who had served during my presidency. Accordingly Roelf Meyer and I discussed the matter one evening with President Mandela at his home in Johannesburg. He had called Mr Sidney Mufamadi, the Minister of Law and Order, to be present during the discussion. I recall Mufamadi kicked off his shoes and was barefoot throughout the meeting. I was convinced the case would not result in a guilty verdict and felt that taking the matter to court would be a travesty of justice. However, my ability to pursue the matter was also limited by Magnus Malan's insistence that I should not attempt to stop the prosecution. He said he preferred to put his case in court so that he could expose the ANC.'

Malan was always confident that he would be acquitted. 'I contacted the Foreign Press Association and said I was prepared to address them,' he said. 'They arranged a breakfast. There were about 80 of them and even my so-called friend Alastair Sparks was there trying to feed them with all the poison he could. I addressed them for an hour, then said they could ask me any questions they liked. If I'd been involved in anything I would have been worried about ending up in jail but the pressure was being on television and in the newspapers daily. It was fantastic to watch the seven teams of lawyers at work – they were some of the most brilliant people I've ever seen. In the end I was very emotional when the Judge said: "Not guilty." It was a very, very positive not guilty he gave us.

'Before the trial I spoke to the lawyers of the various teams – we were sub-divided, you see – I said to them: "Gentlemen, I don't want to get out of this case, I want 20 people out of it. So please don't go for each others' clients. All 20 of us have to get out of here. If one is found guilty then I'm afraid we've failed in this court case." They worked as a team. So I wasn't worried. After July you could see the definitions like: "being offensive" and so forth started falling into place. You could see when our side started testifying the positiveness coming through. You could see the lies and differences of the state witnesses and how the police did things they shouldn't have. All those things came forward,' said Malan. 'When you get arrested for 13 murders of innocent people, hell, it's scary. I was accused number 19, but my friends stuck with me 100 per cent. I had the military and the generals with me. It was the top echelon involved, and we kept the military with us. We had meetings with them and reported back, reported our strategy. So we had the "family" with us.'

On 11 October 1996 Malan and the other senior SADF officers were acquitted, but despite the court's findings the media and many others failed to believe that the generals were innocent. The TRC was one of the most sceptical. Its report reads as follows: 'Although the accused were acquitted, the Supreme Court found that Inkatha members trained by the SADF in the Caprivi were responsible for the massacre and that the two state witnesses, being members of the SADF Military Intelligence, were directly involved in planning and execution of the operation. The court was not able to find who had provided backing for the attack.

' ... Witnesses who did not testify in the 1996 criminal trial testified before the hearing, and the Commission has made a comprehensive finding on the Caprivi trainee project (see Volume Five). In brief, the Commission found that the South African government provided Inkatha with a hit squad, and provided training, financial and logistical management for the project. Further, the Commission found that accountability for the human rights violations that flowed from the establishment of the hit squad lay with twenty-two people from the State Security Council, Military Intelligence, Inkatha and the KZP.

'The Commission finds that in 1986, the SADF conspired with Inkatha to provide the latter with a covert, offensive paramilitary unit (or "hit squad") to be deployed illegally against persons and organisations perceived to be opposed to both the South African government and Inkatha. The SADF provided training, financial and logistical management and behind-the-scenes supervision of the trainees, who were trained by the Special Forces unit of the SADF in the Caprivi Strip. The Commission finds furthermore that the deployment of the paramilitary unit in KwaZulu led to gross violations of human rights, including killing, attempted killing and severe ill treatment.

'The Commission finds the following people, among others, accountable for such violations: Mr P.W. Botha, General Magnus Malan, Chief Mangosuthu Buthelezi, Mr M.Z. Khumalo, Mr Pieter Groenewald, Vice Admiral Andries Putter, Mr Louis Botha, Mr Cornelius van Niekerk and Mr Mike van den Berg.'

To the generals it was just another example of TRC bias. They responded to the TRC findings in an additional submission to the TRC in which they said: 'The alacrity with which the TRC is prepared to accept [the 200 Caprivi trainees] are a hit squad is astonishing ... Although the TRC appears to be timorous to come out and say so directly, the result is the following: Genl Malan sold the concept of a hit squad to Buthelezi, who accepted without demur. Genl Malan then went to the State President and reported his ghastly deed. Instead of being shocked at the horrible turn of events, the State President miraculously turned into a demon and applauded what had been accomplished. These findings are so incongruous that they hardly merit a reply.

'In a thoughtless stroke of a pen these men are relegated to the ranks of murderous criminals. Is it really to be believed that these men of high position and apparent integrity were prepared to place their futures, nay, their very lives in the hands of one Buthelezi and 200 totally unknown uncontrolled and uncontrollable Zulus? This supposition merely has to be stated to be rejected out of hand. And what of Buthelezi? Without any justification at all he is also labelled a conspirator in this ghastly scheme. Could he conceivably have been bona fide? The TRC doesn't even consider the possibility ... The uncontested evidence is that the trainees received the same counter-insurgency military training as countless thousands of other trainees. Why the former should become a hit squad, and the latter not, is not considered or explained.'

The simple fact is that Judge Hugo found that the training was lawful. What the TRC also failed to note was that the Caprivians were never equipped with weapons or ammunition by the SADF. 'It is therefore apparent that the TRC steadfastly refuses to have regard to any evidence of circumstances which may conflict with or detract from the desired result,' the former SADF generals' response reads. 'Unrelated matters are cast into a pot and the desired result is extracted. It becomes plain that the TRC has not considered the matter at all. It rather appears that the TRC has arrived at a finding which appears to be attractive to it.'

The SADF seems to have a point. There are many who believe the TRC had decided on the guilt of the SADF long before the first witness appeared before the Commission. Its co-chairman, Dr Alex Boraine, has long been considered anti-SADF – as were the vast majority of its members. Archbishop Desmond Tutu, Chairman of the Truth Commission, is quoted in an article that appeared in *The Citizen* of 12 October 1996 – shortly after Malan was acquitted – as having said: 'The Court has weighed up the evidence and the accused have been found not guilty, and we would certainly not quarrel with its decision. But the outcome of the proceedings demonstrated our conviction that the processes of the commission offer a better prospect of establishing the truth about our past than the criminal trials ... The commission has not yet decided whether it will conduct its own investigation into the issues raised in the Malan trial. But as with any other investigation, if we were to go ahead we would not hesitate to invite or subpoena those involved in this trial, including those who have been acquitted.'

There are many examples of TRC bias against the SADF:

- The TRC agreed that the former SADF members could make a second presentation to the Commission on 2 September 1997. Shortly before that date the TRC decided to cancel the presentation and instead have a 'Forces Hearing' on 8 October, during which time the second submission could be made. The SANDF Nodal Point (the group co-ordinating the submissions by the former SADF members) was later informed by the TRC that only one hour would be allowed for the formal prepared presentation. General Constand Viljoen was elected to make the presentation, but he was constantly interrupted by Boraine to remind him he had to confine himself to one hour. During the presentation it was obvious some of the commissioners were not at all interested in the proceedings – one of them slept and was repeatedly photographed by a media photographer while doing so.
- At the 'Forces Hearing' in Cape Town in October 1997 an Apla official testified that it was Apla policy to steal and rob, as these actions were legitimised as being mere repossession. These occurrences were not listed and investigated and the incidents of murder, maiming and injury are not recorded. This was in sharp contrast to the aggressive and hostile questioning of the SADF members.

In fact one commissioner, the head of the Investigative Unit of the TRC, formerly defended Apla criminals in court and warmly called them 'comrades' when they appeared before the TRC.

- The TRC has done little to investigate murders committed in the name of a 'just war' – the almost 600 necklacings and torchings, the damage or destruction to some 7 000 private homes carried out in support of the liberation movements.

In January 1998 the SADF Contact Bureau, comprising a panel of the three former Chiefs of the SADF, generals Malan, Viljoen and Geldenhuys, as well as Major General Dirk Marais and WO1 Jan Holliday, submitted a complaint to the Public Protector in which they complained about the TRC's apparent reluctance to pursue the investigation of ANC punishment camps. The TRC replied on 24 April 1998 saying it was not opportune to reply to the Contact Bureau's observations in detail at that stage as they were busy drafting a response to the complaint lodged with the Public Protector. It was the first shot fired in what appeared to be a salvo of delaying tactics. By June the TRC had still not replied, despite requests to do so by the Contact Bureau. This was then followed by a harshly worded letter dated 15 July 1998 from the Committee's chairman, Archbishop Desmond Tutu, who wrote: 'Let me make it quite clear that the TRC has not sought to ignore or cover up any violations that happened in the ANC camps. I would hope that people would stop making opportunistic political capital and scoring points when we should all be striving to engage seriously in the process of healing our land through getting to the truth and so advancing reconciliation. In Johannesburg Mr Mandela attended one of our Human Rights Violations Committee hearings and he arrived just as a witness was testifying about alleged violations he suffered in the ANC camps. We didn't stop him. We should have if we were ANC lackeys, because his tirade was an embarrassment to the President of South Africa and of the ANC as he then was … I hope you will, like a reasonable person, concede that where there is pressure for time, we have enough evidence, oral and written, to make findings about violations in the ANC camps and you will desist from suggesting that no hearing has been held.'

On 29 July 1998 the Public Prosecutor informed the Contact Bureau that the TRC's response had once again been delayed as a result of the chemical and biological warfare hearing relating to the SADF, 'which might be relevant to the reaction by the TRC regarding the issues you have raised. However, the TRC has indicated its response will be soon.' On 19 September 1998 the former Chiefs of the SADF once again asked for a response from the TRC and once again nothing happened, except that the TRC's final report was released 'without any note-worthy response to our "Assessment" or the "Complaints" except for a few humiliating references to the efforts by the Contact Bureau'. According to the generals the TRC report is littered with inaccuracies and unsubstantiated allegations from unreliable sources. They still want to know:

- Who was the Military Intelligence member who was in Kosi Bay, who alleged that they all thought: 'This is it, fuck the kaffirs, this is the time to sort them out'? Who were the 'we' he claimed to quote?
- Who was the faceless Military Intelligence operative quoted regarding train violence, taxi wars, Boipatong and the creation of anarchy? Why was his evidence accepted for inclusion in the report without any further substantiating evidence or examination?

Perhaps the most blatant example of including unsubstantiated and uninvestigated evidence in the report is the case of the amnesty submission of SADF conscript Kevin Hall. The extract from the TRC final report reads: 'In an amnesty application, SADF conscript Mr Kevin Hall … provides an insight into the brutal nature of the conflict with Swapo as well as the routine use of torture. In May/June 1975, he was stationed at the Mapungeerela base in northern South West Africa. He recounts an incident where he was sent out on a seven-day patrol with instructions "to eliminate or arrest any terrorists". On the first night of the patrol, the group was "attacked by unknown forces and came under heavy gun-fire". A lengthy gunfight ensued. In the morning, several bodies were discovered, as well as three badly wounded combatants. According to Hall: "I realised that none of them could survive and to save them any further suffering I shot and killed the three of them. When I shot them, I turned my head away as I could not bear their suffering any more." Hall's action in killing the three was a gross violation of human rights for which he applied for amnesty. His commanding officer, whom he names but whom the Commission cannot identify as he has not applied for amnesty, is likewise accountable. So too is the command structure of the SADF at the time.

'A day or two later, while on the same patrol, the group came across four unarmed "terrorists" and arrested them. On their return to base, the four were placed in a hole in the centre of the base "approximately eight foot square by about seven foot deep" which served as a place of safekeeping of all arrested terrorists. They were the only ones in the hole. "Whilst I was guarding them some of the troops poured boiling water over their heads; another troop of whom I cannot remember the name jumped into the hole and cut off the left ear and centre finger of the right hand of one of the [still-living] prisoners."'

Did Hall have an axe to grind with the SADF? You bet he did. According to his personal file, Hall did his basic training at D Coy, 2 SAI BN, Walvis Bay, during the period 7 January to 14 March 1975. He served at the Equestrian Centre, Potchefstroom, from 17 March 1975 until completion of his one-year military service on 6 January 1976. He joined the Pogietersrus Commando in April 1976, where he attended a number of camps as a member of the Citizen Force, including five one-month camps in the Northern Transvaal border area, and one three-month camp at Sector 20 (Kavango) in the north-eastern area of SWA/Nambia during the period 19 August to 7 November 1982.

Hall's service record reveals long stints of light duty/hospitalisation, starting during basic training and continuing when he was a member of the Potgietersrus Commando, and poor training results:

- he failed his theoretical tests and practical weapon practices during basic training;
- he failed his basic equestrian course (24 March to 2 May 1975) and came last in a group of 49 students (he subsequently qualified as a trainer of horses); and
- he failed all practical progress weapon tests during his Citizen Force camps.

It also reveals a questionable disciplinary record. Descriptions regarding Hall's behaviour varied from 'not trying his best' to 'average'. He was convicted on two charges under the Military Disciplinary Code, namely being absent without leave and failing to comply with a lawful command at the Equestrian Centre. While serving at the Potgietersrus Commando, he received a written cautionary note after failing to attend compulsory shooting exercises.

The simple fact is that Rifleman Kevin Hall, border-fighter-wannabe, never served on the border in 1975. A border service record completed by Hall himself also makes no mention of such a stint of border duty. Added to that small detail, he forgot to mention to the TRC Commissioners that:

- No incident such as the one described by Hall took place anywhere on the border in 1975.
- Mapungeerela base never existed.
- If the incident Hall described had taken place it would have established a record for Sector 20 and would undoubtedly have been reported in the media.
- Captured insurgents, particularly the wounded, were the most valuable

sources of information. The killing of wounded as described by Hall would have resulted in severe disciplinary steps against him and his superiors.

- Hall's patrol would have been replenished or withdrawn after such a contact. The incident would almost certainly have been exploited for propaganda purposes by the SADF.
- Captured insurgents were never kept in holes in the ground but rather were evacuated to the Sector HQ for secondary phase questioning by intelligence experts. This would have been done as a matter of urgency to assist in follow-up operations.

The truth is that Rifleman Hall would never have been considered suitable to serve in a position of authority. A national serviceman rifleman (the lowest rank possible) able to make a unilateral decision like that? I think not!

13

A NEW SOUTH AFRICAN
NATIONAL DEFENCE FORCE

With the unbanning of the ANC and other liberation movements, negotiations towards a new democratic government and a new defence force began in earnest. Once again the military was asked to step into the breach. 'When I took over from Kat Liebenberg [as Chief of the SADF] at the end of October 1993, he'd started a process that began around February of that year,' said General Meiring. 'The Codesa negotiations appeared to be deadlocked. The two main parties couldn't reach an agreement, so he tried to resolve that by offering to talk to MK. In April that year he, myself as Chief of the Army, James Kriel, who was chief of the Air Force, Joffel van der Westhuizen, who was then Chief of Staff of Intelligence, and a few staff officers went down to Cape Town to Admiralty House where we spoke for the first time to the ANC. Joe Modise and Ronnie Kasrils were there, as was Mathews Phosa. Their legal boffin was there looking after Modise and a few others. We started to talk there, to clear the air, to see if this thing could lead to some solution that we could reach together. These talks went both badly and well from time to time – they almost followed the Codesa pattern,' said Meiring.

What was it like talking to people who'd been their sworn enemies? 'If you remember correctly, we never actually fought the ANC,' said Meiring. 'We as the military never really fought with them. There was the odd occasion where we bombed a place in Maputo and a base near Lusaka, but we never fought them in battle. They were hit and run, they came and placed mines and they were really terrorists at the time in that they instigated terror amongst the black population, more than anything else, and planted the odd mine and so on. So we actually assisted the police in many cases in maintaining law and order, more than anything else. We had a good intelligence situation about them, but there was no occasion like when we fought Swapo. It wasn't the same thing as meeting with Swapo.

'With [the ANC] we had an open mind. We had the mindset – okay, this is going to happen, so let's go and talk to them. Kat was instigating and we were towing along. It was strange, but it wasn't completely out of this world. We kept an open mind and said: "Okay, let's talk about this thing." The talks were in fact very friendly,' Meiring explains. 'They were very easy to get on with, especially Modise. Some were sharp and intelligent; others were not. But the point of fact is we didn't expect a lot and we didn't find a lot. It wasn't like speaking to Savimbi: he was a very sharp bloke. These were medium-type people. Right from the beginning I got on very well with Modise, we sort of clicked and spoke to one another easily. I never got to see eye to eye with Kasrils. He was a strange sort of a bloke. Phosa I liked, he was a nice chap and I could also speak to him easily. Yes, some of them were sharp, some were not so sharp, but that wasn't the whole thing. As personalities they were not bad, they were actually fine people to talk to.

'So when I took over from Kat Liebenberg, this process was still ongoing. It had progressed to the point where we were planning to make a plan for the new SADF, the Defence Force of the future. We started to plan in earnest when I took over from Kat. We had a committee on which sat people from the ANC, observers from the homelands armies at the time and us, from the Defence Force. The PAC was invited, but they never wanted to come because they were not part of Codesa. We asked them to send observers, but they didn't. Eventually this thing boiled down to a real structured planning session where we sat and planned the new Defence Force of the future – a tedious story that took a long time,' said Meiring. 'We started with a pukka military planning cycle. We found they didn't bring a lot to the table, they were very good at criticising but not very good at initiating.

'It was a very interesting but also very difficult time. All at the same time we were busy with the planning process with the ANC and the military people from the homelands, and then that thing that happened in Bophuthatswana where we, as the Defence Force of the RSA, had to step in to prevent further bloodshed. At the same time we had to continue driving the military. If anything went wrong with the negotiations, we still had to have a good and running Defence Force. I had a difficult job, a sort of semi-quasi political and military planning cycle on the one hand while talking to the opposition, and on the other putting contingency plans in place and managing the Defence Force on a day-to-day basis,' said Meiring. 'During this process Mandela one day came to talk to the (as he called it) high command – the Defence Command Council. After addressing us he asked to see me personally. We went into a little office and he asked me if they [the ANC] came to power, would I be available to accept the post of the Chief of the new Defence Force. I replied: "Yes, I'm doing it at the moment, so I would certainly be happy to continue." If I said "yes", I could look after the interests of everybody and try to maintain calm rather than step away and end up creating a vacuum and perhaps a lot of chaos in the process.' (Interestingly, Mandela never once raised the point that Meiring had been named in the Steyn Report.)

'After the election we prepared for the inauguration of the new State President, which was a major job – it was one of the biggest military operations ever in South Africa,' Meiring explains. 'We planned to ensure that nothing sinister was going on because with such a lot of foreign people, things could have turned into a bloodbath very suddenly. We flew armed air-cap over Pretoria continuously with two Impalas – if anything had come near it would have been shot down. There were armed Impalas in the sky all the time. We had armed reconnaissance people right around the area. Any bloke playing around with a stovepipe that day would have been dead; it could just as well have been a mortar and it was within mortar distance from the other side of that hill. Nobody was allowed on top of the hill. We really sterilised the area around it completely. It was a major operation, we used five brigades of troops that day just to control and sanitise the entire area. It was close to 9 000 people that we had there,' said Meiring.

'After the inauguration I was asked to sit at the table of the President. I don't know why I was selected. F.W. de Klerk also sat at the main table – he said to me while watching the fly-past and other proceedings: "We really needn't have given in so easily" – his words. I said to him: "But you never used your strong base to negotiate from, you never used the military as a base for strength, which you had available to you, you never wanted to use it." He just stopped [speaking] and we didn't speak after that any more. There haven't been very good vibes between us since that day. The "Night of the Generals" started it. I didn't like him very much', said Meiring.

'Joe Modise became the Minister of the new Defence Force and we worked together fairly well. We showed him around, trying to tell him what a modern army/defence force looks like. I don't think they really understood the workings of the Defence Force. I think that's the case even now: people do not understand how a defence force should be managed. You know you can train a bloke as much as you wish but 10 years' experience takes round about 10 years to acquire. They came from a completely different environment, not even completely guerrilla. Some of them were trained in aspects and facets of guerrilla warfare – for example, one bloke was trained to lay mines, another to carry the mine from here to there. That was his training. I spoke to many of the Russians and Germans [on official visits] who trained them, and they did not have much that was good to say about the training. They had to "sausage machine" them through and never got to train them for the whole picture. For these reasons it was difficult to get them to understand the way in which a modern defence force works. You can't just say "I want to do this". You must go through a planning cycle – and in order to spend money there must be a plan and an approved fund for it. Many of them were perhaps good leaders, but they led people in the field. Money came from somewhere. Logistics was to get this stuff to those people, it was carrying stuff, transporting it. It wasn't really logistics. Somebody else did that; they didn't plan, they didn't budget, they just got it. We had a nice plan, a military plan of about 80 000 people (down from 120 000), but it never came to that because in the planning post, everybody wants to keep his own,' said Meiring.

Integrating armies with such diverse cultural, training and political backgrounds was, however, no easy task. 'What was very difficult was the fact that whenever some people on the ground didn't make the grade, almost every time they would throw in the race card. We had to go to great lengths to try to prove to the politicians, the minister, the deputy minister and the defence committee in Parliament that that was not true,' Meiring said. 'You could never do a proper command and control job where you used your people to the best of their ability, for both your and their benefit. Many a time I said: "It would be very nice if we could say the best man for the job gets the job, it doesn't matter who he is." It never worked like that – but it was supposed to work like that.

'In the beginning we must set the wrong things right. We put people through all their courses, we'd deploy two who were on the same course at the same time and one bloke would come up to expectations and the other not. If you then wanted to promote the bloke who was performing and if he was white and the other black you'd be accused of discriminating against him because he's black. In fact it was usually the opposite. We gave [the black guys] two or three chances to pass a course – something we never did with the whites – because we felt, perhaps as a result of his background he was disadvantaged,' said Meiring. 'We trained them, we trained them as far back as possible. I put Siphiwe Nyanda [the current Chief of the SANDF] on a company commander's course at the time to give him the background. He went through it, I must give him credit, and he didn't do badly, he's quite a sharp chap – but he hasn't got the necessary experience to guide him with the knowledge he now has, and many others are in similar situations.

'[In the SADF] we always did a promotion planning exercise where a bloke was given the experience of first being a battalion commander, then a brigade commander, before he became an army commander. It was a route he had to walk with a lot of other people, and in the end you selected the best person for the job and the right person for the right job,' said Meiring. 'That sort of planning could never be achieved because we were forced to put people in these places and just let them do the job. I said – let's do it the other way around: let's put commanders and deputy commanders together. For example, if you put a previous cadre in a command post then the bloke under him must have come from a statutory force. That way, there would always be a mentor, whether it was from down or from up. If he's the commander, then the 2I-C must teach him how to command, etc. That would have worked well, but due to a lot of things it didn't happen. It was political. Most of this was a political thing,' said Meiring.

But despite the enormous challenges he faced, Meiring had some good and exciting times. 'Our recce troops trained together with the British, the French and the Israelis, and we could measure ourselves against them,' he said. 'We had exercises with other people, with people in Africa, they came on our courses and the whole thing was internationalised. We got subjected to and exposed to international scrutiny and viewing. We also learned a lot from other people – but many people learned a lot from us. That was a grand feeling, which we didn't have previously because we were always the polecat of the world.'

But then the political intrigue and pressure started. Top cover for the military supremo disappeared. In the past the Minister would form a shield against criticism, but that was no longer the case. 'Now this was all gone,' said Meiring, 'and we had to appear before the parliamentary committees where they shat on us and that wasn't nice. We appeared before the standing committee on this and that and nobody understood. Then came the worst of everything – the Truth and Reconciliation Commission. This should never have happened. I think this should be said (it's my deduction): because of the fact that Kobie Coetsee and Roelf Meyer never saw eye to eye, the question about [general] amnesty never came to be discussed. In the beginning the ANC pressed for [general] amnesty.'

Magnus Malan claims that Mathews Phosa went to see Kobie Coetsee to discuss the possibility of a general amnesty, but that Coetsee refused, saying that the government's side did not need amnesty. 'It was not just Phosa,' said Meiring, 'everybody wanted to have amnesty and Coetsee didn't want it because he wanted to use it as a lever and because he didn't see eye to eye with Roelf Meyer. Meyer wanted to get things moving, Kobie wanted to retard him because he wanted more leverage by using the amnesty question – and then the window of opportunity closed.

'The TRC was the worst thing that could ever have happened to unity in this country,' Meiring said. 'We worked really hard on that and gave them the facts, which they never published and never believed. The more we told them the truth, and the fact they couldn't find what they were looking for, the more convinced they were we had to be hiding something. You can't prove a negative, it's not possible. That thing worked up my spleen in words I can't explain and, what with the political top cover taken away in Parliament, really soured the time I spent as Chief of the National Defence Force. It wasn't that easy, and the deputy minister really worked on my tits.

'Then came the thing that started about a year before, the so-called report, which led to my demise. Dirk Verbeek, the Chief of Staff Intelligence, came to me some time between April and June in 1997. He said they had a very good source very near Winnie Mandela who'd given information about a plan to usurp the power of the government. I wanted to know if we had proof. He said: "We've got this one guy: he was Winnie Mandela's driver and at one stage a body guard, so he saw and heard a lot of things." We tried hard to prove or disprove what he was saying. It went on for quite some time. He would for example mention the existence of a camp – insurgents would have operated from bush camps particularly in Mozambique, as the government in Maputo would have been hostile towards them – near the Crooks Corner area, where people were trained and armed to be used as an insurgent force. We flew over the area, took pictures, saw a camp and sent people in, but there was nobody there. It was a camp, but there were Portuguese there. There was a vestige of truth but it was not completely disproved or proved,' said Meiring.

'Then he would say: "There's a cache in a certain area in Soweto." Now you can't just go and look because you'd immediately blow your source, so you have to plan with the police to sweep the area and "accidentally" come upon it. We found a place where a cache was but it was empty. So once again it was true but also not true – but a picture was starting to develop. I decided that somehow we had to get definite proof and went to see the minister. I said: "I've got a problem and I'm going to send recces into Mozambique to prove something specific." I gave him a broad idea of what was going on but told him we had no proof yet. He said: "Okay, keep me in the picture." I only spoke to him, not to Kasrils. So we sent recces into Mozambique. That bloke who was eventually caught, [Robert] McBride, was the courier of the monies and things like that. Winnie Mandela's bodyguard cum driver accompanied him from time to time and we got photos of them together at the old Polana Hotel, but we had no firm proof. We were trying to get him to buy arms with cash we'd tagged and then planned to follow them and see where they went. We had people waiting at the border posts and at Durban and Richards Bay to tag the ship or lorry with a transmitter.'

But then McBride was arrested by the Mozambicans and Meiring faced a major problem. He still had no firm proof he could lay on the table about the planned coup, but if he said nothing about it and it later came out, he'd be accused of having knowledge but doing nothing about it. 'I went to see the Minister and he agreed with me that I should go and see the President,' Meiring said. 'I told him the whole story of this unproven source, we compiled the report and I wrote it in big letters so he could read it himself and no one had to read it for him. I told him it wasn't proven yet but that we were busy with the operation. He thanked me and said he would look into it. When the McBride thing broke, still nothing happened, but it was as though someone had thrown the cat amongst the pigeons – and there were a lot of pigeons flying around. Kasrils wanted to know why I hadn't told him about the report, so I knew the report had found its way to the ANC.

'When McBride was arrested I told our people to pull back and abort the operation. The story of the report broke over the weekend and Mandela called me in. Present at the same time were some of the people mentioned in the report [Siphiwe Nyanda and other senior people]. Mandela told them I'd given him a report a month before in which their names were mentioned, and while he did not know how true it was he was going to look into the way in which it was leaked. He appointed a judicial commission of three judges and they questioned us. We told them the whole sequence of events was written up and kept at Military Intelligence Headquarters because of the need for intense secrecy. We invited them to come and look, something they did not do, yet they formed their own conclusion that the report was false and leaked by somebody.

'After they reported their findings Mandela called me to his house again. Everyone else was there again. He said it appeared the report was false but then he did a very good political thing – a black political thing. He said to each and every one there things like: "Now listen, I knew your father well, you will never plan against me, will you?" … "Of course not, Madiba." To the next bloke he said: "We were on Robben Island together, you will not plan against me, will you?" … "Of course not, Madiba." He went through everyone like this, so he diffused from his point of view the potential threat that there was against him.

'I was left standing like the bloke who told on his juniors,' said Meiring. 'Siphiwe then got up that day with a very good speech I'm sure Kasrils wrote, and said they felt there was a trust problem; they felt they could not work with me because of the breach of trust. Mandela listened to him, I listened to him, and then the President said we could leave. I didn't speak to the others, but went back to consider how things could be salvaged. It is a possibility the report was leaked to get me out. I think for a long time certain factions within the ANC got frustrated with my being the Chief of the NDF and they wanted me out somehow or other. I think this presented them with a window of opportunity.'

Meiring was requested to retire by Mandela, which he agreed to, subject to certain conditions – one of which was that he would say goodbye to the troops in a proper way as the Chief of the SANDF. Mandela went to great pains to tell everyone how the only man to command both the old and the new Defence Forces had acted absolutely properly and had tried to protect him and the State. He explained to the media what had happened and that circumstances beyond Meiring's control had conspired to make the situation untenable and that rather than create further problems, Meiring had offered to retire.

'He acted honourably,' said Meiring. 'He went out of his way to explain it was not my fault.'

On 6 April 1998 General Georg Meiring retired: the last of the old guard, the end of an era. At the same time, General Chris Thirion, fired in the old South Africa, was still trying to get F.W. de Klerk to do the honourable thing.

GLOSSARY

ACK-ACK: informal military term for anti-aircraft gunfire or guns

ALDEAMENTOS: controlled settlements to which rural villagers were forcibly removed; set up in Mozambique by the Portuguese

BANTUSTAN: black homeland set up in terms of apartheid policy of separate development.

BRAAI: barbecue

BROEDERBOND: literally 'brotherhood'; highly influential, exclusive secret society formed in 1918 to secure Afrikaner control in government, culture, finance and industry

CASSPIR: an armoured, mine-proofed military vehicle

KAFFIR: derogatory term for black person

KWÊVOËL: an armoured military vehicle

A MOER OF A: a hell of a

MUTI: colloquial South African term for medicine (from the Zulu word for medicine, *umuthi*)

NAT: member of the South African National Party

NECKLACE: rubber tyre filled with petrol, forced over a victim's head and shoulders, and then set alight; mainly used in the apartheid era against alleged 'informers' and 'collaborators'

OLIFANT: the South African tank in use in the Armoured Corps (from the Afrikaans word for elephant)

OSSEWA BRANDWAG: literally 'ox-wagon sentinel'; an Afrikaner organisation formed in 1939 in opposition to South Africa's declaration of war on Germany

PLATTELAND: rural areas

RATEL: a six-wheeled, high-speed armoured vehicle that carries a crew of three plus eight infantrymen (from the Afrikaans word for honey badger)

RECCE: informal term for reconnaissance

TROOPIES: colloquial military term for national servicemen holding the lowest rank

VOETSTOOTS: Roman Dutch term for 'as is' or 'as it stands'; used to describe items for sale

VOLK: the Afrikaner people

SELECT BIBLIOGRAPHY

This book is the result of interviews with former SADF generals and many other men and women who were involved. However, a wide range of books, publications and Internet documents were also consulted. The following is a partial list of some of the references:

Robert B. Asprey, *War in the Shadows – The Guerrilla in History, Vol I & II* (Doubleday)

Ray Bonds (ed.), *The Illustrated Directory of Modern Soviet Weapons* (Salamander)

Fred Bridgland, *The War for Africa – Twelve Months that Changed a Continent* (Ashanti)

Barbara Cole, *The Elite – The Story of the Rhodesian Special Air Services* (Three Knights)

Ron Reid Daly, *Selous Scouts – Top Secret War* (Galago)

F.W. de Klerk, *The Last Great Trek, A New Beginning* (Pan Books)

Paul Els, *We Fear Naught But God – The Story of the South African Special Forces* (Covos Day)

Edward Clinton Ezell, *Small Arms of the World* (Stackpole)

Jannie Geldenhuys, *A General's Story* (Jonathon Ball)

Evelyn Groenink, 'On the twisted trail of Dulcie's Death', *Electronic Mail & Guardian*, 12 January 1998, (http://www.mg.co.za/mg/news/98jan1/12jan-dulcie1.html. and http://wn.apc.org/wmail/issues/980109/NEWS16.html)

Robert Kirby, 'There was no Machel crash conspiracy', *Electronic Mail & Guardian*, 19 June 1998 (http://www.mg.co.za/mg/news/98june2/19june-machel.html)

Helmoed-Römer Heitman, *War in Angola – The Final South African Phase* (Ashanti)

Ian V. Hogg and John Weeks, *Military Small Arms of the 20th Century* (Arms and Armour Press)

Jim Hooper, *Koevoet* (Southern Book Publishers)

South African Defence Force Review 1989 (SADF Publication)

Debora Patta, 'How Machel signed his own death warrant', *Electronic Mail & Guardian*, 14 July 1998 (http://www.mg.co.za/mg/news/98july1/14july-machel.html)

F.J. du T. Spies, *Angola – Operasie Savannah* (SADF Publication)

Peter Stiff, *Nine Days of War* (Lemur Books)

———, *The Silent War – South African Recce Operations 1969–1994* (Galago)

Willem Steenkamp, *South Africa's Border War* (Ashanti)

John Stockwell, *In Search of Enemies – A CIA Story* (W.W. Norton & Co)

The following publications were also consulted:

Rand Daily Mail, Sunday Times, Sunday Express, The Star, Washington Post, Mail & Guardian, Janes Defence Weekly, Soldier of Fortune, Time, Newsweek, Der Spiegel, Stern, The Citizen, Rapport, Scope, Sechaba, The African Communist, AIM dispatches, SAPA reports, Institute of Soviet Studies Reports (Stellenbosch University), *Daily Dispatch, Christian Science Monitor,* TASS reports, *New York Times, Boston Globe, USA Today, Wall Street Journal* and others.

INDEX